ELIZABETH BISHOP

Elizabeth Bishop

QUESTIONS OF MASTERY

Bonnie Costello

Harvard University Press
Cambridge, Massachusetts
London, England

Pages 257–258 constitute a continuation of the copyright page.

Publication of this book has been aided by a grant from
the Andrew W. Mellon Foundation.

First Harvard University Press paperback edition, 1993

Library of Congress Cataloging-in-Publication Data

Costello, Bonnie.
Elizabeth Bishop : questions of mastery / Bonnie Costello.
p.   cm.
Includes bibliographical references and index.
ISBN 0-674-24689-6 (alk. paper) (cloth)
ISBN 0-674-24690-x (paper)
1. Bishop, Elizabeth, 1911–1979—Criticism and interpretation.
I. Title.
PS3503.I785Z63 1991
811'.52—dc20
91-2354
CIP

to Frank

Contents

Acknowledgments

My greatest debt is once again to Helen Vendler, who read an early version of the manuscript and who has inspired and supported me throughout my career. A fellowship from the Rockefeller Foundation and an office at the Bunting Institute helped me to get started on the book. I am grateful to Alice Methfessel not only for permission to quote from Elizabeth Bishop's unpublished writings but for providing me with some wonderful slides of the poet's artwork and of the "sketch" which inspired "Poem."

ELIZABETH BISHOP

Quotations from Bishop's published poetry are from *The Complete Poems, 1927–1979* by Elizabeth Bishop (New York: Farrar, Straus and Giroux, 1983). All references are abbreviated as CP, with the page number cited in the text. Quotations from Bishop's published prose are drawn from *The Collected Prose* by Elizabeth Bishop (New York: Farrar, Straus and Giroux, 1984), abbreviated as CPR throughout the text.

Introduction

In "One Art" Elizabeth Bishop confronts her reader with a paradox central to her work: "The art of losing isn't hard to master" (CP, 178). The villanelle form enumerating losses strikes some readers as sardonic. What sort of mastery does this Job-like speaker really profess? Even her meter almost yields to the pressure of personal loss at the end.

> —Even losing you (the joking voice, a gesture
> I love) I shan't have lied. It's evident
> the art of losing's not too hard to master
> though it may look like (*Write* it!) like disaster.

But the art of losing follows from an essential insight: "things seem filled with the intent / to be lost." Bishop's poetry helps us "accept the fluster" of a Heraclitean world and calls upon us to "look" and "watch" as it goes by. In such a world the ownership we crave is illusory. Bishop organizes her villanelle not only to broaden the scope and intensity of loss, but, conversely, to explore the concept of mastery. One may indeed "own" a thing such as a mother's watch (as a substitute for the inevitably lost mother), but one certainly does not own "the hour badly spent" (or, for that matter, well spent), or even control one's intentions ("what you meant to do"). One may "own" a house and its keys, but not a continent and certainly not a "realm." Least of all, the poem implies, can one own another person, though one may wish most intensely for that possession. The "joking voice" warns against melodrama.[1] Poetry is one of the few places where limited mastery is possible. This "one art" depends on control and unity. But Bishop sets it to expressing the flux and variety of things.

In this book I argue that Elizabeth Bishop concerned herself, throughout her career, with questions of mastery—artistic, personal, and cultural. Her poems portray both the desire for mastery and the dangers and illusions to which such desire is prone. Throughout Bishop's poems we find a strong urge for order and dominance confronting a recalcitrant world and volatile inner life. Bishop sometimes expresses dismay, even aristocratic disdain, over an untidy or barbaric world. But the same poet forces herself and her reader to encounter the mess of life, at times even to exhilarate in it. How much imaginative, cognitive, or political control can we have over a diverse and changing reality? What are the pleasures of relinquishing control? What limited forms of mastery remain necessary and viable? Bishop is a profoundly visual poet with an eye for the particular and mutable. Thus these questions of mastery promote new ways of seeing in time.

The traditions—devotional, romantic, and modern—out of which Bishop wrote often made the image a means of unifying experience and transcending time. Visual schemata might reveal a higher spiritual authority or concentrate experience in a unified aesthetic moment. Bishop's work responds to a broad and dynamic tradition of seeing and beholding—imitating, revising, challenging its claims and techniques. Her visual experience and the spatial and visual poetry which communicates it do not resist history and diversity but rather disclose it, challenging her position as a detached creative subject. She sets her eye not on the transcendental fade-out or on the modernist fixed object, but on the panorama and minutiae of a changing world which she tentatively orders and interprets.

Critics have long appreciated Bishop's visual accuracy and the spiritual and psychological expressiveness of her images. They have admired her skill in turning description to the task of mapping an inner life. "Everything has written under it—'I have seen it,'" wrote Randall Jarrell.[2] John Hollander, on the other hand, calls Bishop's images "tropes of psyche, not mere reports from the psyche."[3] What has not been sufficiently explored is the complex, unresolved relationship in this poet's images between observation and metaphor. To read Bishop's poetry is to be caught up in its descriptive vitality and its psychological and philosophical wisdom. But it is also to find the balance between them shifting and unstable. This fluency between description and trope relates, I will argue, to the questions of mastery that pressure her imagination.

A decade of criticism has established that Bishop is far from being the mere describer that early critics took her to be. But it is wrong, too, to present Bishop's attention to detail as mere coyness meant to distract us from her "higher" rhetorical purposes. Of course the images and experiences she records are rhetorical; they echo and challenge the major myths of the lyric tradition. But Bishop's particularity and preference for looks over vision are not, as John Hollander has suggested (in an otherwise illuminating essay on the poet), "an evasion of the consequences of visionary seriousness."[4] She bases these qualities on a directed resistance to idealism and its quest for mastery over nature's plurality and flux. Bishop's observations are her imagination's caress of the natural world; they free her from herself as much as they may reflect back. Fact gives more to the imagination than the imagination gives to fact.

Bishop kept a journal during and after college in which she recorded her reflections about the strategies and purposes of poetry. In one entry she explores this relationship between descriptive material and spiritual meaning:

> It's a question of using the poet's proper materials, with which he's equipped by nature, i.e., immediate, intense physical reactions, a sense of metaphor and decoration in everything—to express something not of them—something, I suppose, *spiritual*. But it proceeds from the mate-

rial, the material eaten out with acid, pulled down from underneath, made to perform and always kept in order, in its place. Sometimes it cannot be made to indicate its spiritual goal clearly (some of Hopkins', say, where the point seems to be missing) but even then the spiritual must be felt. Miss Moore does this—but occasionally I think, the super-material content in her poems is too easy for the material involved,—it could have meant more. The other way—of using the supposedly "spiritual"—the beautiful, nostalgic, the ideal and *poetic,* to produce the *material*—is the way of the Romantic, I think—and a great perversity. This may be capable of being tested by a mere studying of similes and metaphor—This is why genuine religious poetry seems to be about as far as poetry can go—and as good as it can be—it also explains the dangers of love poetry.[5]

This passage is remarkably discriminating as the product of such a young mind. Bishop understood not only her own direction but her difference with the past. Intense physical sensation is the material, not the aim, of Bishop's art, yet as the material it provides the basis of and sustains the spiritual aim. Bishop continually yields to this unmastered material, through which she nurtures and revises her poetry. At the same time, her poems testify to the urge for creative dominance.

Bishop's awareness of flux and plurality has many consequences for her portrayals of human consciousness, action, and desire. In an early notebook Bishop wrote: "Freud the perfect interpreter of *touch* only . . . For sight, sound, etc. draws false conclusions."[6] Bishop set out herself to be the interpreter of sight. The eyes provide a source of knowledge and pleasure for Bishop, but they serve the yearnings of the will. Bishop's critics have variously noted her critiques of mastery but have not seen them in their broader relation. Feminist critics have written of Bishop's challenge to patriarchal mastery over nature and the female. Psychological critics have pointed to her distinctions between a solipsistic dream world and external reality.

Others have brought out her developing interest in place and history as counters to her early symbolist internalizations. Critics with an eye for the formal qualities of poetry have noted her ways of modulating meter and rhyme to contain emotion and also give a sense of the naturalness and spontaneity of a mind in action.

This book adds to these and other arguments by exploring more inclusively what it means to be a visual poet. What ways of seeing does Bishop devise, and how are her modes and critiques of mastery related to her way of seeing in time? Bishop found distinctive means of adapting her temporal vision to poetry. Her poems are records of beholding in which the wish to engrave and frame experience is expressed, checked, or revised. In this book I study certain aesthetic devices—antimimetic manipulations of perspective and scale, violations of associative norms, iconographies of vertical and horizontal—which challenge visual and conceptual frames. I also consider some of Bishop's central motifs and themes—travel, memory, art—in which she presents the impulse to master plurality and flux. In all of these ways Bishop might be characterized as an early postmodernist, though she resisted labels. She sometimes presents a static, hierarchical view of the world or a conservative attitude, but at the same time her eye is drawn to a life that challenges norms. An heir to high modernism, she reveals a temperamental distrust of its idealism. She tried in her poetry to represent a way of observing and experiencing that could give vent and even satisfaction to our desire for pattern, meaning, and continuity without static orders or illusions.

Bishop wrote in a letter to Marianne Moore: "I used to have relatives with glass eyes when I was small and for some reason I worried because I thought they wouldn't go to Heaven. I don't think I was ever fully reassured until I read in Herbert something about— 'Taught me to live here so, that still one eye / Should aim and shoot at that which is on high.'"[7] Bishop's remark mockingly endorses the optimistic tradition of transcendent seeing she inherited from British and American Romanticism. A later version of this ancestral anecdote found a different "poetic justice" for the limits of natural vision.

In "The Country Mouse" Bishop wrote of her grandfather: "He was walleyed. At least, one eye turned the wrong way, which made him endlessly interesting to me. The walleye seemed only right and natural, because grandmother on the other side in Canada had a glass eye."[8] Bishop questions both ways of rationalizing away the limits of human vision—transcendental and communal. Whatever delight there may be in imagining a balanced world, careful observation throws it off again. But between the parallel distortions of the transcendent gaze and the walleyed glimpse Bishop found her own distinct peripheral vision.

Bishop attempts in her poetry to loosen the relation between the eyes and an imperious or transcendental "I" that would master or possess what it sees by ordering it around a center. Again in her notebook she writes, perhaps quoting Pascal: "Nature has made all her truths independent of one another. Our art makes one dependent on the other. But this is not natural. Each keeps its own place."[9] The eye perceives but also resists this natural diversity. Bishop's poetry attempts to display that diversity by confronting the ordering imagination with mutation and mutability. Whatever syntheses or resolutions her poetry offers contend with this peripheral vision.

Emerging from a tradition of seeing that idealizes it to Vision, Bishop's is a poetry of looks. She dismantles the transcendent gaze of Romanticism and relaxes the immanentist gaze of objectivism, offering in their stead a temporal, particular glimpse in which imagination plays a crucial but not a hierarchical part, expressing itself as peripheral rather than centered. Vertical heights and depths yield repeatedly to the waves and tremors of the iridescent surface of the earth. In Bishop's verse, consciousness throws its broken nets or wields its awkward pickaxe over this surface, turning up tentative orders or meanings, at least things that seem important or produce affects of joy or terror.

The glimpse, concerned with transient things, is more visual than the penetrating or transcendent gaze of mental mastery. The visual was always displaced in Romanticism by a supersensible voice or mind; Wordsworth and Coleridge showed disdain for the merely visual. Rivers and cascades were "the types and symbols of Eternity." There is no metaphysical counter to duration in Bishop. By contrast, she projects into the fixed objects of perception a knowledge of their transience. Denis Donoghue has called this her "historical geography."[10] But the phrase suggests a topographical mastery of the past which she would disavow.

Bishop's sense of time as a special problem for the ordering imagination is clear as early as her college writing. "Time's Andromedas," an essay she published in the *Vassar Journal of Undergraduate Studies*, exemplifies her early attempt to combine her visual and temporal awareness and to explore the relation between the mind's stasis and drift. At this early point in her career she aimed, through spatial concepts, to unify time around a fixed idea. Bishop describes a contemplative moment which is not immune to but alive with change, a scene of reading, disrupted by the flurry of her own thoughts and subsequently by the intervening sunset from the window. Drawn toward this window by a "faintly rhythmic irregularity" of bird sounds, she watches a migration and gradually becomes aware that the individual irregularities of groups of birds express together "a sort of time-pattern or rather patterns." At this stage, so much under the spell of T. S. Eliot, the poet feels compelled to refer all these coincident "time-patterns" to a "still and infinite" absolute, to an epiphany of some "static fact of the world." Yet even here Bishop's spatial image of time articulates a movement of "*passing* the time along" which will increasingly become the object of her attention.[11] For the human beholder, as she writes in "Gerard Manley Hopkins: Notes on Timing in his Poetry," "the target is a moving target and the marksman is also moving."[12]

Yet Bishop shows sympathy as well as skepticism toward the search for teleologies, origins, and ends. The movements of hope, nostalgia, revelation springing from the visual occur throughout her poetry. She was raised in the pervasively Protestant culture of rural Nova Scotia, bred on church services and hymns. The rhetoric of religion—its mode of questioning, its expectations and desires, and especially its approach to visual experience as a sign of the invisible—remains basic to her view of the world. This rhetoric influenced her further through its literary versions (Herbert and Hopkins in particular) and its secularized versions in English and American Romanticism. To Robert Lowell she wrote: "On reading over what I've got on hand I find I'm really a minor female Wordsworth at least, I don't know anyone else who seems to be such a Nature Lover."[13] And later, to Anne Stevenson: "I also feel that Cal (Lowell) and I in our very different ways are both descendants from the Transcendentalists—but you may not agree."[14] The breadth of this visual tradition, which includes Ruskin as well, made seeing a form of religious revelation. But Bishop is not, finally, a theological poet, as David Kalstone has suggested, or even a late Romantic prophet like Wallace Stevens. To Robert Lowell she writes: "I believe now that complete agnosticism and straddling the fence on everything is my natural posture—although I wish it weren't."[15]

The movement of hope springing from the visual, characteristic of quest literature, occurs throughout Bishop's poetry. The eye, searching out in the receding or dismantled surface some line of pursuit, finds a road disappearing into mountains, a figure edging toward mist, birds dissolving into pinpoints of sky. Such images tease the sight; Bishop knows with the landscape artist that nothing excites so much as that which is hidden. Yet she does not sanctify blindness or succumb to illusions of depth. The discovery and acceptance of transience form a major plot of Bishop's descriptive poems. She often begins by approaching a scene or landscape as a timeless tableau, masterable and uniform. Such static observation quickly yields to an iridescent, fluent reality, exhilarating but also threatening. The emotional logic of such description leads to a focus on something dark and impenetrable in the landscape, the antithesis of the image of timeless order. But Bishop's attention seldom rests in this abyss; her feeling is lightened in the experience of being in time and her eye delights in the particular. Variations on this visual and emotional plot appear throughout Bishop's poems and together present an alternative to the Romantic plot of transcendence.

If Bishop's poetry questions some forms of mastery and transcendence offered in devotional and Romantic traditions, she is equally skeptical about the symbolist and objectivist absolutes which shaped modernist thinking. Again, her differences with their claims to mastery do not erase the importance of these influences or their temperamental affinities. Bishop's early poetry, especially, shares Eliot's eschatological yearnings and his alienation from a world that has ceased to express spiritual vitality. In her ideal houses and imaginary icebergs, Bishop entertains the possibilities of aesthetic totality and pure interiority which high modernism offered as retreats from the disorder of a godless world. She was intimately familiar with Stevens' poetry and tempted by his supreme fiction. But she would gradually eschew the abstraction and idealism of this view and immerse herself in the observable world, sometimes in disdain toward its social forces, but with delight in its natural beauty. Williams, the spokesman for that world, raised other questions for Bishop. The objectivists aimed at a camera-like mastery of objects. In Bishop's poetry, by contrast, the observable world recedes from our gaze. She experiences knowledge as glimpses on the periphery of vision.

I begin this book by exploring Bishop's optical strategies, especially her approach to perspective as it relates to problems of mastery. Bishop is well known for her unusual perspectives, but they have not been fully interpreted. Sometimes they portray the inevitable solipsism of human awareness. But taken together, they amount to a critique of the single vantage point of integrated, timeless subjectivity. Her use of multiple, angled, liminal, and inverted perspectives is reminiscent of symbolist and surrealist techniques but sometimes has a different outcome, leading away from abstraction rather than toward it. Bishop gradually developed an approach to perspective which stressed the dynamism of engaged vision. Bishop's images and metaphors similarly tend to resist stasis and challenge normative frames, as I show in the second chapter. She explores margins and boundaries of association, juxtaposes the sinister and the beautiful, and introduces the strange into the familiar. Bishop particularly applies these techniques to her representation of organic process and the forms of resistance to it. An emotional ambivalence and rhetorical instability attend these juxtapositions and suit her themes of mastery and mutability. These ruptures often reflect nature's own violation of static form, producing feelings of both loss and creative freedom.

The Romantic and symbolist traditions responded to natural limits with a rhetoric of sublime transcendence. Ruptures in the rational ordering of the finite world become openings for imaginative expansion into a higher, absolute power. In Chapter 3 I show how Bishop displaces the vertical sublime with her own horizontal accent. While the religious pull toward a supersensible, transcendent focus retains its hold on her, she repeatedly turns away from it. Her alternative is not alienation but a renewed, sometimes painful but often grateful identification with the natural world and recognition of her own inchoate psyche. Along these lines, she shifts her iconography to emphasize the volcano rather than the iceberg. A volatile flow of internal heat into the external world displaces her earlier epiphanies and static, antivital ideals.

Travel is Bishop's major trope of this horizontal condition, the spatial equivalent of her temporal awareness. Chapter 4 is devoted to Bishop's excursive vision as she expresses it both thematically and formally. Questions of mastery become focused in this motif as the desire for conquest or escape yields to the struggle of perception and the delights of discovery. Bishop's models for this genre include not only literary journeys but popular and scientific ones as well. In keeping with these models she employs the rhetoric of the catalogue, the postcard, the journal notation—open, tentative forms of representation. Travel is a constant challenge to the boundaries of culture and selfhood and an expression of their frailty. Horizons vanish, not into an interiorized or sublime infinite but into new horizons or into a void. Bishop is not the privileged beholder of a new, unmediated Genesis, but a victim of her own belatedness, her archaic codes and assumptions. But defeat is not the only condition of travel; Bishop finds pleasure in the uneasy heightening of sensation which accompanies travel and brings surprise, delight, and engagement with the world.

The travel genre is, for Bishop, closely tied to themes of memory, which concern me in the fifth chapter. From her early, symbolist poems, full of nostalgia and irony, Bishop developed a more positive view of memory. The traveler through space becomes a traveler through time as poems of witness become poems of remembrance. Bishop explores the impact this retentive faculty has on the experience of time. Memory is not, for her, a form of mastery over time; indeed, it often arises as an involuntary force. Bishop possessed a nearly eidetic memory, or at least invents a rhetoric of exact recall. Iconic events in her personal history shape her acts of beholding. Thus memory remains for her a major force of identity. The self which has neither transcendent identity nor grounding in the present achieves, through the rhetorical force of memory, a principle of continuity. This remains true even when the memories are disturbing or dislocated from their origins.

As memory is primarily visual, so visual art becomes the subject within which she explores art's alliance with memory. My sixth chapter examines Bishop's stance in the ekphrastic tradition, poetry's long yearning for the condition of the visual arts. Her work shows ample evidence of influence from the visual arts (which I discuss throughout the book). And what is more important, it joins the celebration of art's power to conserve a moment while suggesting its vitality and movement. But "the moment" preserved in art is fictional and moves laterally through time, subject to its conditions, rather than beyond or outside it. Art is less a form of immortality than of commemoration.

The areas of concern I have just described overlap in most of Bishop's poetry. While I have taken up whole poems under individual rubrics, my aim is to provide a matrix of considerations through which to read the poetry. Each of these rubrics draws together thematic and formal approaches to the work. Although the study is not chronological, I do emphasize early poems most in the first and third chapters, while the fourth chapter concerns later poems. All other chapters explore the span of Bishop's career.

Since her death Bishop's reputation has risen dramatically. Her work has now received praise and commentary from a number of perspectives—thematic, stylistic, historical, biographical, feminist. Anne Stevenson's early study *Elizabeth Bishop* laid the groundwork of isolating themes and aesthetic characteristics, and began to place Bishop's concerns in the larger context of twentieth-century thought and art. A great deal of criticism since then has been dedicated to describing and debating the nature of her "descriptive" art and its mythopoetic strategies.[16] This book continues that discussion, putting renewed weight and meaning into the perception of Bishop as a visual poet while at the same time providing psychological and epistemological interpretations of the poems. Bishop's visual thinking is deeply self-conscious, but her images are not merely rhetorical or transparent. The power of the visual sensation—to awaken desire, stimulate interpretation, elude possession, provoke association and feeling, relieve and tantalize the mind—is often the matter of her art. Yet this sense of the visual particular is deeply complicated by her awareness of the mediation of signs, the abyss of representation in which we are conscious.[17] The other major concern which joins Bishop's forms to her themes is temporality. Few critics have acknowledged the full impact of Bishop's temporal consciousness on her visual presentations and her choice of modes, or understood it as the unifying principle of her poems of travel, memory, and art.[18] The first four chapters take up major aesthetic strategies within which Bishop considers problems of perception and meaning.[19] The last three chapters invert this relation, exploring how Bishop's predominant subjects express a mode of consciousness. These subjects are obvious and have been repeatedly noted.[20] I have tried to add to the perceptions of previous critics by showing how these subjects emerge as questions of mastery, and how they affect her style of representation.

Any choice of emphasis is necessarily an exclusion. The matter of gender has laid great claim on our attention in recent criticism and is certainly relevant, at times inescapable, in the study of Bishop's poetry. A number of critics—Joanne Diehl, Lee Edelman, Lorrie Goldensohn, Dale Robert Parker, among many others—have written well on the psychosexual aspects of Bishop's work, freeing me to pursue other topics except where the female body is the primary subject of a poem.[21] More broadly, Bishop's poetry is ideologically complex, and critical discussion has begun concerning the politics of her poetry. My interest remains primarily on her poetics and vision, though her politics obviously had an impact on her way of writing and seeing, and informs her questions of mastery.

My aim in this book has been to integrate and thereby deepen readers' understanding of various strategies and themes in Bishop's work. Her stylistic features, interesting in themselves, imply assumptions about human awareness. I have treated whole poems whenever possible, since the movement of the poem itself expresses the attitude toward mastery. I attempt to trace the emotional structure of the poems as it is visually articulated. Many poems previously neglected in the criticism reveal Bishop's development of visual and temporal awareness.

My reading of Bishop's poetry has been enhanced by the letters, manuscripts, journals, and other materials available in the archives at Vassar College and elsewhere. In using these materials my intention has been to provide not a biographical but rather a compositional and meditative history of the poems.

"Active Displacements in Perspective"

One of the great forms of mastery in Western art was central perspective, in which nature appeared rationally aligned with art and art could claim, through the isometric design of space, to express the unity of nature. The invisible basis of that unity was the static position of a single, impersonal beholder. The modernist challenge to such illusions of mastery had become doctrine by the time Elizabeth Bishop began writing. Her early poem, "The Monument" (CP, 23), confirms this:

> The view is geared
> (that is, the view's perspective)
> so low there is no "far away,"
> and we are far away within the view.

But Bishop's perspectives, though often disturbing in their effects, affirm visual thinking. Against the paralyzed gaze, her active displacements of perspective keep the mind open and affirm the presence of a creative subject. Mastery by perspective gives way to engagement by constant readjustment. To choose a single perspective, writes the painter David Hockney, is to be dead: "For perspective to be fixed, time is stopped—and hence space has become frozen, petrified. Perspective takes away the body of the viewer. To have a fixed point, you have no movement; you are not there, really."[1]

Bishop does want to be there, and she wants her reader to be. Early in her career she employed modernist techniques of fragmented, distorted, and multiple perspective to break up illusionary space and emphasize the limits of the central beholder. But she resisted both the movement toward perspectiveless abstraction and the movement toward perspectiveless presentation of things for themselves. Bishop achieved her greatest strength as a realist poet employing antimimetic devices, a poet for whom perspective is the interaction of subject and environment. But her particular realism portrays the instability of her point of view, the challenges to her mastery. Sometimes the poet depicts a world of very limited beholders, including herself, who see and act according to their own unique purposes. Some poems offer little possibility, within experience, of comprehending the world from anything but one's own narrow perspective. One alternative of modernism was to idealize the alienated. But Bishop's vision multiplies or shifts perspectives, aware of life at the peripheries of our interpretations. Her attitudes toward that life may at times be critical, but she acknowledges values alternative to her own. Bishop's multiple perspective is often connected with temporal changes or alterations of light. She enacts this openness through dynamic perspective within the poems. Bishop's realism not only allows the world to make an actual, recognizable appearance; it makes the poet-beholder an essential, dynamic part of that appearance rather than a mere vehicle of ideas. Conversely, the abstract element of her poetry—its metaphor and mind play—never abandons its engagement with the real.

Bishop's earliest experiments with perspective occur within a symbolist and surrealist rhetoric, and I will begin with an examination of this rhetoric in "Love Lies Sleeping," "Anaphora," "Sleeping on the Ceiling," and other poems. But she soon found ways of introducing her antimimetic devices into a more descriptive mode. In such poems she demonstrates her greatest originality and power. "Seascape" and "Pleasure Seas" are early examples; these anticipate the perspectival shifts in "Twelfth Morning; or What You Will," "Filling Station," and "Invitation to Miss Marianne Moore," in all of which the poet's pessimism is countered. In these later poems she achieves a vision at once immediate, even intimate, and yet directed to the world and questioning a single perspective or self-hood.

"Love Lies Sleeping" (CP, 16–17) provides an excellent example from Bishop's early work of devices of perspective, scale, and light which she would refine in her later descriptive poetry. The poem deals with the stress of urban life and culture on the inhabitants of a city in which the environment is toxic and love is perverted to predation. It explores these stresses through the perspective of a beholder trying to fend off brutality and gain imaginative control over this life. The beholder, looking out her window after a night-mare, moves from a perspectiveless inward vision to focused, shap-ing vision, opened to other, less benign perspectives. The tender window-vision of the city as a miniature chemical garden in a glass never becomes fixed or detached from the real visual experience, though the window marks both a boundary and a surface.[2] The vision gradually accepts other inhabitants (half-awake workers, birds, street cleaners) and even their perspectives as it moves through a subtle emergence of day. The poet does not attempt to unify these views; the metaphor of the chemical garden in fact reverses and becomes toxic as the day progresses. The inverted or distorted vision of a drunk or dead pariah ends the poem. The pressure of urban life undermined, for Bishop, the recuperative power of observation. The vision here is more awful than cheerful. But Bishop begins to find in this poem the delicate middle ground between imaginary, solipsistic control of the world seen and sur-render to the "entire night" of inwardness and despair.

Several contrasted points of view define the shifts in perspective through "Love Lies Sleeping." The perspectiveless nightmare be-longs to an indeterminate "we"; the window vision to a single first person; the final, ambiguous gaze to a third person. But these are not strictly alternative ways of seeing either. They define an emo-tional and perceptual continuum and merge into one another to enhance the dynamic awareness of the poem, a vision flowing and, eventually, flown in a temporal unfolding.

Bishop's beholder usually confronts an inchoate darkness in the middle of her poems, but in "Love Lies Sleeping" this is where the poem begins and ends. Thus the recovery of sight which redeems the beholder in other poems seems here but an interlude in the gloom. We enter the poem in a transitional moment, when the memory of the nightmare state is still present as outward sight is restored:

> Earliest morning, switching all the tracks
> that cross the sky from cinder star to star,
>   coupling the ends of streets
>   to trains of light,

Even the dream space of the sky offers no retreat from the mechanistic, sooty world of the city. The "coupling" of streets and light evokes the love theme in a disturbing way. The train track metaphor also describes a perceptual process. Bishop does not illustrate a sharp transition from an inner infinity of dream to outer contingency; the inner landscape is influenced by external signals. In the nightmare state an unarticulated world of "twitching signs" presses "down the gray avenue between the eyes" as a neon glare, and the self is overtaken by an undifferentiated "we" which at the outset has no feeling in it. As she wakes the poet's glance changes direction and becomes more individualized. She casts her eye creatively out, ordering the world and placing herself above it. What is "revealed" is both visionary and visual, imagined and actually seen.

> From the window I see
>
> an immense city, carefully revealed,
> made delicate by over-workmanship,
>   detail upon detail,
>   cornice upon façade,
>
> reaching so languidly up into

a weak white sky, it seems to waver there.
    (Where it has slowly grown
    in skies of water-glass

from fused beads of iron and copper crystals,
the little chemical "garden" in a jar
    trembles and stands again,
      pale blue, blue-green, and brick.)

The "immense city" is reduced to "a little chemical 'garden' in a jar," so that the beholder can feel tenderness rather than fear (such as the ubiquitous nightmare produced). But this miniaturization is not finally a stance of power so much as a precarious transference of pity from the self to the world.[3] The little garden "trembles and stands again." The fragility projects what she feels after the nightmare. Throughout the poem the terrors that implicitly caused the nightmare reassert themselves. Indeed, the scene is "carefully revealed" because the shaky beholder must put the world back together after a breakdown of ordinary seeing. Visual articulation becomes a way of releasing the excess inner pressure. The garden metaphor offers an interesting inversion as the artifice of the imagination converts an inorganic, urban reality (the neon world) to an image of organized nature.

But instead of converting the city to a pastoral garden, the metaphor of the chemical garden anticipates the later danger, exposing mortal nature to chemical poisons. In stanzas seven and eight Bishop draws on the fear which had been suppressed in the charm of the "delicate" scene. The metaphor which had been generated by the first perspective now suggests a different perspective.

Then, in the West, "Boom!" and a cloud of smoke.
    "Boom!" and the exploding ball
    of blossom blooms again.

(And all the employees who work in plants
where such a sound says "Danger," or once said "Death,"

> turn in their sleep and feel
> the short hairs bristling
>
> on backs of necks.)

Bishop introduces two perspectives at once here, inviting irony. The window-viewer in her garden reverie sees industrial explosions as "blossoms." The sleeping employees, for whom the blossoms represent the subliminal threat of death, remain in the state described at the opening of the poem (the world, pressing in, has not been successfully distanced by trope or conscious sight). Bishop renders anxiety in terms of hearing (the "boom" of the explosion) and feeling (on the backs of necks) so that she can sustain her visual detachment while noting its fragility.

But the poet does not permit dread to overtake other emotions or to block perception. As in so many of her poems, Bishop soothes as soon as she shocks. The water wagon enters the scene, making, on the street, "the pattern / of the cool watermelon," another visual metaphor of natural refreshment that softens the pitiless pavement.[4] Yet again, and throughout the poem, visual pleasure is undermined by tactile and auditory signals. The "day springs" of the beds and the "alarm clocks" break the spell this time. The oxymoronic phrase "alarms for the expected" captures, in understatement, the routine oppression of the industrial culture. Love is depicted as something that consumes urban dwellers, all the more because they are "dragging in the streets their unique loves." We are prepared, then, for the terrible reversal of the speaker's reverie in the gaze of the figure at the end of the poem. He has not managed to convert urban terror into aesthetic pleasure. His inversion is, indeed, a form of trope, like the speaker's, but the city is "revealed" to him quite differently, not as something "clear" but as something "distorted."

> for always to one, or several, morning comes,
> whose head has fallen over the edge of his bed,
> whose face is turned
> so that the image of

the city grows down into his open eyes
inverted and distorted. No. I mean
    distorted and revealed,
      if he sees at all.

The poem returns at the end to the inverted perspective with which it began. The city "grows down" with its oppressive weight rather than "reaching languidly up." This "one" who closes the poem does not see outwardly. But Bishop does not idealize his blindness as a timeless epiphany. "I think the man at the end of the poem is dead," Bishop wrote to Anne Stevenson.[5] This victim of the city's psychic violence is the focus of the poem's disturbing benediction, "Scourge them with roses only, / be light as helium," which echoes the ambiguous metaphor of the chemical garden. Bishop rests the perspectives of the poem in a dead-drunk gaze, far from an idealized inner vision as we might expect in a dream or allegory. If he sees at all, he sees outwardly. But if he sees, his distorted and inverted gaze is revelatory.

We can see the uniqueness of Bishop's approach to representation if we compare this poem with the work of two poets who had a major influence on her work. Whereas Eliot worked through multiple perspectives toward a unifying myth or allegory, Bishop remains within the observable world. Conversely, her emphasis on active displacements of perspective affirms the importance of the beholder against the extreme claims of objectivism in Williams and others.

"Love Lies Sleeping" is one of the many early poems influenced by Eliot (Bishop frequently acknowledged her absorption in his poetry during her college years). The high modernist poet provided not only a set of themes and landscapes but rhetorical strategies as well. His "impersonal" voice and metonymic style could, while still directing the attention outward, upset customary vision and suggest the mind's eye. His anti-similes, fragmented images, and shifting points of view remained essential to Bishop's work even as she moved toward a more descriptive and anecdotal style. But she resisted Eliot's tendency to move from broken surfaces to mythic and symbolic unities. Whatever unity Bishop claimed would remain tied to the perceptual and temporal world.

Eliot's "Preludes" (glimpses of city life at early morning and evening, which shift from impersonal to first- and second- and third-person utterance) may be the model for "Love Lies Sleeping," especially the third prelude:

> You dozed, and watched the night revealing
> The thousand sordid images
> Of which your soul was constituted;
> They flickered against the ceiling.
> And when all the world came back
> And the light crept up between the shutters
> And you heard the sparrows in the gutters,
> You had such a vision of the street
> As the street hardly understands:

In "Love Lies Sleeping" Bishop also awakens as the world comes back, complete with sparrows; she too has a vision of the street which the street hardly understands and is, in Eliot's phrase, "moved by fancies that are curled / Around these images," though hers are more sympathetic than repellent. Both poets awake in a mechanized world where human beings behave like automatons. Bishop hears "the day springs of the morning strike / from stony walls and halls and iron beds. . . . / queer cupids of all persons getting up, / whose evening meal they will prepare all day." For Eliot:

> The morning comes to consciousness
> Of faint stale smells of beer
> From the sawdust-trampled street
> With all its muddy feet that press
> To early coffee-stands.
> With the other masquerades
> That time resumes . . .[6]

Both poets enter their daylight vision from a perspectiveless, time-less night vision in which the shadowy, flickering images of the city "press upon the brain," or in Eliot's terms "constitute the soul." But Bishop's poem is much closer than Eliot's to the traditional aubade, the expression of love in the transition from night to day. Indeed, in an early draft Bishop used the title "Morning Poem." The vision is open to the daylight and to others. Bishop's morning revelation is sharply distinguishable from the obscure hallucinations of night, even if inspired by night terrors. For Eliot the perspectiveless night "reveals" the truth about day. Bishop merges Eliot's sordid vision with the aubade's purifying one.

Bishop's major device for presenting her characteristic mixture of hope and anxiety is the manipulation of perspective and perspectival metaphors. In this regard at least her poem is superior to Eliot's, which moves arbitrarily through pronouns toward an abstract, im-personal soul "of some infinitely gentle / Infinitely suffering thing" which bears little relation to the images that come before it. Bishop does not make this shift from multiple perspectives to a perspective-less allegory, but instead offers a logic in her shifts of perspective that allows vision, though kept within perspective, to be open and inclusive. From the collective terror of the night ("draw us," the poem pleads, "into daylight") an "I" emerges which is not solip-sistic but urges the morning, the moon, and especially "Love" to treat gently "all persons getting up." But she does not shift to an allegory of Love such as her title suggests. And where Eliot ends in epiphany, Bishop remains within the partitive world of the shifting perspectives through which "morning comes." Thus, too, while Eliot's speaker concludes with abrupt ironic detachment, Bishop ends with a very qualified benediction.

Williams' "The Attic Which Is Desire" offers fewer parallels to "Love Lies Sleeping" (and his influence on Bishop is in fact much looser). But the poem does suggest how Williams' movement to-ward perspectiveless objectivism contrasts with Bishop's treatment of observation.

the unused tent
of
bare beams
beyond which

directly wait
the night

and day—
Here
from the street
by

```
        *  *  *
        *  S  *
        *  O  *
        *  D  *
        *  A  *
        *  *  *
```

ringed with
running lights

the darkened
pane

exactly
down the center

is
transfixed[7]

There are many virtues to this presentational style which certainly
would have attracted Bishop. But she chose not to imitate the
objectivism, the transparency of the beholder. In Williams' poem
"Here" indicates perspective, but it is unclear whether it refers
backward or forward in the poem, to the attic or the street. Even
agency among the various objects he introduces is ambiguous, the
syntax of "by" in the middle of the poem suggesting both proximity

and causation (is transfixed by). Their symbolic displacement of human feeling relies on the title and a pun on "pane" and "pain." As in Eliot's poem, the vision yields to a kind of epiphany, though in Williams the abstraction cleaves to the concrete details. Bishop's details are embedded in human perspective; they neither rise to the status of pure metaphor nor bare themselves as objective reality. Their fluency and connectedness are a matter of perspective.

As Bishop imagines what the drunkard with his head over the side of the bed sees, she offers a qualified and embedded conclusion. It wrenches the aesthetic control that set the poem's metaphors in motion, but it does not become a detached, final position. Instead, her ending recalls the beginning of the poem. These represent the alternative to the dominant "upright" perspective, what the nightmare might have led to: something disturbing though also perhaps consoling in its lucidity. Bishop integrates the final moment of her poem into the continuum of the meditation, not only by a visual and emotional logic but by a consistency within the stanzaic form (five stanzas of two pentameter and two trimeter unrhymed lines). The cooperative relationship between syntax and line provides a unity of eye and ear where the poem's narrative suggests a tension. Thus while Bishop's poem describes the failure even of imaginative mastery (except in the brief interlude between sleep and entire wakefulness) and rejects the idea of a controlling perspective, she achieves an aesthetic mastery through form and image.

Bishop's "Anaphora" (CP, 52) resembles "Love Lies Sleeping" in theme and structure, but it provides an interesting contrast in terms of the level of representation the poet would later pursue, and the consequences of that choice in the treatment of perspective. Both poems record an early morning vision whose dreamy optimism is gradually displaced by the pressures of day. For both this involves dynamic shifts in light and angle of vision. But "Anaphora" telescopes this process into a movement more rhetorical than observational. Indeed, it treats nature's cycles as a kind of rhetoric, its title marking not only the syntactic repetitions in the poem, but "endless" repetition of the cycle it describes. This theme of repetition makes the symbolic treatment eloquent and appropriate.

Each day with so much ceremony
begins, with birds, with bells,
with whistles from a factory;
such white-gold skies our eyes
first open on, such brilliant walls
that for a moment we wonder
"Where is the music coming from, the energy?
The day was meant for what ineffable creature
we must have missed?" Oh promptly he
appears and takes his earthly nature
    instantly, instantly falls
    victim of long intrigue,
    assuming memory and mortal
    mortal fatigue.

More slowly falling into sight
and showering into stippled faces,
darkening, condensing all his light;
in spite of all the dreaming
squandered upon him with that look,
suffers our uses and abuses,
sinks through the drift of bodies,
sinks through the drift of classes
to evening to the beggar in the park
who, weary, without lamp or book
    prepares stupendous studies:
    the fiery event
    of every day in endless
    endless assent.

As in "Love Lies Sleeping," the imagination actively tropes on what
it sees, yet obeys a temporal sequence. At the beginning the speaker
proposes some "ineffable creature" who might be the audience to
the brilliant "ceremony" of daybreak, but vision quickly shrinks to
mortal proportions. Articulated human sight becomes associated
with memory and fatigue, with a fall into time. The poem makes

the relation of beholder and beheld ambiguous. The "ineffable creature"—now incarnate humanity—"falling into sight," is both seen and seeing. He becomes, at the end, a Christian-Wordsworthian beggar-visionary who "without lamp or book prepares stupendous studies." As in "Love Lies Sleeping," we come full circle. The particular beggar, much reduced from the "ineffable creature," converts the "eternal ascent" to an "endless assent." But this is not a negation of the first ceremony so much as a shift to a different light, a different reality. The "fiery event" is a non-apocalyptic sunset, the image of an ending, to be repeated, against the day's idealized beginnings. Bishop distinguishes an "anaphora" of nature's cycles from an epiphany of first causes.

The poem achieves a seamlessness through anaphora, broken only by the shift from rising to falling action, where the first sentence ends at the stanza break and the second and last sentence begins. The poem's fourteen-line sentences and asymmetrical rhymes achieve a fluency of thought and funnel into the inverted ending rather than creating an abrupt reversal. But what it gains in rhetorical mastery it loses in realism, not only of the world illustrated but of life in the poem. Bishop would ultimately refuse this sacrifice.

But early on Bishop examined questions of mastery in isolation from questions of observation. The dream and the mirror world seem to define frames of meditation which preclude problems of perspective. Yet perspective is important even here as a challenge to static ideas of self-identity.

Early in her career Bishop looked to surrealism (more of the visual arts than of poetry) for solutions to the problem of integrating symbolic rhetoric with the realism she sought for her poems. Bishop's decision to live in France immediately after college (1934) was inevitably a decision to explore surrealism, the vital aesthetic of the thirties. While in France, she told Ashley Brown, she read "a lot of surrealist poetry and prose."[8] Her library, which contained volumes of Apollinaire, Baudelaire, Char, Corbière, Jacob, Proust, Reverdy, and Rimbaud, corroborates this statement. She also kept fliers of numerous exhibitions at the Julian Levy gallery in New

York, which attest to her continuing interest in surrealist art. The visual artists de Chirico, Klee, and Ernst (all of whom she mentions in poems and letters) were even more important than the writers in suggesting ways of including several vanishing points (de Chirico), suspending figurative portraits in abstract space (Klee), and allowing associative play with objects (Ernst). Dream imagery and distortion are the most conspicuous features of this influence. John Ashbery notes as a "special" element in Bishop's art "the life of dreams, always regarded with suspicion as too 'French' in American poetry."[9] When Bishop described "Varick Street" to Anne Stevenson, she wrote: "I use dream-material whenever I am lucky enough to have any and this particular poem is almost all dream—just re-arranged a bit."[10]

But as many critics have observed, Bishop's surrealist images and subjects do not constitute a surrealist technique or testify to shared beliefs about the nature of the creative unconscious. She would ultimately refuse to differentiate conscious and unconscious forms of awareness, or to entertain a notion of perspectiveless inner life. In these early poems dream life and nocturnal perception are primarily rhetorical devices. Their perspectives, while contrasting with ordinary perception, are fixed. They do not embody the reality of the dreamer or a dynamic visual reality, but narrate the dream vision to illustrate an idea. Nevertheless, these perspectives generate striking metaphors that contain their own descriptive and narrative logic.

"Sleeping on the Ceiling" (CP, 29) describes a dream in which the ceiling of the dreamer's room becomes the Place de la Concorde, her wallpaper the Jardin des Plantes, her photographs animals. The dream animates objects, inverts orders, and transforms the scale of the domestic space, all techniques that Bishop would use in later, more realistic poetry. Objects are enlarged to heroic proportions, or, conversely, the dreamer diminished to "insect" proportions as she proposes meeting the "insect-gladiator" under the wallpaper "to battle with net and trident." The poem becomes a fairy tale in which the ceiling represents an ideal space which the warrior aspires to, but from which he is closed off by dark forces with which he must contend. It expresses, mock-heroically, her feeling that ordinary existence is itself a matter of closed-off ideals and gargantuan struggle rather than of mastery even over one's private domain. Even sleep is a middle region of contention rather than a gravity-free respite from daily troubles. That middle region occupies the middle stanza of the poem, which is denied the neat rhymed couplets that round off the first and last stanzas. Yet surely Bishop also intended the reader to remember that the Place de la Concorde, the scene that opens and closes the poem, was the site of the guillotine and the end of utopian views of the French revolution. Dream and sleep provide opportunities for manipulation of perspective and scale easily naturalized in the theme.

Bishop produced more interesting results when she employed the surrealist device of the mirror. Indeed, the mirror became a lasting motif in her poetry. Within this motif Bishop was able to explore many aspects of representation and, especially in the early poetry, self-reflection. Within the mirror the self could no longer be defined as a region of interior, perspectiveless infinity. If the mirror objectified and divided the self, it also reversed the natural order, suggesting an imaginative space in which necessity was not master. But even more than dream, the mirror image remains tied to its antecedent reality, not a fixed image but one constantly affected by the fluency of the world before it.

"The Gentleman of Shalott" (CP, 9–10), Bishop's comment on Tennyson's famous poem, particularly reveals the limits of reflective doubling as a tool of mastery. The Lady of Shalott sees the world as "shadows" in her mirror, which she then weaves into her fixed tapestry; her demise comes when Lancelot enters the mirror scene and compels her gaze down to Camelot. This encounter with reality, this turn away from the detached, controlled world of shadows, shatters the mirror and leads to her death. But she was already "Half sick of shadows," and thus her rejection of the mirror is inevitable. Tennyson tells a story of art's failure to resist destiny, of the danger of living in the half-life of reflection. The Gentleman of Shalott sees things a little differently, and Bishop treats her subject with benevolent humor rather than melodrama. The question of outer reality does not even arise for him. For the Gentleman, who thinks he is half mirror, at least "at present" "half is enough." He lives straddled between reality and the mirror, between, perhaps, an experiential and reflected self, even before the world outside the self is considered. And because the anterior self is not stable or unified but subject to flux, the reflected self is never fixed in a single perspective or merged with the source of reflection. This self-division is one theme of "The Gentleman of Shalott." Bishop clearly mocks him for his narcissistic self-absorption (touted as modesty), and one reading of "half is enough" might be that self-reflection has actually diminished him. He cannot even clearly distinguish reality and illusion. He might better seek his other half in the world, as the Lady did, though that positive encounter with the real destroyed her. While the poem dramatizes the perils of narcissism, too many lines in the middle of the poem suggest Bishop's positive identification with the Gentleman. "That constant state of readjustment" accounts for the exhilaration in many of her poems, and the realism they project. Bishop is sympathetic with the notion that our sense of reality is somehow destabilized by the phenomenon of the mirror and by the representational nature of mind which vainly aspires to the mirror's reflecting powers. As symbolic creatures, we are indeed "half looking-glass."

By contemplating himself in this way the Gentleman evades the impact of the actual mirror on the self. He avoids recognizing his existence in the world. The speaker in the riddle poem "To Be Written on the Mirror in Whitewash" (CP, 205) shows less confidence than the proud Gentleman who "wishes to be quoted." Here the mirror has the disturbing effect of presenting the self as something out there, subject to what else is out there, rather than the neatly contained, "economical" identity of the interior being.

> I live only here, between your eyes and you,
> But I live in your world. What do I do?
> —Collect no interest—otherwise what I can;
> Above all I am not that staring man.

While a slight poem in its own right, this epigram introduces the concern about self as subject and object, as conscious and represented being, that is central to many later poems, particularly "In the Waiting Room." Here the mirror raises the question of who the "I" is "between your eyes and you" but does not supply the answer. Indeed, in raising the question it resists confining answers. "Above all, I am not that staring man" (presumably, the image in the mirror). But this disavowal invites us to include rather than exclude the notion of the self as external being. The "here" the writer designates has no spatial register, however. The "I" seems to exist only as an effect of the writing itself and is thus inherently unstable.[11]

In "Insomnia" (CP, 70) the mirror becomes explicitly tied to displacements of perspective. In this poem Bishop welcomes rather than rejects the mirror image, for in it she can contemplate a "world inverted" where the facts of reality are transformed. She imagines a point of view from the mirror out into the world. This proves a very unstable projection, however, and the mirror image itself ultimately contradicts it.

> The moon in the bureau mirror
> looks out a million miles
> (and perhaps with pride, at herself,
> but she never, never smiles)
> far and away beyond sleep, or
> perhaps she's a daytime sleeper.
>
> By the Universe deserted,
> *she*'d tell it to go to hell,
> and she'd find a body of water,
> or a mirror, on which to dwell.
> So wrap up care in a cobweb
> and drop it down the well
>
> into that world inverted
> where left is always right,
> where the shadows are really the body,

where we stay awake all night,
where the heavens are shallow as the sea
is now deep, and you love me.

The shifts in scale and perspective in this poem ultimately lead away from the sense of mastery that generates them in the speaker's imagination. The cosmic moon is brought into the space of the speaker's room, but instead of absorbing the moon's imagined power of defiance, the speaker finds her loneliness given cosmic proportions. Care may be wrapped up in a cobweb, but the well in which it is dropped becomes the deep sea by the end of the poem. By multiplying the mirrors, making the desired world an infinite regress, Bishop ultimately corrects the ideal inversion the moon boasts and brings the speaker ironically back to her own real deprivation. The moon, on which the speaker projects a solution to her loneliness, is already reflected in the bureau mirror. So if the moon finds "a mirror on which to dwell," the speaker is even further away from an original light. Other features of the poem mark its resistance to the neat inversion the speaker longs for. The ballad form is disturbed in the first and last stanzas by final lines that deviate from the set rhythm and rhyme. Even in the middle stanza the three rhymes (hell, dwell, well) are hardly optimistic ("well" a kind of pun which cancels positive meaning). The infinite well of reflection in which she plunges her cares becomes itself a kind of hell. We expect the closing couplet to complete the inversion, to tie off the alternating rhymes in a neat antithesis. But Bishop forestalls this closure by the surprising enjambment which brings the poem back to present reality from a conditional future. "Where the heavens are shallow as the sea / is now deep, and you love me." And even that conditional future is not strictly oppositional. Certainly in the mirror image "left is always right," but more invention is required to claim that "the shadows are really the body" (if anything, the mirror would have the opposite effect, turning body to shadow, so she is describing an inversion of the mirror, not the mirror inversion). And since the poem is called "Insomnia" presumably the speaker herself is already "awake all night," so that inversion is not at issue so much as inclusion (she would have her unrequiting lover stay awake with her). This contradicts her earlier identification with the moon's solution to its cosmic loneliness (rejection of the world), a solution the speaker, in her particular human and emotional situation, cannot embrace. Indeed, Bishop's poetry, especially in *Geography III,* becomes a critique of the idealization of solitude. The moon does not become a focus of identification and alternative companionship for the insomniac speaker, but rather a force reminding her just how impossible her desires are. The haughty moon herself (in the bureau mirror) finds solace by looking out "a million miles" at her own face. The speaker remains undoubled. Sir Philip Sidney found, by projecting himself onto the moon, a fellow sufferer who might recognize the injustice done to him in a sublunary world of inverted values (*Astrophel and Stella,* no. 31). Bishop's "Insomnia" answers that the modern poet, or the female poet, finds no such narcissistic company in her misery.

These and other images of reflection, like dream images, offered Bishop opportunities to explore shifts of scale, inversions of natural order, and the division or doubling of the self. They also opened up unsettling questions about the relation of inner to outer self, of imagination to reality, questions suggesting that representation offered only precarious and dependent shadows. Stylistically, dream and mirror devices offered Bishop early opportunities to introduce antimimetic elements into a mimetic context, a major feature of her later style. But such mechanical tropes are far less persuasive than the fluent exploration of spatial and temporal perspective that characterizes Bishop's descriptive poems. She does not attempt to map the various angles of vision and casts of light onto some aggregate truth of representation or some controlling myth outside time and space. The objects of the visible world, freed from customary sight, become open to imagination while still belonging to reality. Rejecting distinctions between inside and outside, unconscious and conscious states, so insistent but problematic in the dream and mirror poems, Bishop's descriptions spread subjectivity out across a visual surface rather than centering it in opposition to the visual, as something absolute which can endow it with meaning.[12] She turned, that is, to "glimpses of the always-more-successful surrealism of everyday life."[13]

Among the early descriptive poems, "Pleasure Seas" (CP, 195–196) shows the direction of Bishop's later work. The poem begins with a kind of liquid mirror, a swimming pool, in which the world is fluent but framed. As in "Insomnia," the poet turns from the mirror to the sea, still a reflective surface, now deep and unmasterable. But the shifts of perspective arise first in the representation of an outer reality rather than serving simply as tropes of an inner reality.

The poet moves through several perspectival frames on her way to the infinite perspective of the sea. While no single beholder speaks in the poem, the movement through various perspectives creates a dynamic of visual thinking that gives a reality to the poem and the poet as beholder. The poem presents the careless, dangerous atmosphere of human "pleasure" and affection, but this concern remains bound to a description of the resort landscape in which such pleasures and dangers are cultivated. "Pleasure Seas" follows a visual and emotional rhythm which Bishop takes up more self-consciously in later poems, but which even here gives a continuity to the fragmented point of view. Its logic of color—from variegated to opalescent to white—parallels the opening of perspective from discrete frames to indeterminacy and flux. Thus she achieves a pattern for the poem without establishing a mastering perspective.

Before it directs the mind's eye out, first to the view of an airplane overhead, then to the solitude of the reefs where the holiday fantasies are shattered, the poem describes a resort scene.[14]

> In the walled off swimming-pool the water is perfectly
> flat.
> The pink Seurat bathers are dipping themselves in and
> out
> Through a pane of bluish glass.
> The cloud reflections pass

Huge amoeba-motions directly through
The beds of bathing caps: white, lavender, and blue.
If the sky turns gray, the water turns opaque,
Pistachio green and Mermaid Milk.

As in "Love Lies Sleeping" and so frequently in later poems, Bishop begins with a highly artificial, controlled image (often described in terms of a visual artist's forms) which she immediately sets about dissolving. Here she communicates the unreality of the scene in the pictorial flatness and fairy-tale coloring. At first reality is broken down into distinct colors, as in Seurat. The funny "amoeba-motions" of the clouds pass through but do not affect the pretty garden formed by the beds of bathing caps. This opening suggests Stevens' "Sea Surface Full of Clouds," and, like Stevens, Bishop will move out from this frame to other, darker, and less stable interpretations (though visually based, rather than grammatically based, as in Stevens.) These are already hinted in the graying of the bright water as clouds pass over. Bishop's travel notes indicate that the description assigned to the swimming pool originally belonged to the sea, so we may think of the swimming pool as a very controlled version of the sea (since the poem is called "Pleasure Seas"). On September 6, 1938, she records: "The sea lay, a flat, indifferent floor of pistachio-green, reflecting the sunset a little," but she chooses to transfer this color to the pool. On November 24, 1938, for instance, she writes: "At the swimming pool the sky was heavy blue—huge clouds—the water pale opaque green. *In* it, looking only at the surface, it was whitened and grayed by clouds." On November 25 she continues: "At the swimming pool cloud-reflections like huge amoebas—amoeba-motions in the water." March 4, 1938, reads: "Swimming at the pool the water was the palest, opaque green— Mermaid Milk."[15] But all this effort to establish exact coloring is yielded up to a dazzling, iridescent sea. The eye abandons this focus and visual control. It moves "out among the keys" where the water is not walled off but goes its own way "mingling currents and tides / In most of the colors that swarm around the sides / Of soap-bubbles, poisonous and fabulous." The passage anticipates the dissolution of pictorial colors in "Over 2,000 Illustrations and a Complete Concordance" (CP, 57–59) into the "watery prismatic white-and-blue" which leads to the disorder of memory. But this is not a Baudelairean mingling of correspondence. The image of the soap bubble suggests how fragile controlled perspective is; as the previously distinct colors swarm on it, they almost explode it. The bubble is "fabulous," imagining the unreality of the scene, but also suggesting a freedom from boundaries and determinate measures to which Bishop will often be drawn. Here, having moved from framed to apparently frameless space (as a soap bubble bursts in the air), Bishop entertains another mastering perspective, that of the airplane. From this view reality looks like a map; the beholder sees "the water's heavy sheet / Of glass above a bas-relief." But this perspective, which celebrates expansion ("the sea means *room*") without yielding control, is threatened by the sudden intensity of the red bell-buoy, though again there is a certain attraction in this danger. Bishop treats danger pastorally here, as if one could play dangerously within a fantasy of space: the sea is a well-ventilated ballroom, another soap bubble. But the clouds, shadows, and warnings which have been part of the surface attraction are also foreboding. Increasingly the poem's comic mood becomes ominous, its diction more somber, though always detached.

Bishop does not locate the consciousness of danger within any single perspective of the poem. In order to entertain it she must revert to a perspectiveless, allegorical language of Love and Grief. The highly irregular tetrameter lines that run throughout the poem become more conspicuous:

> Pleasures strike off humming, and skip
> Over the tinsel surface: a Grief floats off
> Spreading out thin like oil. And Love
> Sets out determinedly in a straight line,
> One of his burning ideas in mind,
> Keeping his eyes on

The bright horizon,
But shatters immediately, suffers refraction,
and comes back in shoals of distraction.

The poem ends with a recapitulation of its various limited perspectives (in which the world seemed controlled) and then adds another, inhuman one which shatters the rest. Such a moment will recur in later poems, in which Bishop imagines a perspectiveless, frameless freedom equivalent to obliteration.

And out there where the coral reef is a shelf
The water runs at it, leaps, throws itself
Lightly, lightly, whitening in the air:
An acre of cold white spray is there
Dancing happily by itself.

At its close, the poem rests outside human concerns, turning instead to nature's easy tolerance of mutability, and to the white color of obliteration. The perspective of the poem does not offer an alternative to these forms of blindness and indifference. The unhappy perspective of the omniscient reader, for whom all love's dreams are shattered, is only allegorically and ironically presented.[16]

Many of Bishop's early descriptive poems lack an individual perspective. The poet is like the storm in "Little Exercise," "roaming the sky uneasily / like a dog looking for a place to sleep in" (CP, 41). Rather than sustaining one perspectival identity which can then shift or reorient itself, she seems to drop in on a number of limited perspectives, and then abandon them. And yet this poetic freedom never becomes entirely detached or abstract; it seeks an orientation and makes the poem the scene of that search.

Indeed, the ambition of the poet to tolerate multiple and fluent perspectives is often cast as something outside the world of actual beholders. More often, the contention of perspectives in a struggle for dominance is the subject of Bishop's poems. In such poems irony substitutes for inclusive and dynamic vision. "Seascape" (CP, 40), for instance, provides a simple, ironic contrast of two limited perspectives, one celestial, one diabolical, one representing day, the other night. The first half of the poem, a "L'Allegro" vision of the "celestial" seascape, directs all the lines of the description upward. Bishop subverts this optimistic perspective by comically revealing its rhetoricity—"white herons got up as angels, / . . . bird-droppings / like illumination in silver." We are many removes from ocular precision in "this cartoon by Raphael for a tapestry for a Pope," this freehand artifice toward celestial ornament. Description here defines everything according to one perspective, making bird-drop-pings into illuminations in silver. Bishop juxtaposes to this view the mutually intolerant and similarly excessive downward view of aus-terity and "weightiness." The light-house view refuses to enjoy the details of life and concerns itself with moral depth. The "skeletal lighthouse," obsessed with danger and warning, is "got up" "in black and white clerical dress," to preach damnation. Darkness as a source of truth gets no more credence in the poem than does light: "and when it gets dark he will remember something / strongly worded to say on the subject." The poet's point of view here can only be one of impersonal irony, but the source of the poem suggests a different perspective. According to Bishop's notes for a poetry reading, she was "out in a small inboard motorboat, fishing in the evening, in that harbor where Stevens dreamed of living on a houseboat." This view from the midst of things is forfeited in favor of ironic detachment. But later Bishop will present experiential perspectives that shift and merge rather than merely compete.

Two poems of Bishop's mid-career, "Filling Station" (CP, 127–128) and "Twelfth Morning; or What You Will" (CP, 110–111), demonstrate her development of immediate beholders. These poems record feelings and emotions in response to direct observation rather than detached reflection or description. They express strong per-spectives and attitudes, yet remain open to deviating details and alternative views of reality. These do not lead to a third, integrated perspective, nor to ironic awareness, but rather to questions and uncertainties.

Bishop begins "Filling Station" (CP, 127–128) in an attitude of class revulsion. She views the world of the filling station from outside it, with an air of superiority, and her first two sentences suggest a mind made up, a rigid, uniform perspective on the world she beholds:

> Oh, but it is dirty!
> —this little filling station,
> oil-soaked, oil-permeated
> to a disturbing, over-all
> black translucency.

From a fastidious, female perspective she observes the male world of greasy sons and their father with an initial response of disgust and caution, accented by trochaic variations in the iambic trimeter. "Be careful with that match!" But gradually she imagines the scene from behind it, as a plausible home. An attempt, however comic or pathetic, has been made to modify the over-all black translucency. The humor in the poem is as much at her own expense as at the expense of the crude gestures of mother-love she observes.

The scene is already less brutal in the sight of the poet as she discovers it is a "family filling station." Her eye recedes from the coarsely sexual "pumps" to the porch and its "grease- / impregnated wickerwork." Masculine "grease" invades the feminine world, but also softens it, judging by the "dirty dog, quite comfy" on the porch. This is a place of nurture and shelter, not immunity. The poet cannot quite reconcile these elements as her missing maternal counterpart presumably does, but her puzzled attention to decorative details betrays her attraction to this family despite class differences. She can recognize the sensibility behind the details, thus can specify the taboret and see that it is part of a set, the doily, rhyming as it does with oily, nevertheless "Embroidered in daisy stitch / with marguerites." The begonia is hairy, the crochet is gray, but they are not preposterous. The feminine, marked by differences of diction and image, becomes the extraneous element in this greasy world (whereas the filling station had suggested a brutal affront to the speaker's propriety). The invisible mother is a kind of poet, who makes a shabby beauty in and from filth. The poet has begun to entertain this point of view. Doily, taboret, extraneous plant indicate a creative impulse, a "note of color" rather than a controlling or disguising impulse. The humble character of the ornaments and the sampler rhetoric they inspire in the speaker ("Somebody loves us all") do not undercut their value. These are not signs of mastery but of small attempts at aesthetic order which express affection.

To those who wish to read Bishop as a poet of terror and darkness, these comforts along the highway form a significant challenge. There is something redeeming about these naive efforts at decoration. The poem's final observation, "Somebody loves us all," may be sardonic ("only a mother . . .") but "Somebody" might, in a broader sense, imply a divine perspective in which the filth and the ornament are reconciled. But this final assertion does not really answer the questions raised in the penultimate stanza:

> Why the extraneous plant?
> Why the taboret?
> Why, oh why, the doily?

The observer tries to make sense of what she sees, revising her perspective. "Somebody" still leaves the question "who?"

In "Twelfth Morning; or What You Will" (CP, 110–111) the issue contrasting perspectives is explicitly one of class. The poem turns on a Shakespearean comparison of perspectives between classes. It also invokes, mock-heroically, the traditional Christian inversion in which the meek shall inherit the earth and a poor infant become King of the Jews. Bishop names the poor black child Balthazar, after one of the three wise men. He bears on his head a can which shines like the star of Bethlehem. The poet, from the dominant class but not a landlord, sees poverty as a kind of chaos threatening the order of things. But her dominant perspective is "dozing," and through the haze of it she entertains another, alternative outlook.

> Like a first coat of whitewash when it's wet,
> the thin gray mist lets everything show through:
> The black boy Balthazar, a fence, a horse,

a foundered house,

—cement and rafters sticking from a dune.
(The Company passes off these white but shopworn
dunes as lawns.) "Shipwreck," we say; perhaps
    this is a housewreck.

Instead of the "overall black translucency" of "Filling Station" we
have a "whitewash," exposing the exploitative intention of the
white-owned company that would pass off dunes for lawns. The
dominant public "we" shakes its head condescendingly at the plight
of the poor blacks, and gloats in its candid renaming of the village
as a "housewreck." But as the poet becomes more individual her
stance is less complacent and her perspective changes. As she opens
herself to the apparent disorder of the scene, she gets unexpectedly
involved with the alternative vision of the poor. At first this shift is
rendered as an aural pathetic fallacy—the scene is no longer an
affront but, against the backdrop of the indifferent sea, an uncertain
source of pity and fellow feeling.

The sea's off somewhere, doing nothing. Listen.
An expelled breath. And faint, faint, faint
(or are you hearing things), the sandpipers'
    heart-broken cries.

As if marking her new attunement to sounds in the landscape,
Bishop introduces more punctuation into the middle of lines,
marking an attentive, hesitant voice attempting to connect with the
scene in new ways.

As she returns to visual experience without the defenses of class
detachment, she describes a scene which won't be fixed in a certain
point of view. The fence no longer defines fixed differences, but
becomes "dotted lines" which waver and turn, making a mockery
of the company's pretense of "lawns." The big white horse, possibly
a parody of the company, is "bigger than the house," but his
dominance, indeed his placement, is dubious.

Don't ask the big white horse, *Are you supposed*
to be inside the fence or out? He's still
asleep. Even awake, he probably
   remains in doubt.

Bishop often makes brilliant use of her pallette to define the moods
and qualities of her poems. Here she marks the gradual ascendancy
and dignity of the poor through a gradation from whitewash mist,
to a "pewter-colored horse," to the tin can turned star in the
imagination of Balthazar. From his innocent perspective (which for
the poet is highly dubious), "the world's a pearl, *and I, / I am / its*
highlight." The indifferent sea is now "slap-slapping" water in the
can, and the heartbroken cries of the sandpipers have been drowned
out by the boy's proud singing.

What is the final perspective of this poem? Is this Blakean irony,
innocence juxtaposed to experience, in which Balthazar cannot see
the oppression that afflicts him, and the speaker sees only the
oppression? Or does Bishop attempt to establish a dignity for
poverty even as she protests the structures that perpetuate it? As in
several of her poems, Bishop holds a unique point of view here,
critical of the landlord class and what it perpetrates, yet detached
from the fantasies of the poor as well. What kind of epiphany does
the poet experience on this "twelfth morning" (the traditional Feast
of the Epiphany)? Balthazar makes his claim for happiness despite
the poet's scorn of the mess that surrounds him. The fence cannot
keep him out. "Twelfth Morning" presents a rather bleak view of
life in Cabo Frio, but entertains that view with a humility that
acknowledges alternative perspectives not its own.

Point of view and perspective are fundamental aspects of the
observational poetry Bishop created. She began with simple perspectival studies that offered thematic possibilities: a highway in
"From the Country to the City" (CP, 13) imagined at night as a
demonic clown, a "View of the Capitol from the Library of Congress" (CP, 69) in which the pompous, imperial ceremony dissipates
in the breeze. She worked with simple juxtapositions—gull, cloud,
and man viewing the sea with varying degrees of false confidence

or panic in "The Unbeliever" (CP, 22), man and man-moth differently viewing the moon and its effects in "The Man-Moth" (CP, 14–15). In these poems the poet remains fairly detached from the various perspectives she considers. Her early descriptive poems often roam cinematically, taking on several angles of vision but settling on none, though I do not agree with David Kalstone that they seem therefore without a beholder. Yet as Bishop developed, the taking on of perspective seemed increasingly necessary to poetic identity and to the realism of the poem (as an experience rather than an illustration). At the same time, she was not satisfied with fixed or centered perspectives. What she gradually created were points of view that discovered or acknowledged their inadequacy, that expressed uncertainty or need and could not account for everything before them. Such open or unresolved perspectives allowed the poet to define the limits of despair as well as complacent optimism.

Even in poems which are not particularly visual, Bishop's tropes tend to be perspectival ones. The world can be inverted, imagined from a detached height, seen from the impassive, immobile stance of a mountain, or judged by a solipsist. Conversely, her special perspectives tend to generate trope in the poems, as when a city seen from an airplane looks as if it were burning, or when a suspension of scale allows a typewriter to appear as a besieged village. Thus Bishop's imagination both determines angles of vision and invents through them. This perspectival basis of interpretation and metaphor means that the imagined world is always connected to the seen world. I will examine a number of these shifts in perspective as I consider later poems under different contexts. But one relatively early poem, "Invitation to Miss Marianne Moore" (CP, 82–83), reveals Bishop's ability to entertain perspectives other than her own, indeed, to acknowledge the need for them without simply embracing them.

An "invitation" (like the many letters Bishop would explicitly or implicitly write in the form of poems) implies the interaction of two points of view. In this case the poet's point of view is one of confusion and vulnerability. She invokes Moore's stance of moral and perceptual mastery. The gesture of invitation rather than challenge or homage is itself significant in relation to an earlier poet. This is not a contest of perspectives, in which one voice must dominate another, but an acknowledgment of lack and a call for support. "From Brooklyn, over the Brooklyn Bridge, on this fine morning, / please come flying." Indeed, Moore becomes a kind of aerial spirit, bringing lightness into a drab world. But Bishop's perspective makes Moore's meaningful. Both are important.

The poem readies the world for the ceremonial visit. The ordinary scene is metamorphosed in expectation of poetic presence. Bishop is absorbing Moore's own sensibility, already defining nature as art:

> Enter: two rivers, gracefully bearing
> countless little pellucid jellies
> in cut-glass epergnes dragging silver chains.

Moore herself appears oxymoronically as a good witch or necessary angel, at once gracing the world with imaginative glitter and casting a moral eye over its stains. She has a "slight censorious frown and blue ribbons," wears an austere black cape "full of butterfly wings and bon-mots." Such Mozartean conjunctions of light and dark, of moral seriousness and aesthetic delight, mirror Moore's art. Bishop admires her ability to see the world as it is without being crushed by it, admires her "natural heroism" by which she can hear a higher music and connect the good with the beautiful.

> Mounting the sky with natural heroism,
> above the accidents, above the malignant movies,
> the taxicabs and injustices at large,
> while horns are resounding in your beautiful ears
> that simultaneously listen to
> a soft uninvented music, fit for the musk deer,
>   please come flying.

Moore's art tames the brute world and raises it out of lassitude: the lions outside the library follow her through the doors to the reading rooms, the grim museums "behave like courteous male bower-birds." Moore believes in a divine order (heard in the uninvented music), and her perspective is thus a confident, optimistic one.

But Bishop seems less confident about what ultimate impact such a "daytime comet" will have on the world. When she offers her invited guest various entertainments, they seem incommensurate with the pleasure of her company:

> We can sit down and weep: we can go shopping,
> or play at a game of constantly being wrong
> with a priceless set of vocabularies,
> or we can bravely deplore, but please
>   please come flying.

Is this Bishop's reminder about the limits of art? The options are not as arbitrary as the list makes them sound. They describe the sadness of the world, its consumerism, but also the pleasure Moore takes in picking and choosing. They describe Moore's relentless accuracy (which to Bishop, as to Stevens, may have a tragic dimension), and they describe her courage.

Bishop manages to be similarly specific, in this apparently whimsical piece, about the techniques she admires in Moore which facilitate her transformation. The "inaudible abacus" is of course Moore's syllabic method. The "dynasties of negative constructions" are Moore's double negatives which render positives and her ironic reversals. Moore's poetry generates something indeed "unnebulous" (not yet obvious), but still celestial. Yet Bishop has maintained her own perspective in this poem as well, not only visually but aurally, in a form (borrowed from Neruda but made her own) unlike anything one would find in Moore's poetry. Out of Moore's enchanting presence, Bishop sees, as in all her poems, a corrupt world seething underneath compelling surfaces. But her skepticism never dampens her genuine appreciation of Moore's spirit and perspective—rather, it heightens the need for them.

Bishop is not Marianne Moore, the daytime comet above the world, reimagining it in terms of moral and aesthetic ideals. Her glance is always within the world, partial, troubled, inquiring. Repeatedly her eye confronts a terrifying darkness, an "entire night" along its path, but turns from it, toward life and movement. These perspectives suggest a way of knowing and experiencing the world which mediates between the darkness of utter skepticism and dread, on the one hand, and the solipsistic illusion of mastery or transcendence, on the other.

Bishop's experiments with odd and multiple perspectives, with radical shifts of frame and scale, with temporal conditions of observation, provide her with the visual language for representing a fluent, temporal subjectivity. Through her inventive use of scale and perspective she brings the eye into the poem, rather than making description an illustration of the eye's prior experience, or a posture of the self or the mind. She creates a dynamic pictorial reality rather than an illustrative realism.

Attractive Mortality

Nothing disarms us like the violation of categories we assume are secure ("life/death, right/wrong, male/female"). Bishop's poems are full of little revolts against decorum. Questions of mastery arose in the last chapter with regard to perspective. Those addressed here concern images and associations that cross conventional boundaries to challenge complacent or repressive thought. In particular, this chapter considers poems about organic process and our ambivalence toward it. Bishop presents objects undergoing convergence and mutation in a way that is disturbing, even frightening, but can also be exhilarating. She further presents the forces—psychological, social, political—that work to suppress such a process.

Bishop objected, in a letter to Robert Lowell, to the overemphasis of her contemporaries (Lowell in particular) on "this suffering business."[1] Her own way is not to deny suffering or one's distaste for a brutal world, but to locate it in terms of the larger world of change. And in a letter to Anne Stevenson she wrote, alluding to George Herbert: "My outlook is pessimistic. I think we are still barbarians . . . But I think we should be gay in spite of it, sometimes even giddy,—to make life endurable and to keep ourselves 'new, tender, quick.'"[2] It is this effort to remain "new, tender, quick" (and perhaps, as a consequence, to relinquish mastery), that accounts for much of Bishop's use of the grotesque. We tend to associate this style with Poe or Mary Shelley, with nightmares of uncontrollable, unnatural, demonic power, whether from inside or outside the human soul. Bishop's style is more deeply ambivalent and undecidable than this tradition of morbidity and horror.[3] Certainly there is a subversive element in her violations of decorum, but most often it is tied to a representational aim. She emphasizes the betweenness of seeing form against conflicting form, the perceptual challenge of the world as process. The grotesque style brings together (without resolution) the categories our minds and our culture like to keep apart. Bishop expresses mixed feelings of attraction and revulsion toward the subversions of form that mark the organic world. Her appeal as a poet includes this honest expression of mixed feelings, a matter both of tone and representation.

With disarming nonchalance Bishop confesses in "Memories of Uncle Neddy," "I am very fond of molds and mildews" (CPR, 228). Like anyone else she does what she can to keep them back, wiping off the portraits often, to preserve them for posterity, yet she admits to a certain delight in the advance of these transmogrifying growths over the domestic protections of walls, furniture, clothing:

> I love the dry-looking, gray-green dust, like bloom on fruit, to begin with, that suddenly appears here on the soles of shoes in the closet, on the backs of all the black books, or the darkest ones, in the bookcase. And I love the black shadow, like the finest soot, that suddenly shows up, slyly, on white bread, or white walls. The molds on food go wild in just a day or two, and in a hot, wet spell like this, a tiny jungle, green, chartreuse, and magenta, may start up in a corner of the bathroom. That gray-green bloom, or that shadow of fine soot, is just enough to serve as a hint of morbidity, attractive morbidity—although perhaps mortality is a better word. The gray-green suggests life, the sooty shadow—although living, too—death and dying.

That complex hint of mortality is everywhere in Bishop's poetry, intruding with its gray-green bloom and black soot upon the white world that the mind and the culture set up against it. Unruly life, which includes death and dying, asserts itself despite our efforts to contain it. Bishop's grotesque style reveals her ambivalence about opening protective forms to life's processes: repellent and attractive, awful and cheerful, frightening and beautiful at once. Pain often accompanies this openness, yet the rewards are amply displayed. If Bishop expresses the inevitable shock and resistance before that which challenges fixed perceptions, she also expresses an exuberance and freedom in that challenge. Her attention rests on the margins and thresholds which designate the limits of the known and the burgeoning of new orders from the contradictory ones.

Bishop's earliest poems are not concerned with organic process as such. Instead, they tend to take natural images as symbols of the human spirit asserting itself against fixed forms and forces of mechanization. "Cirque d'Hiver," "The Man-Moth," and "The Weed" form a sequence toward the increased identification of the human spirit with natural flux. In "The Fish" and "Roosters" Bishop confronts the urge to master nature; together these poems contrast the consequences of relinquishing or asserting power. All of these early poems form around central icons, but challenge the conceptual unity of the icon through their metamorphic and hybrid features. Bishop is better known as a descriptive poet, but her mimetic surfaces are similarly full of contradictions. Her observations—in "A Cold Spring," "Faustina, or Rock Roses," "The Shampoo," "The Armadillo," and others—represent a variety of responses to the mutable body. In each poem Bishop juxtaposes the beautiful with the awful, the morbid with the vital, aesthetic pleasure with moral indignation, in ways that challenge our conventional responses to life. Through Manuelzinho, the Pink Dog, and other misfits she confronts her own ambivalence about spiritual and corporeal deviance. She can write with sympathy about the desire to order or transcend the mess of life; but she writes with even more passion about the terrible, "barbaric" implications of our efforts to deny life or suppress it.[4]

In the early poems of *North & South* the grotesque style arises, rather conventionally, to describe an inner being asserting itself against material and social limits. The mechanical toy of "Cirque d'Hiver" (CP, 31) suggests Bishop's early sense of dichotomies in human experience which are uncomfortably joined. The toy grimly mimics a horse and dancer from the Paris Winter Circus:

> Across the floor flits the mechanical toy,
> fit for a king of several centuries back.
> A little circus horse with real white hair.
> His eyes are glossy black.
> He bears a little dancer on his back.
>
> She stands upon her toes and turns and turns.
> A slanting spray of artificial roses
> is stitched across her skirt and tinsel bodice.
> Above her head she poses
> another spray of artificial roses.
>
> His mane and tail are straight from Chirico.
> He has a formal, melancholy soul.
> He feels her pink toes dangle toward his back
> along the little pole
> that pierces both her body and her soul
>
> and goes through his, and reappears below,
> under his belly, as a big tin key.
> He canters three steps, then he makes a bow,
> canters again, bows on one knee,
> canters, then clicks and stops, and looks at me.
>
> The dancer, by this time, has turned her back.
> He is the more intelligent by far.
> Facing each other rather desperately—
> his eye is like a star—
> we stare and say, "Well, we have come this far."

The yearning marionette and the mechanical dancer are stock figures of Romantic and symbolist imagination, suggesting the captivity of an infinite human spirit in deterministic being. Hoffman and Kleist come to mind as well as de Chirico. Here, more specifically, Bishop depicts the problem of the artist, who can perhaps achieve a gleam of the genuine but whose aspirations exceed his formal means. She hobbles her form with monosyllables and identical rhymes as if to turn the poem itself into a clumsy machine which winds down at the end. "I think the title referred more to the mood than anything else," Bishop told Anne Stevenson.[5] This is indeed a wintry poem. The little horse seems doomed, even if he is more comic than tragic.

The poem turns to include the speaker at the end, and to suggest a mutuality between herself and the horse, whose "glossy black" eye is now "like a star," a symbol, perhaps, of the speaker's aspirations.[6] "We have come this far," remarks the little horse at the end of the poem. The "we" may refer to the horse and the speaker, in which case they are collaborating intelligences. Or perhaps the "we" refers to the artist and the shadow of himself and his aspirations that gleams through the artifice of the work and exceeds the performance of its formal devices, symbolized in the dancer. The little horse has "real white hair," here marking his authenticity rather than his corporeality. He is controlled by a "big tin key," perhaps symbolizing forces which also bind him to the duller and entirely artificial dancer, his burden and his pride. Thus his look is "desperate," implying he has come this far but may go no farther in realizing his sublime ambition. The beholder shares his desperation, suggesting that the big tin key runs through the artist as well as her work. Hers is no more a position of mastery than is the horse's. This opposition, of a transcendent ambition desperately curtailed by a mechanical universe, will be considerably altered in Bishop's later work, where natural flux is associated with freedom.

"Cirque d'Hiver" represents an extreme dichotomy already modified in "The Man-Moth" (CP, 14–15). While constructed of similar symbolic elements, the latter poem explores the terrors of the inner and outer life more complexly. The Man-Moth gets a step beyond the impasse of the little mechanical horse through a series of cracks and openings in the dehumanized surface, beginning with the title and its annotation : "newspaper misprint for mammoth."

The poem describes an imaginary creature, perhaps a symbol of the repressed psyche of urban man, which comes "to the surface" at night when the influence of conscious "man" diminishes. Like "Cirque d'Hiver," the poem contrasts a mechanized human figure and an animal endowed with human feeling and aspiration. But they are kept apart here for rhetorical purposes, permitting a more complex and ambivalent relationship at the end of the poem. Anesthetized "Man" is finally displaced by the reader, who may appropriate some emotion from the personified animal.

"The Man-Moth" begins with another image that could, with its manikins and shadows, be "straight from Chirico":

> Here, above,
> cracks in the buildings are filled with battered
>   moonlight.
> The whole shadow of Man is only as big as his hat.
> It lies at his feet like a circle for a doll to stand on,
> and he makes an inverted pin, the point magnetized to
>   the moon.

Doll-like "Man," brother to the artificial dancer, is here estranged from and unfamiliar with his desire. (Bishop's striking phrase "battered moonlight" describes the atmosphere of the modern imagination.)[7] Having suppressed his unconscious life to a mere hat-sized shadow, he is, paradoxically, paralyzed by his desire, "magnetized to the moon." An "inverted pin," he is not a mechanical pointer but an image of latent pain. He "does not see" the moon, and he is baffled by its "vast properties" because they cannot be recorded rationally. Bishop was interested in the comic hero of silent film, and "The Man-Moth" certainly owes a debt not only to Charlie Chaplin in his baggy black suit but to Buster Keaton in his big-brimmed hat. A draft Bishop wrote for a poem called "Keaton" suggests a prototype of "Man":

I will be good; I will be good.
I have set my small jaw for the ages.
and nothing can distract me from solving
the appointed emergencies
Even with my small brain
—witness the size of my hat-band the diameter of my
    hat band
and the depth of the crown of my hat.[8]

The Man-Moth scaling the building may in turn suggest Harold
Lloyd on his clock-face. The antithetical Man-Moth, all shadow, is
Bishop's earliest Pierrot and a significant variation on the stock
figure of grotesque literature. He is a more hopeful figure than
"Man," despite his absurd idealism.

                    But when the Man-Moth
pays his rare, although occasional, visits to the surface,
the moon looks rather different to him. He emerges
from an opening under the edge of one of the sidewalks
and nervously begins to scale the faces of the buildings.
He thinks the moon is a small hole at the top of the
    sky,
proving the sky quite useless for protection.
He trembles, but must investigate as high as he can
    climb.

                    Up the façades,
his shadow dragging like a photographer's cloth behind
    him,
he climbs fearfully, thinking that this time he will
    manage
to push his small head through that round clean
    opening
and be forced through, as from a tube, in black scrolls
    on the light.
(Man, standing below him, has no such illusions.)

> But what the Man-Moth fears most he must do,
>   although
> he fails, of course, and falls back scared but quite
>   unhurt.

Bishop employs a humorously inverted rhetoric in which rational man is "above" the diminutive, unmammoth-like Man-Moth, yet emotionally ignorant. But the adjustment of value is by no means absolute. While engaging our sympathy for the Man-Moth, Bishop repeatedly distances herself from his Romantic intensity. His vertical ambition is illusory, and man, now "below" him, is right not to believe that the moon is a small hole (the pinhole made by man, the pinhead?) through which he can transcend the finite world, defy gravity, and transform himself to pure inscription. The poem draws back from the agonistic vision of Shelley and Keats, whose psyche-moths immolate themselves on the flame of their desires, though it owes a great deal to both poets. But Bishop will establish the martyrdom of the Man-Moth on other terms.

The Man-Moth is more sympathetic as the post-Freudian under-ground figure, compelled to return to "the pale subways of cement he calls his home," obsessed with the past into which he is jolted "without a shift in gears or a gradation of any sort." He is drawn to a suicidal electric charge, figured as the third rail. Again Bishop resists melodrama, and undercuts romantic intensity, by humorously introducing the rational, practical world. "He has to keep / his hands in his pockets, as others must wear mufflers." The reduction of the suicidal urge to a fidget does not erase our sympathy, even our admiration for the Man-Moth. But it keeps us from thinking his shadow life can be a whole life, his idealism an appropriate vision or his inwardness a sufficient dwelling.

The success of this poem is established in the last of its six eight-line stanzas.

>   If you catch him,
>   hold up a flashlight to his eye. It's all dark pupil,
>   an entire night itself, whose haired horizon tightens

as he stares back, and closes up the eye. Then from the
    lids
one tear, his only possession, like the bee's sting, slips.
Slyly he palms it, and if you're not paying attention
he'll swallow it. However, if you watch, he'll hand it
    over,
cool as from underground springs and pure enough to
    drink.

Here Bishop gets beyond the antithesis of man and his shadow life and achieves an image of connection and expression alternative to the idealized "scrolls of light" because more real sacrifice and relief are involved. The impersonal, phallic but impotent "Man," the inverted pin, is displaced by the still distanced but more personal "you," a generalization offered to the reader of the speaker's own experience. The inverted pin is turned over to the Man-Moth, in whose possession it becomes a potent, vaguely phallic but also feminine tear, "like the bee's sting," painful to the receiver, perhaps fatal to the bestower, yet "cool as from underground springs and pure enough to drink." The beholder is now the questing hero, drinking the redemptive waters of expressed feeling. The introduction of two natural images (bee and underground spring) in this world of black, moonlight, and cement opens the poem's world even though these are only symbolic images. The Man-Moth is the sacrificial victim (the artist martyr?) in this ritual rejuvenation, however, since he puts all his ingenuity into hoarding the tear. He may not be "quite unhurt" this time, when self-expression replaces romantic idealism. But his "entire night" must be brought to light, must converge with the conscious life, whatever the consequences. He cannot hoard his emotion any more than he can transcend his physical world.

The intense ambivalence of Keats's "Ode on Melancholy" finds modern expression in this last stanza, in which the psyche-moth suffers after all. The beholder gazes into the Man-Moth's night eyes as Keats peers "deep, deep" upon the "peerless" eyes of his raging mistress. The beauty and joy the beholder extracts, in Keats "turning to Poison while the bee-mouth sips," combine with melancholy. The tear is both the draught of poison earlier evaded (in the subway scene in Bishop's poem) and a sign of redemptive waters. Like Keats, who warns "go not to Lethe," Bishop resists the usual association of melancholy with pain and death, only to rediscover its poison at the site of pleasure, to find danger associated with purity.

In "The Man-Moth," a poem born of hyphenation and error, Bishop creates a more truly liminal vision than was possible in the composite figure of the mechanical toy. The divided worlds of man and Man-Moth, of feeling and rationality, converge in the tone, imagery, and narrative of this poem. Their convergence is not a synthesis but a dynamic tension of frames that keep the mind "new, tender, quick." Bishop faces her undecidedness and ambivalence directly in "The Weed" (CP, 20–21). The experience of being divided is here the narrative focus; it effects the poem's tone and representational style. Indeed, there is almost no aspect of the poem which does not involve some form of convergence or division. While nature is still symbolic of a timeless, inner landscape, the details of the poem pressure its boundaries.

The poem describes a dream of death-like composure suddenly disrupted by inner turmoil. In the dream, a mental state of resolve and finality is represented as bodily stasis, even entombment. But the relationship between mind and body (here tenor and vehicle) is highly unstable.

> I dreamed that dead, and meditating,
> I lay upon a grave, or bed,
> (at least, some cold and close-built bower).
> In the cold heart, its final thought
> stood frozen, drawn immense and clear,
> stiff and idle as I was there;
> and we remained unchanged together
> for a year, a minute, an hour.

The spark of conflicting frames of meaning arises in the first two lines of the poem: "I dreamed that dead, and meditating / I lay upon a grave, or bed." Such ambiguities of inner/outer, conscious/unconscious, dreaming/waking states continue throughout the poem. The tension is temporarily suspended here by the motionless self who contemplates a "final thought" in a timeless dream. The uncertainty of "a year, a minute, an hour" seems only to emphasize the measureless quality of eternity. But the ambiguity of "grave or bed" and the contradiction in "dead and meditating" plants the seed of active division without a clear Christian context to resolve the paradox. As though to reinforce the effect of the words, Bishop introduces incidental rhymes into the much halted tetrameter lines, making the reader uncertain of what she will hear next.

Bishop represents the agency of the turmoil as a weed that springs up from the dreamer's breast:

> Suddenly there was a motion,
> as startling, there, to every sense
> as an explosion. Then it dropped
> to insistent, cautious creeping
> in the region of the heart,
> prodding me from desperate sleep.
> I raised my head. A slight young weed
> had pushed up through the heart and its
> green head was nodding on the breast.

While remaining a symbolic, abstract space of "final thought," the scene's disruption is felt "to every sense." The weed introduces narrative sequence into this eternal space. The dead self then raises her head without reviving (the heart changes but does not beat). These insistent contradictions express the ambiguity and ambivalence of the dream life, but Bishop repeatedly breaks the dream frame which tolerates them with parenthetical remarks of the conscious, remembering subject who struggles to resolve them. The weed releases two rivers ("with my own thoughts?") and ultimately divides the dreamer's previously frozen heart. The symbolic underground spring, expressed into "one tear" in "The Man-Moth," becomes a cascading river of thoughts which washes over the dreamed body and threatens to wash away the very weed-self that released it. Bishop controls the high drama of the dream with a matter-of-fact observer's voice (the wakened speaker's) chillingly detached from her own inner turmoil. That voice also suggests another line of division in this divisive poem.

"The Weed" still posits an inner region of perspectiveless self-hood, designated by the darkness of the dream space. But that region quickly becomes subject to penetration, flux, and even illumination. Bishop vaguely suggests gender distinctions here. In "The Weed" the male space of mental finality, of "stiff and idle" thoughts, is transformed to a female space of "the heart," its broken membranes and cascading streams associating the heart with the womb ("it split apart / and from it broke a flood of water"). She treats the weed as a newborn baby or a poem from the heart. The very dynamic, contradictory, and open nature of that psychological space denies static oppositions, of male/female, inner/outer, feeling/thought, body/mind, pain/pleasure, any rigid alignments of its images. While the natural imagery remains symbolic, its detail and emphasis predict the complex continuum of inner and outer geography which will characterize Bishop's mature work. At this point the natural imagery serves to emphasize the idea that inwardness is no retreat from mutability.

The most discomforting contradictions in the poem arise as Bishop details the physical features of the psychological space. While mind and body meet on a third, metaphoric plane of geology, they converge rather than synthesize. Two arterial or amniotic rivers flow into the externalized "black grains of earth," but also shower the weed with "thoughts." They also "glance" off from the sides, as if they were eyes, and the drops on the dreamer's eyes empower her with sight, even in the dark. Sight cannot simply be made a trope of insight; the dream is "in the dark" yet intensely visual.

The images continue to divide, as do the emotions they evoke. These streams also provide a sudden illumination within the darkness. "Assuredly, smooth as glass," they turn out to be mirrors and are themselves made of racing images.

> (As if a river should carry all
> the scenes that it had once reflected
> shut in its waters, and not floating
> on momentary surfaces.)

Having adjusted from the retentive "final thought" to the cascading streams, we discover within that flux a principle of retention. The weed is an unwelcome intruder upon the heart enclosed in antivital permanence, in "a close built bower." But while the violation of this spiritual stasis is unwanted, the untidy, tormenting weed is associated with refreshment and fertility. ("A few drops fell upon my face / and in my eyes, so I could see.") The bower is a grave, and the sleep in it is desperate. A tenderness develops for the "slight young weed," with its "graceful head" "nodding on the breast," almost washed away by the powerful stream. The stream, in turn, is attractive as it makes its way toward the equally "fine black grains of earth." Yet if a certain exhilaration develops over this inward mutability, it never entirely supplants the original feeling of invasion. A shudder accompanies the thought that this process will be endlessly repeated, that the weed grows "but to divide your heart again."

Bishop's "The Weed" remains undecidable in its representation. By contrast, George Herbert's "Love Unknown," which she acknowledged as the inspiration of this poem, depends upon an immutable force which controls the transformations of the heart. For Herbert, bodily torments remain symbols of the soul's torments, explainable within a specific tradition of Christian redemption. In Bishop, the inner life is defined by and inclusive of corporeal life; they are not simply parallel. No immutable force controls either. Herbert's imagery is violent (the heart is plucked from a bowl of fruit and thrown into a bloody font, then immersed in a boiling cauldron, then forced to lie on a bed of thorns). Bishop retains a landscape of flowers, streams, and cascades. Yet without the confidence in a higher authority, an ulterior system of meaning and value, this landscape is more disturbing than Herbert's. The weed moves "like a semaphore" whose meanings are not decodable. "The nervous roots / reached to each side; the graceful head / changed its position mysteriously, / since there was neither sun nor moon / to catch its young attention." The baptism does not revitalize anything, so that we cannot make the easy choice of life over death, but can only witness a transition from stasis to change. While Herbert's antagonistic God provides a context of righteous purpose (his apparent aggressions "all strive to mend, what you had marred"), Bishop's weed has no other motive than division. Behind that division may be Herbert's message, though, that change makes us "new, tender, quick."

"The Weed" demonstrates how even within a symbolist aesthetic Bishop binds the mental to the corporeal, which it cannot master. The parallel imagery of the last poem in "Songs for a Colored Singer" (CP, 47–51) reinforces this interpretation with a more explicit movement across the boundaries of internal and external reality. In this case the weed emerges as a consequence of "dew or tears" which have become "black seeds" and form a "conspiring root." What emerges is the "flower or fruit" of a face.

The ambiguity of equating tears and dew goes beyond a pathetic fallacy to link grief to natural metamorphosis. This association of dew and tears, of personal grief and nature's processes, persists throughout Bishop's career (in "Sestina," "Song for the Rainy Season," and several others). The analogy resists self-absorbing sorrow and suggests a more inclusive vision of loss as natural change, a *lacrimae rerum* imaged as rain. The "face" here emerges not as a source of the tears, not as some original realm of feeling, but as its fruit or flower. This face itself becomes quickly plural, "Like an army in a dream / the faces seem," connecting individual grief with the collective suffering of World War II. Thus while the poem remains, like "The Weed," highly figurative, it insists on locating feeling and identity within the world, not the isolate self. The consequence is a tonal tension—a delight and a terror. As dew, seed, and flower, as natural process, the vision is lovely. As tear, conspiring root, and face, it is frightening. The poem insists on this balance to the end, just as it insists on moving freely between human and natural forces and insists that the vision is not securely internal, but rather is (like the weed in the other poem) "too real to be a dream."

Near the time Bishop wrote "The Weed" she recorded a vision in her diary which, although it pursues a different narrative from that in "The Weed," includes some of the same imagery of memory and self-reflection within the larger flux of the world.

> The windows this evening were covered with hundreds of large, shining drops of rain, laid on the glass which was covered with steam on the inside. I went to look out, but could not. Instead I realized I could look into the drops, like so many crystal balls. Each bore traces of a relation or friend: several weeping faces slid away from mine, water plants and fish floated within other drops; watery jewels, leaves and insects magnified, and strangest of all, horrible enough to make me step quickly away, was one large drop containing a lonely, magnificent human eye, wrapped in its own tear.[9]

The image of the windows from which she cannot look out parallels the dream space of "The Weed." The self is projected into the world and, conversely, the mutable world enters the domain of the self. Bishop sees at the threshold, along the pane of glass. Each drop, while it falls, retains an image of some particular lost friend or object. The "crystal ball" raindrops reveal lost human connections, which fall along with vegetation, insect and animal life, in a general course of loss which neutralizes it. The vision returns to the human center, but in the most surreal manner, at the end. The human eye metaphysically "wrapped in its own tear" causes a shudder, for that organ of perception turns back to reflect the "lonely" perceiver, suddenly conscious of the passage of her own life, yet isolated by her grief from all the "watery jewels" she contemplates. Moments of self-reflection such as this send Bishop to "that self-forgetful, perfectly useless concentration" on the physical world. But just as the self, even in these early meditations, is conceived as but another space of mutability and metamorphosis, so also her most outward gaze is subjective; it bears the image of the eye as an organ of grief as well as sight.

These early poems exemplify Bishop's iconic imagination. They also show the tremendous pressure the poet places upon the conceptual frames of these icons, through conceptual paradox and naturalistic detail. In "The Weed," as we saw, Bishop conceived an icon the very agency of which is divisive and metamorphic. The next step in this direction toward natural flux was "The Fish" (CP, 42–43), half image and half symbol, "half out of water." Where "The Weed" offers a symbol of inward change, "The Fish" presents a symbol of nature uncannily suggesting home. He makes a heraldic appearance, concentrating plurality and history into his bulk. But he remains a contradictory figure and returns to the flux he never entirely leaves. Questions of mastery are basic to this poem, a fish tale not about the one that got away, but about the one that was let go.[10]

> I caught a tremendous fish
> and held him beside the boat
> half out of water, with my hook
> fast in the corner of his mouth.
> He didn't fight.
> He hadn't fought at all.
> He hung a grunting weight,
> battered and venerable
> and homely. Here and there
> his brown skin hung in strips
> like ancient wallpaper,
> and its pattern of darker brown
> was like wallpaper:
> shapes like full-blown roses
> stained and lost through age.

Bishop's description of the fish alludes, through simile, to a fading domestic world. But the fish is brought only halfway into this world, simile itself being a half-measure trope. The description turns from these allusions to record the actual exterior of the fish and to imagine its flesh, now in more gruesome terms:

> He was speckled with barnacles,
> fine rosettes of lime,
> and infested
> with tiny white sea-lice,
> and underneath two or three
> rags of green weed hung down.
> While his gills were breathing in
> the terrible oxygen
> —the frightening gills,
> fresh and crisp with blood,
> that can cut so badly—
> I thought of the coarse white flesh
> packed in like feathers,
> the big bones and the little bones,
> the dramatic reds and blacks
> of his shiny entrails,
> and the pink swim-bladder
> like a big peony.

Simile returns "like a big peony" to redomesticate the images, but the description remains uncanny. The "homely" fish is also "frightening." What is most frightening, and also visually dramatic, is what lies beyond the visible, the fish's flesh and entrails, which contrast, at least in the speaker's imagination, with the dull browns and faded pinks she sees. And the apparent discreteness of the fish, with its "grunting weight," is challenged by the "tiny white sea-lice" and barnacles, as well as the multitude of bones and the "coarse white flesh / packed in like feathers" (making him half bird).

It is not surprising, given the instability of the initial personification, that Bishop's encounter with this animal is much more constricted than that with the little circus horse or the Man-Moth, or even the weed. The fish will not become a counter-self with whom she might interact. The eye of the fish is shallow, "more like the tipping / of an object toward the light." This objectivity is reinforced by the turn of the description, which retains the sense of age, but in an impersonal, less "homely" context.

> the irises backed and packed
> with tarnished tinfoil
> seen through the lenses
> of old scratched isinglass.

Bishop was very interested in optics. She had read Newton's *Optics*, had worked in a factory in Key West making lenses for binoculars, and generally delighted in instruments of visual precision. Thanking her physician, Anny Baumann, for a gift of binoculars (June 18, 1965), she wrote: "The world has wonderful details if you can get it just a little closer than usual."[11] But Anny Baumann was the poet's psychological counselor as well as her physician, and the "getting closer" suggests imaginative grasp and personal intimacy as well as optical accuracy. The poet does not simply relinquish her desire for imaginative contact with the fish. But her attention shifts from spatial to historical imagining. History is no longer distant and figurative but "still attached" in the form of "five old pieces of fish-line, / or four and a wire leader / . . . with all five big hooks / grown firmly in his mouth." Five wounds on a fish make him a Christ figure, but the epiphany he brings the poet has nothing otherworldly about it. The domestic images at the beginning of the poem, followed by the battered body of the fish, evoke the poet's unconscious life, the uncanny return of the repressed which can "cut so badly." The final letting go is then a victory because the unconscious material has been "remembered" so that it can be released, forgotten. But Bishop can entertain such self-reflection now within the larger context of the life of nature and the beholder's tentative grasp of it. She no longer has to define a discrete interior space through dream or symbolic abstraction in order to explore her subjectivity; she has brought the self out of nocturnal seclusion and explored its relation to everything under the sun.

There is also a pervasive but ambiguous sexual quality to the fish. An untamable, corporeal energy violates the domestic world of wallpaper and roses. The fish, a he, hangs like a giant phallus, yet as the beholder imagines his interior, its "pink swim-bladder / like a big peony," he takes on a female aspect. Indeed, the hooks in his mouth suggest that phallic aggression is the fisherman's (woman this time) part. This hermaphroditic fish challenges the conventional, hierarchical antithesis of female nature and male culture. Here there is no struggle, and the victory is not exclusive.

For Bishop, nature mastered as static knowledge is a fish out of water. Its beauty and venerability belong to time. Yet it can be entertained, with a certain humility and lightness (such as simile registers), for its figurative possibilities. The poet "stared and stared" even though the fish did not return her stare. Her imagination transforms a "pool of bilge / where oil had spread a rainbow" into an ecstatic (and perhaps deliberately excessive) "rainbow, rainbow, rainbow!" Such an epiphany, set as it is in the highly ephemeral space of the rented boat with its rusted engine, must be of mortality. The grotesque is the style of mortality not because it makes us turn away in horror but because it challenges the rigid frames of thought and perception through which we attempt to master life. All the conceptual and emotional contradictions that emerge within the description of the fish point to the letting go.

Bishop employs her iconic imagination most dramatically in "Roosters" (CP, 35–39). The roosters, traditional symbols of patriarchal power, stand, at first, for masters of war. The poem was inspired by the Nazi invasion of Norway; there can be little ambiguity in the poet's feelings toward that subject. She relishes the demise of the roosters, ironically "flung / on the gray ash-heap" where their prowess means nothing. "Those metallic feathers oxidize" along with all that is mortal, including the "courted and despised" hens. But the roosters come, in the end, to represent Christian forgiveness as well. Thus questions of mastery apply not only to subjects within the referential world of the poem but to poet and reader as they attempt to absorb the political and spiritual significance of that world. Through the initial image of a barnyard scene in Key West, Bishop deals not only with World War II but with the nature of aggression and the failure to resist it. Male arrogance and female submission become a subtheme of militarism. But the greatest challenge of the poem arises as the symbolic context and the moral import of the roosters reverse, from war in modern Europe to Peter's betrayal of Christ. The result is an icon which resists idolatry to provide an open, dynamic response to the world.

As in "The Fish," the iconic nature of the image emerges indirectly, through description. Bishop again directs her meanings through a controlled pallette—here the "gun-metal blue dark" of four o'clock in the morning suggests the grimness of military occupation.[12] Later the metallic glitter of the roosters' iridescent feathers suggests "green-gold medals," and "glass-headed pins, / oil-golds and copper greens, / anthracite blues, alizarins," the arrogance of military glory, "the vulgar beauty of iridescence." The tendency of roosters to perch high, and their emblematization on weather vanes "over our little wooden northern houses," connects them in Bishop's mind with militarists "marking out maps." They divide up the world into domains of power, each seeing the world in terms of his own interest and authority, "each one an active / displacement in perspective" rather than a tolerance of many perspectives. The metallic glitter of the rhymed "medals" also combines with the brilliant synesthesia of the rooster's inflammatory crow, which "grates like a wet match. . . . / flares, and all over town begins to catch." A slow-burning fire of oxidation ironically destroys him later.

The roosters serve not only to parody evil, however. They remind us that a terrible evil can "wake us" from indifference and dream-indolence, "here" (in America, away from Europe) "where are / unwanted love, conceit and war." The sleepers are implicated, by the incongruous sequence "love, conceit and war," in denying mortality. No one wants conceit and war (though perhaps we should be criticized for our indifference to their force in the world). But surely a place where "love" is "unwanted" must awake to human compassion. For Bishop, indifference to violence goes hand in hand with indifference to love. This brief shift (from the combatants to those who would sleep through brutality and love) permits the abrupt reversal in the symbol of the roosters. Bishop recollects an "Old holy sculpture" (likely of Northern derivation) which depicts St. Peter.

> St. Peter's sin
> was worse than that of Magdalen
> whose sin was of the flesh alone;
>
> of spirit, Peter's,
> falling, beneath the flares,
> among the "servants and officers."

Magdalen's sin arises here to contrast with both the loveless populace and the scene of the decomposing bodies which precedes it. Her indulgence of the flesh (her acknowledgment of the weakness of the flesh) is nothing against the merciless, arrogant denials and hatred of the flesh displayed by both sleepers and patriarchal roosters. Indeed, Bishop associates spiritual sin with indifference to or denial of the body.

Bishop subtly links the two scenes of her poem and the two emblematic meanings of the roosters. The heavy, irregular trimeter triplets which suggested the grim force of militarism now take on the sacred meaning of the trinity. The flares of the "servants and officers" (in quotation to denote the official mask evil wears) remind us of the flame-feathers of the barnyard roosters. But the rooster himself is now not the perpetrator of sin but a "pivot" between denial and the remorse which brings on forgiveness. While Bishop links the two parts of her poem both imagistically and thematically, she makes this pivot deliberately shocking and never resolves the two versions of the symbol. Its contradictory force remains to pressure our understanding within aesthetic, moral, and conceptual frames. Thus Peter, figured on the sculpture, "still cannot guess" the full meaning of "his dreadful rooster."

Bishop's reader must accommodate yet another turn in the description, back to the barnyard where the light of day is appearing. The iconic roosters are "now almost inaudible." The poet brings the vision down from its heraldic "pillar" to meet the iconoclastic sun. Its light is "low" and comes "from underneath / the broccoli" "gilding the tiny / floating swallow's belly." The sun is, like Peter, like the sleepers, "faithful as enemy, or friend," yet different in lying outside the moral sphere of the icon, challenging its boundaries. The Christian meaning, which supplanted the military meaning of the poem, is now in turn supplanted by the noniconic force of nature.

That predominance of nature over our symbolic defenses informs many poems after *North & South*. Bishop confronts organic processes more directly in these poems. Yet the tension of frames continues. Through various antimimetic devices Bishop expresses the force of nature against perceptual norms. Her constant conjunction of life and death within a single image disturbs our will to separate them. "Nature" is a central concern of Bishop's poetry now, not only a detached, observed environment, but the growth and degeneration of the body.

By imagining organic processes in the landscape, where they can be confronted and affirmed, Bishop reduces the fear of life, the horror of the body. The most personal anxieties are released into visual awareness. "A Cold Spring" (CP, 55–56) exemplifies Bishop's grotesque realism within the pastoral mode. This is indeed pastoral poetry, not because it idealizes the landscape, but because it provides, through the landscape, a way of accepting human change and loss. Bishop's later, more direct confrontations are less emotionally resolved.

It is tempting to read the epigraph from Hopkins, "Nothing is so beautiful as spring," ironically, given the title and the series of inauspicious beginnings which follow it.

A cold spring:
the violet was flawed on the lawn.
For two weeks or more the trees hesitated;

the little leaves waited,
carefully indicating their characteristics.
Finally a grave green dust
settled over your big and aimless hills.
One day, in a chill white blast of sunshine,
on the side of one a calf was born.
The mother stopped lowing
and took a long time eating the after-birth,
a wretched flag,
but the calf got up promptly
and seemed inclined to feel gay.

All the images here arise in a precarious balance of life and death. The calf and mother intensify the grotesque conjunction as the birth occurs within a "chill white blast." Yet this is a blast of sunshine, not the blast of winter wind which lingers in memory. Similarly, the afterbirth signifies both the beginning and the end of a process. But this tension is already apparent in the flawed violet and the "grave green dust" of budding spring, which settles over the "big and aimless hills" like a mold over the dead. In the next stanza, which describes the next day, it is clear that nature is not dead, only sleeping, and the vague personification of the landscape becomes explicit; the sleeper awakens, "stretching miles of green limbs from the south." Yet the poem continues to resist a one-directional conception of this seasonal sequence. "In his cap the lilacs whitened, / then one day they fell like snow." The landscape continues to present the conjunction of birth and death, growth and decay, though without reversing the onward process. The lilacs do fall, but they are only "like" snow. Yet the dogwood which redemptively (as a traditional symbol of Christ's wounded body) "infiltrated the wood" has itself suffered, been "burned, apparently, by a cigarette-butt" and "The infant oak-leaves swung through the sober oak." Though in the first stanza the "little leaves" were "carefully indicating their characteristics," the beholder does not sustain this vision of definition and distinction. The "blurred redbud," though motionless, is paradoxically "almost more / like movement than any place-able color." The unframable force of change overwhelms the distinct outlines of objects. Bishop does for spring what Keats did for autumn, resisting the monolithic association with birth as he resisted the monolithic association with death. Her poem is as affirmative as Keats's; indeed, "nothing is so beautiful" to her as this metamor-phic life of nature in which no object or being can remain "stiff and idle."

Against this seasonal instability and temporal advance the be-holder possesses the stabilizing power of recollection and anticipa-tion. The poem makes a successful transition from spring to summer through the shifting attention of the beholder, from the past, to the present, to the future. Yet the present and future are imagined in the evening and the pastures are shadowy, thus countering the sense of seasonal beginnings with the brief passing of a single day. Bishop presents the dark and light negative of the passing landscape at the end, against the burgeoning color of oncoming summer. This summer evening landscape is strikingly different from that of spring. The directives are now vertical, in contrast to the shifts from fore-ground to background that characterize the earlier sections of de-scription. The coloring is now luminous rather than pastel; the hesitant spring gaiety has become a wild party with bull-frogs playing bass, moths as Chinese fans, and fireflies like bubbles in champagne. Yet even these "glowing tributes" are uncertain and metamorphic, so the poem reaches no stable destination.

It is easy to pass over this poem, just as Keats's "To Autumn" was once passed over, as "mere description." But it is feeling and thought perfectly realized in sensation. I have mentioned its visual complexity: its shuttle from foreground to background, its shift to verticals, its carefully constructed coloring in which bright colors and lights set off the seasonal pastels and the nocturnal shadows to resist a static conception of the landscape. Through visual details Bishop registers a temporal awareness. Equally impressive are the aural images and effects, from the synesthetic "blast" of sunshine and whip-cracking red (or sharp call?) of the cardinal to the invisible but aurally blatant bull-frogs. Within the open form of the free verse the poem is densely alliterative, assonant and rhythmic, allowing an undersong to persist within the casual voice.

In "A Cold Spring" Bishop achieves a vision of generation and decay which is indeed beautiful. This is not a beauty of symmetry but of convergence and mutation, the beauty Darwin beheld and through which he developed new concepts of nature's evolution. But when our eye is turned to the processes of our own bodies it is less easy to embrace the metamorphosis. Indeed, our instinct is to resist, as the dying woman in "Faustina, or Rock Roses" does.

In the world of "Faustina, or Rock Roses" (CP, 72–74) the rose, symbol of life, beauty, love, has become calcified in the effort to stay its passing. Bishop shows us a nameless, even faceless old woman surrounded by pills and powders and attended by her detached, mildly complaining black maid. As a visitor brings roses to the dying woman, we are reminded how futile, even grotesque, the efforts to resist the aging process can be. In this fetid, airless indoor world, nature makes a bizarre appearance. Bishop employs a reduced pallette of inorganic colors: white on white, black and metallic, offset only by "rust-perforated roses" at the end. The tacks in the wallpaper have an eerie intensity, "glistening / with mica flakes." A "dew glint on the screen" and "glow worms / burning a drowned green" ("drowned" like corpses) offset an "undazzling" white on white to create an uncanny effect of imminent death.

It is not nakedness but its opposite, disguise, which is embarrassing here: the enamel, the "towel-covered table" which "bears a can of talcum / and five pasteboard boxes / of little pills, / most half-crystallized." The poem barely acknowledges the humanity of the old woman, focusing instead on inhuman surfaces and the coverings of flesh: white hair, undershirt, fan. The poem moves to the attending Faustina only two-thirds of the way through, making her "sinister kind face" the funnel of uncertainty into which the other details flow as the petrified becomes petrifying. The antithetical, black Faustina is in a sense the emblem of her mistress's deterioration, the enigmatic face of death, its "coincident conundrum." From this face the questions of the poem seem to generate:

Oh, is it

freedom at last, a lifelong
dream of time and silence,
dream of protection and rest?
Or is it the very worst,
the unimaginable nightmare
that never before dared last
more than a second?

When the beholder looks at eyes for an answer to her questions, she does not designate whose, as though the two women in the house had become one. Faustina is strangely at home in this scene. She is the one uncovered element, but also the one mystery. The servant's cruel and sinister enigma gives her a moment of mastery over her supposed mistress, like that of Melville's Benito Cereno over the ship's captain, in the tale Bishop admired. The poem is one of many in which Bishop explores class relations and their connection to mortality. For her, class power provides a feeble illusion of power over nature, but the fact of the mortal body continually threatens such illusions. Since the poor have fewer barriers against nature's force, they obtain a kind of power over those deluded by their class status. By her name Faustina perhaps also reminds of futile attempts to master the course of nature alchemically.

The visual tensions and ambiguities of the poem return us to the gaze of the visitor, a distancing surrogate of the narrator (whose discomfort and anxiety in this scene are registered in the tense trimeter stanzas, each closing with an indrawn, shuddering dimeter). Bishop's notes for this period suggest how she may have projected herself as the third-person visitor in this scene. Her first experience of it was distant: "Lying on my bed in the dark. I can look across into the bedroom of the people whose back-yard adjoins ours. The blinds are up and the light bulb hanging above the double bed must be an *80 watt,* the room is so bright."[13] This becomes, in the poem, "Meanwhile the eighty-watt bulb / betrays us all." What it betrays are all the disguises and denials—talcums, gowns, and fans—leaving exposed the paralyzing enigma of death, whether it is dream or nightmare. Uneasy in this enigma (which is detached from the dying lady and floats, becoming "helplessly / proliferative" as life itself), the visitor "proffers her bunch / of rust-perforated roses." The roses have been there from the beginning, in the "vaguely roselike / flower-formations" on the chipped enamel, in the pattern of the disordered sheets, "like wilted roses." They remind us of mutability even when they are inorganic (make them of enamel, they will chip; of metal, they will rust). They remind us, too, that life is "proliferative," not something to be hoarded or mastered. The final query of the poem—"whence come / all the petals" (a whence now rather than a what or why) is much gentler and less demonic than the first, "snake-tongue" question. Rock roses are, after all, not roses made of rock but a shrub that grows in rocky soil, something vital and mutable, defying the barren whiteness of the scene.

These roses do not emerge again in Bishop's published poetry, but unpublished manuscripts reveal her preoccupation with the image and her unconventional use of it. They also make much more explicit her association of roses with the mutable female body and her challenge to the sad sentence women receive under the *carpe diem* tradition. These are poems of homoerotic desire in which beauty and mortality are juxtaposed. The detail and tenderness with which they describe the aging human body provide an alternative to the sinister vision of "Faustina" and suggest that Bishop was able to sustain an open, realistic vision not only of the changing landscape but of the human body.

In the unpublished prose piece "After Bonnard" Bishop sustains a visual and aesthetic disinterestedness toward the aging body, displacing her own desire to touch onto a personified "Time."

> The small shell-pink roses have opened so far, after two days in their bottle of water, that they are tired. The pink is fleeing—it is more mauve this afternoon.—The centers stick up further and are faded, too, almost brown. Still delicate, but reaching out, out, thinner, vaguer, wearier—

like those wide beautiful pale nipples I saw somewhere,
on white, white and strong, but tired nevertheless,
breasts.—Time smeared them, with a loving but heavy
thumb—[14]

Ostensibly modifying roses, the breasts become the real focus of
this piece, their erotic immediacy buffered by the foregrounded
roses. The tired breast is attractive, and time's thumb is loving as
the beholder would like to be. The image remains ambivalent—the
attraction to the delicacy of flesh combines with a fascination in its
decay; the gesture is both loving and wounding. But in this im-
pressionistic world the ambivalence is light and the desire is tran-
quil. In another unpublished piece, "Vaguely Love Poem," Bishop
attempted a more hard-edged, cubistic vision (as in William Carlos
Williams' "The Rose") to describe a less mediated, not at all
"vague" passion. But this is a "vaguely love poem" in the sense
that love and harshness uncomfortably converge. The roses here
are "rock roses" because they proliferate toward some intense erotic
center both physical and emotional, rapturous and exacting.

Just now, when I saw you naked again,
I thought the same words: rose-rock; rock-rose . . .
Rose, trying, working, to show itself,
Unimaginable connections, unseen, shining edges,
(forming, folding over,)
Rose-rock, unformed, flesh beginning, crystal by crystal,
Clear pink breasts and darker, crystalline nipples,
rose-rock, rose-quartz, roses, roses, roses,
exacting roses from the body,
and even darker, accurate, rose of sex—[15]

While there is a grotesque effect in the convergence of hard and
soft images, the hard images do not suggest an antivital ideal, but
rather strong sensation at once pleasurable and violent. The symbolic nature of the rose icon suggests a unity of sensation rather
than of emotion. This is not an image of petrification or of Bonnard-

like gentleness but of rose and rock modifying each other in a momentary bodily coalescence.

Among the published poems of this period only "The Shampoo" (CP, 84) offers a real counterpoint to the terrified vision of the mortal body presented in "Faustina, or Rock Roses." While the focus is on "hair" rather than sexual "breasts," the washing becomes a loving ritual. In the first two stanzas the lover is compared to nature. This nature is not idealized or timeless but metamorphic. As in "A Cold Spring," Bishop finds spatial registers of imperceptible processes.

> The still explosions on the rocks,
> the lichens, grow
> by spreading, gray, concentric shocks.
> They have arranged
> to meet the rings around the moon, although
> within our memories they have not changed.

The association of the lover's hair with the lichens in the next stanza has a grotesque effect, but again there is no repulsion. The shocks in the visually accurate oxymoron "still explosions" turn out to be imperceptible and harmless, making the aging process more acceptable. But the sense of alarm remains. The temporal sequence is not abrupt, but the revelation of change may shock us. The grotesque is not a register of ugliness but a challenge to fixed ways of associating beauty and nature. In an inverse of the courtly trope the lover surpasses nature, not by being more ideal ("Shall I compare thee to a summer's day . . .") but the reverse. Though the lichens seem not to have changed, are slow in their ascendancy to the moon, the lover has been "precipitate and pragmatical" in her aging process. But this is a backhanded compliment. Her gray hair, now "shooting stars," will reach the moon faster than the lichen. But the moon itself is "battered and shiny," not a transcendent object but part of a cosmic metamorphosis, a symbol of mutability. This simile works inversely, just as the lichen metaphor does. The moon ostensibly modifies "the big tin basin" (with rings around it?). But the simile serves to bring the moon (associated with lovers) into the domain of time, with the easy swing of the rhyme which sustains the relaxed, variant line lengths of the poem. There is none of the cramped rhythm of "Faustina" here. "The Shampoo," which ends *A Cold Spring,* is Bishop's earliest study of the body in time. It challenges the courtly convention (as "Insomnia" does, but now more positively) which recognizes as lovable only what is youthful or immutable. Bishop endows the *carpe diem* rose with many days, many moments in its changing life, but she does not evade the shock we feel in the awareness of our mutability.

One of the most troubling and unresolved tensions in *Questions of Travel* is that between moral and aesthetic responses to mortality. The aesthetic imagination often works against the discriminations of good and evil that the moral imagination insists upon. Aesthetic interest resists the identification with life and the horror of what threatens it. Bishop explores this division most fully in "The Armadillo" (CP, 103–104), in which the drama of the beholder is indistinguishable from the drama of the poet imagining. Bishop describes the St. John's Day carnival in Rio, in which fire balloons are a tradition. She watches them rise exaltedly, but her attention shifts to the effects, once they burst and their flames are released, on the forest and animals below. These effects are first treated with aesthetic detachment, but a strong moral voice breaks in to oppose the stance of transcendence and aesthetic mastery.

Since "The Armadillo" is dedicated to Robert Lowell, it has been read as a critique of his way of making art out of suffering.[16] But the poem is more self-reflexive than that. In earlier poetry Bishop had chosen to see bodily metamorphosis as aesthetically beautiful, to distance herself from the pain associated with mortality. In "The Armadillo" she dramatizes this aesthetic distance and the inevitable return to the rage of the suffering body.

Throughout, we have seen the grotesque as an aesthetic of rupture, liminality, and ambivalence. It forces together the degenerative and creative, the awful and cheerful aspects of life. The urge to domesticate the grotesque, to seek moral and emotional stability within it, to convert it to a stable meaning whether of protest, elegy, or praise, is often overpowering in a writer. The desire for harmony must certainly be as strong as the desire for freedom. The grotesque is caught between the image of freedom and a nostalgia for order and definition. An imaginative struggle is apparent in all grotesque vision; the anxiety and uneasiness of its dualism urge us through its interludes into another moment. This urge is apparent throughout "The Armadillo."

It is not surprising that Bishop should choose carnival as the scene of several poems. Carnival is that state or domain in which the norms of culture are violated or inverted and in which repressed anxieties and desires find expression. But for just this reason it can also be very disturbing. A space of metamorphosis, rebellion, inclusion, and inversion, heightened community and heightened eccentricity, it is a site of both moral and aesthetic contradiction. Carnival is Dionysian in an agonistic as well as in an ecstatic fashion. It is, as Bakhtin saw, a space of grotesque realism. An ambivalence about carnival haunted "The Armadillo" from its inception. When describing it to her New York doctor, Anny Bauman (June 24, 1955), Bishop wrote: "This is Saint John's Day . . . It is pouring rain which is too bad because it's a day for fireworks and bonfires, etc.—but very good, really, because there may not be so many forest fires and accidents. Fireballoons are supposed to be illegal but everyone sends them up anyway . . . They are so pretty—one's of two minds about them." Later the same summer (August 24) she wrote to her friend again: "Now all our scenery, all the mountains, are burned black with what trees survived all singed pale yellow, or white—it looks exactly like the negative of a photograph, awful, but beautiful, in a way."[17]

Drafts of the poem indicate that it began quite differently from the final version. The poem included a sardonic epigraph, an old song: "If St. John only knew it was his day / He would descend from Heaven & be gay."[18] But the epigraph does more than contrast with the subsequent holocaust imagery. It suggests a descent, before the reciprocal ascent of the fire balloons. And in drafts Bishop devoted the first three stanzas to a description of an extraordinary sunset, a natural counterpart to the descent of St. John. From the poem's inception, then, Bishop was interested in the intersection of celestial and earthly perspectives. In its final version the poem contrasts two kinds of martyrdom, one sacred and one profane, which are causally connected. The first involves the self-immolating transcendence of the fire balloons, associated with the praise of the martyred St. John and the vision of the Cross. The second involves the suffering of the profane world and its hopeless protest against the forces that afflict it. The poem also has three distinct and unstable moments, clearly marked in the text through the progress of the beholder's reflection—a moment of transcendence, a moment of worldly disintegration and aesthetic absorption, and a moment of moral outrage. Together these moments represent the intense dividedness of the human spirit. Our wish for spiritual transcendence conflicts with our instinct of survival. Our aesthetic imagination, detached from its object, conflicts with our moral imagination, which empathizes with its object.

The carnival setting of "The Armadillo" admits all of these disparate impulses. Antisocial feelings and moral deviations find a containable expression. Bishop marks the ritual and perennial aspect of this cultural phenomenon by the first line of the poem: "This is the time of year," approached with dread and awe. (This is the only stanza in which first and third lines rhyme as well as second and fourth, perhaps marking the expected repetition of the event). Martyrdom will be both celebrated and reenacted.

In the unfolding of visionary process, one would expect a movement from the devastation of the natural world to a transcendence of it. But this poem moves in an opposite way. It sets a moral weight against the sublime urge the fire balloons express and focuses on consequences rather than aspirations. The gaze of the beholder is downward; the sublime becomes grotesque as the balloons (like the roosters discussed earlier) are brought down to earth.

Bishop seems to privilege the agonism and outrage at the end of the poem by emphasizing it in italics and making the armadillo the title image. Transcendence is a dangerous dream, the poem seems to say, from which we are awakened to a reality of terrible, meaningless suffering. The martyr may endure the agony of the body in the service of a higher strength, but our creaturely being must protest against our affliction. This may indeed be Bishop's intention. If so, the language of the poem is wiser than the poet. The rhetorical excess and single-mindedness of the final stanza make it difficult for the reader to accept its didactic message. Was Bishop aware of this ambivalence between aesthetic and moral vision? Is the imagination repelled by didacticism as the reason is repelled by the grotesque? The poem raises these questions inadvertently, through the play of danger and desire, of violence and freedom, working in the body of the poem. But Bishop's pattern of ambivalence in earlier poems— her many poems in which a will to transcend or master experience competes with an identification with the body, her constant tension between aesthetic and moral responses to mortality—has a bearing on this poem. Is she attempting, finally, to silence her aestheticism, or is she dramatizing an inevitable conflict?

The opening stanzas of "The Armadillo" represent a human desire, which the festival unleashes, to transcend, to explore the cosmos, somewhat like the Man-Moth's urge to push through the sky, here explicitly a forbidden and dangerous desire. The "frail, illegal fire balloons" are compared to hearts, becoming emblems both of desire and, ultimately, creaturely limit. "[T]he paper chambers flush and fill with light / that comes and goes, like hearts." The poet is obviously entranced by the upward journey these balloons make, imaginatively identifying with both their frailty and their aspiration (as one might identify with a martyr). Yet the poem separates this desire from the material existence below (the place of the body), with which the narrator also identifies: the balloons rise

> receding, dwindling, solemnly
> and steadily forsaking us,
> or, in the downdraft from a peak,
> suddenly turning dangerous.

The poet has made room for emotional volatility and for a range of statement by permitting her line lengths and meter to vary considerably from stanza to stanza and within stanzas. Sometimes the rhythm lifts ("rising toward a saint"), sometimes it palpitates ("or the pale green one. With a wind"), sometimes it drags ("receding, dwindling, solemnly"). The imagination is caught between poles or points of view, projecting vulnerability onto the animal world, the world of nature and nurture, yet retaining the transcendent point of view. The next four stanzas of the poem look at the disintegration of natural order as a consequence of the transcendent urge, but with an aesthetic interest only. This is the grotesque center of the poem precisely in its incongruity of treatment and subject matter, and because destruction and creative beauty are identified.

The sublime urge defeats regeneration. But there is an aesthetically recreative moment, if not a regenerative one, in the poet's vision. The falling fire is described as a broken egg; it drops behind a house, and disturbs the owl's nest and rabbit's lair, centers of domesticity. Insofar as the destruction is spectacle and aesthetic distance is maintained, the expiring scene is magnificent. But it is also terrible:

> . . . owls who nest there flying up
> and up, their whirling black-and-white
> stained bright pink underneath, until
> they shrieked up out of sight.
>
> The ancient owls' nest must have burned.
> Hastily, all alone,
> a glistening armadillo left the scene,
> rose-flecked, head down, tail down,
>
> and then a baby rabbit jumped out,
> *short*-eared, to our surprise.
> So soft!—a handful of intangible ash
> with fixed, ignited eyes.

The aesthetic observer notes the ear-length of the ignited rabbit, the rose-flecked scales of the burning armadillo. But as identification shifts from the fire balloons to the scorched animals below, that aesthetic distance is shattered and the poet's rage is more intense for her shame. The distanced images of the natural world are recapitulated and converted to moral meaning in the final stanza, as if in penance not only for the event but for the aestheticism with which it was observed. The owl's shriek becomes a piercing cry, the rabbit's surprise becomes panic, the armadillo's form becomes *"a weak mailed fist."*

In an unfinished poem, "A Drunkard," Bishop imagined another fire with similar dispassion.[19] "I felt only amazement, not fear, amazement . . . perhaps my infancy's chief emotion." Yet we feel her vulnerability on the peripheries of this vision. The child's mother does not answer her call for water, and later, after the fire, when the child picks up a loose stocking on the beach, her mother reacts violently ("Put that down"), indicating a consciousness of death which in the child is not complete. To the child the stocking is first an object of disinterested curiosity. The adult narrator's drunkenness, her terrible thirst, is the expression of the unconscious need, which remained unexpressed in her infant amazement. In "The Armadillo" that identification with the mortal body bursts onto the surface, expressing itself as rage. But the moment of amazement in the middle of the poem, in which the disintegrating or threatened body is imagined without moral closure or personal connection, is essential to the power of the poem. It is not simply refuted by the excessively engaged, outraged, anthropomorphic conclusion.

In "The Armadillo" Bishop addresses our ambivalent will to transcend or aestheticize the body. The ending of the poem is conservative in that it emphasizes protection. If we read the poem as a whole, however, we see the conservative impulse challenged. This ambivalence remains throughout Bishop's work. But more often the conservative, defensive posture will be challenged, rather than the deviant impulse. In such poems deviance is defined not as an escape from the body but rather as an alternative relationship to the body which reminds us of its uncontrollability. In particular, Bishop turns to carnivalesque images of the misfit who resists the social and cultural norms through which nature is disciplined and controlled. "A Summer's Dream" and "House Guest" treat this idea allegorically, but in poems such as "Manuelzinho" and "Pink Dog" the realism of the figures makes their deviance more unsettling. In such poems Bishop takes on the stance of someone living within the fragile norms of the dominant culture, but susceptible to the challenge of the misfit, who embodies the expelled elements of the speaker's life. Bishop's misfits frequently exist within a background of unruly nature and come to represent a creative relationship to their environment. They are "eyesores," like the deviations of nature itself, in a cultivated garden. But they also possess mystical knowledge or power. They are not strictly antithetical but rather live within the community, not across some well-defended boundary. Their effect is not so much to present a pastoral or idealized alternative but to alter community through deviance, to resist the repressions of the official view. They also symbolize the failure of our domestic orders, the inevitable intrusion of uncontrollable elements into our lives, toward which we may react openly and creatively, or defensively.

"Manuelzinho" (CP, 96–99) represents Bishop's most joyous, though still ambivalent, image of the misfit. The speaker, standing in for the poet ("A friend of the writer is speaking"), is open to the inventive vitality of her incorrigible servant. Class differences and hierarchies remain in place, but their stability is shaken. Again the relationship between master and servant is quickly reversed, but with less irritability and resignation. "Half squatter, half tenant (no rent)— / a sort of inheritance," he is hopelessly recalcitrant and fails at the simplest everyday tasks, has bad luck, is desperately poor and more than a little mad. Yet his employer not only provides for him, but takes off her hat to him in recognition that the meek shall inherit the earth, and that the civilized orders she sustains are ultimately futile defenses against the reality in which he dwells.

She indulges Manuelzinho not merely out of pity or resignation, but because his madness has something mystical and rejuvenating about it, something which thwarts predictable orders and thus keeps the soul and the imagination alive. Through him she consecrates inventive freedom and liberates herself from convention. Manuelzinho is quite literally a colorful, outlandish figure, with bright blue pants and painted hat. He is "the world's worst gardener since Cain," letting everything go, yet this fugitive makes gardens that "ravish [the] eyes." These wild, creative orders are never stable alternatives to traditional husbandry; they are ruined and renewed, spectacular displays of mutation. The speaker observes in awe: "you bring me / a mystic three-legged carrot, / or a pumpkin 'bigger than a baby.'" The mystical aspect of this Christ/Cain in his holy/holey hat is reinforced throughout the poem, and is given both comic and serious dimensions:

> And once I yelled at you
> so loud to hurry up
> and fetch me those potatoes
> your holey hat flew off,
> you jumped out of your clogs,
> leaving three objects arranged
> in a triangle at my feet,
> as if you'd been a gardener
> in a fairy tale all this time
> and at the word "potatoes"
> had vanished to take up your work
> of fairy prince somewhere.

Manuelzinho does not represent nature against culture, but rather an alternative ordering of nature that challenges and opens up the dominant one.[20] Here the magical trinity (this poem in trimeter abounds in tridentate figures) is opposed to a solemn Christian ritual by an atmosphere of fancy. But the poem does take on a more serious tone in places. Manuelzinho mystically refuses the boundaries of life and death, not by recourse to symbolic values, but literally: he refuses to recognize that a corpse can no longer be a father. He approaches numbers magically (financial order becomes aesthetic and imaginative order, account books become dream books). The speaker notes his affinity with nature when she nicknames him "Klorophyll Kid" and describes him, in a Yeatsian phrase, as "improvident as the dawn." Manuelzinho's protean quality infects the beholder, who participates through metaphor in the defeat of her old orders and joins his deviant creativity, making a bridge between his world and hers.

> Between us float a few
> big, soft, pale-blue,
> sluggish fireflies,
> the jellyfish of the air . . .

She is beginning to think like him. Again the beholder confronts the grotesque figure (wind-up toy, weed, fish, man-moth, servant) directly at the end of the poem and reveals her ambivalence: "I love you all I can, / I think. Or do I?" She cannot enter his imaginative world entirely, nor does she wish to. His reality is only figurative for her: "I take off my hat, unpainted / and figurative, to you." Her hat is not "holey."

While she tips her hat to Manuelzinho, the landowner remains within her own world, ambivalently open to new potentialities and freed from cliché. But "Exchanging Hats" (CP, 200–201), which Bishop published in *New World Writing* in 1956 but did not include in any collection, describes an anxiety about social roles as well as creative deviance. The "hats" we wear, the social identities we take on, are inherently insecure. Bishop describes a world of sexual anxiety, where men become effeminate and women become the captains. The sportive carnival atmosphere of "Manuelzinho," in which alternative, even mystical orders are tolerated, is here replaced with a more sinister humor and leads to a darker vision at the end. Here the exchange is "unfunny," because it exposes "a slight transvestite twist" in us all, which we suppress. The insistent, end-stopped rhymes and processional tetrameter build to a reeling rhythm that expresses the "madness" acknowledged in the sixth stanza.

> Anandrous aunts, who, at the beach
> with paper plates upon your laps,
> keep putting on the yachtsmen's caps
> with exhibitionistic screech,

the visors hanging o'er the ear
so that the golden anchors drag,
—the tides of fashion never lag.
Such caps may not be worn next year.

Or you who don the paper plate
itself, and put some grapes upon it,
or sport the Indian's feather bonnet,
—perversities may aggravate

the natural madness of the hatter.
And if the opera hats collapse
and crowns grow draughty, then, perhaps,
he thinks what might a miter matter?

Bishop employs a deliberately grating diction and punning sarcasm which cuts through the civilized, mock-poetic voice ("visors hanging o'er the ear / . . . the tides of fashion never lag"). The anandrous aunts who pretend to be at the helm are screeching orders. Bishop's own marginality as lesbian and poet becomes normative in this family where men become effeminate and women become captains. This inherited "natural madness of the hatter" is exacerbated in the fifth stanza as an unnamed "you" (the poet's uncle, and perhaps also the poet herself) tropes further, putting on "the paper plate / itself." This "you" at least acknowledges the arbitrariness of the hats and can enjoy their array. At this point the hats become endlessly exchangeable and the outlandish roles accelerate. Bishop speaks from inside a culture that cannot sustain the norms of gender identity but perceives their instability as "abnormal" or perverse or experimental. In this sense the openly deviant poet who converts role-playing into troping becomes the only potentially joyous member of the family. Her subversion of various forms of masculine power (metonymically shown as Indian's headress, monarch's crown, bishop's miter) can be heard in the alliteration ("what might a miter [meter] matter"?).

The carnival hysteria reaches a pitch in stanza six and turns somber as it moves toward the singular, personal, and retrospective.

Uncle Neddy and Aunt "Hat," remembered as devils in "Memories of Uncle Neddy," are alluded to here: the man who could never establish a successful identity but with whom the poet feels a strong affinity, the "exemplary" woman who dominated, scowled, and disapproved. These dead now wear the figurative hats of darkness ("black fedora" and "shady, turned-down brim") . The poet wonders about the uncle's aspiration ("are there any / stars inside your black fedora?") and about the aunt's judgment of history ("what slow changes"). These stanzas, like the dream of the grandparents in Eternity in "The Moose," take Bishop outside the anxious experimentations of the world she lives in, but without providing any solace. She is not sure there are any stars under the uncle's black fedora, or that the aunt has seen any genuine changes, however slow, within the unlagging tides of sexual and social fashion. The creative deviance of Manuelzinho, whose hat signified the sportive alternative to the conventional world of the speaker, has been displaced by a world of relentless "costume and custom" where roles are exchanged rather than made flexible. The divine, creative madness of the gardener is now the perverse madness of the hatter who has lost all connection to nature. Instead of expressing the freedom from fixed order and identity, the grotesque here expresses the radical instability and inauthenticity of all cultural roles.

This same decadent carnival world of "costume and custom" defines "Pink Dog" (CP, 190–191), one of Bishop's last poems. What makes this exploration of social and physical anxiety so powerful is that she both abhors the enforcement of "costume" and sees its necessity. We are embarrassed here by nakedness and by its opposite. In "Exchanging Hats" the poet may share the "transvestite twist" of the unfunny uncles, may feel inspired to experiment with unstable identities. In "Pink Dog" she urges a costume on a naked dog (a dehumanized image of the body) for the sake of its survival in a culture that wishes to deny the mortal body. The poet writes from the margin, on the divide between culture and nature, a creature of both. It is her empathy for the pink dog, her own sense of marginality, that provokes her terrible advice. In a culture which abhors the body's mutability, disguise is the only alternative to expulsion or annihilation. The dog in us must be dressed up and taught to dance if it is to be tolerated at all. Carnival is now the expression not of freedom but of repression.

In carnival time, when everyone is disguised, the poet sees a naked pink diseased female dog. It is not easy for Bishop to embrace the reality of the pink dog. Her impulse is to hide it, not just from herself, but from the forces that threaten it (which she has internalized). In "Pink Dog" Bishop makes her most complete and successful use of the grotesque; its style, its imagery, and its tone are all intensely ambivalent. Where other poems explore grotesque images but collapse them in thematic reduction, "Pink Dog" sustains its uneasy vision of marginality. In "The Armadillo" Bishop depended upon a dramatic shift of sympathy, from the desire for spiritual and aesthetic transcendence, in the fire balloons, to the will to survive and the rage against oppression. In this poem the two impulses are in more immediate competition. The beholder is herself ambivalent—horrified by and concerned for the grotesque figure, participating in the repressive forces even while she wishes to save the dog. The poem is not simply responding to the depilated dog, an image of disorder and mutability; Bishop also turns the techniques of the grotesque against the culture which the dog offends. If a depilated dog does not look attractive, one in mascara, dressed up and dancing, is truly obscene.

There are two parts to the grotesque in this poem. One part represents the decay and regeneration of the body, to which the poet responds in shock; the other represents the attempt to disguise that process. The opening of the poem introduces both responses:

> The sun is blazing and the sky is blue.
> Umbrellas clothe the beach in every hue.
> Naked, you trot across the avenue.
>
> Oh, never have I seen a dog so bare!
> Naked and pink, without a single hair . . .
> Startled, the passersby draw back and stare.

Nature, including the beach where nakedness is supposed to be displayed, must be clothed. Color here is a sign of disguise rather than festive deviance. The idiots, paralytics, and beggars all exacerbate a body-anxiety by exhibiting their vulnerabilities. The pink dog combines degeneration and regeneration, displays ongoing metamorphosis. But the poet does not sustain the neutral descriptiveness of "A Cold Spring" toward this coincidence. The engaged voice makes this a far more powerful, far more troubling poem. "You have a case of scabies / but look intelligent. Where are your babies? / (A nursing mother by those hanging teats)." Bishop herself suffered from eczema and other skin ailments, and as a schoolgirl was sent home for open sores. She had the constant sense, then, of physical betrayal. Yet a dog without hair is a reductive image of any human form. The dog is female to express woman's greater identification with the body, male culture's symbolization of the body as woman.

Whatever combination of compassion and horror we may feel toward the nurturing, festering body, these feelings are increased as we imagine the impersonal violence wielded against it by society.

> Yes, idiots, paralytics, parasites
> go bobbing in the ebbing sewage, nights
> out in the suburbs, where there are no lights.
>
> If they do this to anyone who begs,
> drugged, drunk, or sober, with or without legs,
> what would they do to sick, four-leggèd dogs?
>
> In the cafés and on the sidewalk corners
> the joke is going round that all the beggars
> who can afford them now wear life preservers.

The black humor of the passage heightens the grotesque effect of the brutal actions it describes. The drowned bodies "go bobbing," forms of suffering are hurled together in the syntax as "with or without legs." Whose crass language is this? The poet does not seem to participate in the brutality beneath the veneer of culture (she exposes the fringes, "out in the suburbs, where there are no lights"). But her own alternative, she knows, is equally grotesque, if more complex.

> Now look, the practical, the sensible
>
> solution is to wear a *fantasía*
> Tonight you simply can't afford to be a-
> n eyesore. But no one will ever see a
>
> dog in *máscara* this time of year.

The poem clearly parodies this proposal. But it also suggests that, in a culture as hysterically repressive as this one has become, the logic of survival leads this way. The contorted language of the poem emphasizes the strain of this logic, however. The awkward enjambments and forced triple rhymes are Bishop's commentary on her earlier attempts to disguise personal dread in elegant forms and tropes. They are also a comment on the fundamental lack of grace inherent in our repression of the body.

The poem offers no clear answer to the public fear of the mutable body, yet that fear and the repressive behavior it provokes are obviously criticized. We are left suspended between sympathy and judgment toward this speaker. Pink dog and speaker appear as two rival aspects of the self—one that would parade its nakedness, whatever the consequences, and one that would cover and protect, since it cannot or does not wish to expel, the body. The pink dog has none of the alterity of the fish or other iconic figures in Bishop's poetry. She lives among us, in our element, as the aspect of ourselves we cannot tame. But by making her central figure a dog rather than a human, Bishop reminds us that she does not represent, in her naked, diseased state, a viable human option. The poet is not the dog but the troubled speaker who must somehow reconcile her culture to the dog it despises.

Bishop's late poetry, with its greater realism in treating biological and social themes, is pessimistic about our ability to remain open to difference and change. The tension which produces her grotesque style is no longer between a beautiful, transcendent, or inwardly infinite self and a mechanistic environment, or, as in the middle period, in the strangely beautiful coincidence of generation and decay in nature. In the end she focused on the untamable body, its needs, desires, processes in time, and the culture's wish to control, disguise, or suppress it. In the landscape we are able to experience joy in the vision of mortality and mutability. Culture can go out to impersonal nature and there symbolize mortality in a solacing way. But when nature parades naked within the boundaries of culture, when "nature" includes our own untamable desires and processes which threaten its stability, the society responds with fear and loathing. Nature, when it intrudes on culture, is an "eyesore"; nor are the forms of culture (the *fantasía,* the *máscara,* rhyme and meter) beautiful when they are designed to disguise or suppress nature. Yet in bringing nature and culture together in the confrontational style of the grotesque, Bishop reminds us that they are not discrete or dichotomous realms, that our imaginations need form and order but must remain open to mutable life. She expresses the necessity (though not always the hope) for a less "barbaric," more flexible, tolerant culture that can accommodate difference and change without anxiety and remain "new, tender, quick."

Imaginary Heights,
Invisible Depths

During a stay in North Carolina, after living in Key West, Elizabeth Bishop wrote in her travel notebook (August 10, 1938):

> I'm not much of a Thoreau—all this loftiness is very depressing particularly in foggy weather. I've never lived in the mts. before. They are all around us, big blue shapes, coming & going through the mist—like recurring thoughts—rather depressing. I miss all that bright, detailed *flatness* of K.W.—.

And a week later (August 26, 1938), she continues:

> Every time I look at the mountains, I think of the expression, "at the back of my mind." This sensation they give is so strong that I feel a physical compulsion to turn my back and then with them *there*, to go on looking at the ferns, roots, etc.
> > "I must lie down where all the ladders start
> > In the foul rag-&-bone shop of the heart."[1]

The passage tells us a great deal about Bishop's relation to the sublime. She resists its vertical thrust, turning instead "to all that bright, detailed *flatness*" of the immediate world. Yet the mountain is there "at the back of my mind," "like recurring thoughts," an obscure but magnetic force in experience. The vertical continues to suggest itself in the quotation from Yeats, for while the lines support a call to immediate, vulgar feeling and sensation, they also assume a ladder of vision, an ascending structure grounded in details. Bishop directs her eye to the visible roots, and these she associates with human, finite experience, but "back behind us" are always those misty thoughts of the ideal, otherworldly or profound. This tension represents one area of difference with both Romanticism and high modernism.

This chapter concerns the place Bishop gives in her poetry to those thoughts of the infinite. She expresses an attraction to the idea of a still point or spiritual center, but continually turns back to the flow of memory and immediate experience. I will examine the role Bishop gives to vertical iconography, and to receding background, in representing them. In previous chapters I have considered Bishop's treatment of psychological and physical realities. Her inventive perspectives express an open, fluent subjectivity and question static correspondences between the outward eye and an inward I. The ruptures and incongruities in her representations, we saw, resist the will to classify reality and express a world as process. In the poems discussed so far Bishop emphasizes a temporal, dynamic vision over the will to master experience in static forms. But she did not simply relinquish all thoughts of the absolute, all wish for transcendence and epiphany. Religious rhetoric of the soul and of divinity haunts Bishop's poems. Even in her most descriptive work, she searches for a supersensible meaning or authority to which she might submit. Repeatedly, however, this modern, skeptical poet questions her own impulse to convert obscurity to essence or idealize what is not plainly visible to The Invisible. She does not dwell in obscure heights and depths as if they presented an alternative to the shifting middle ground of experience. The mind travels toward ideal absolutes, like the fire-balloons in "The Armadillo." But Bishop's primary identification remains with the mutable world, where she experiences, at moments, a coalescence of being. In this she represents a major temperamental shift from the poetry of high modernism on which her imagination was bred.

The focus in this chapter will be on poems from *North & South* and *A Cold Spring.* In these volumes religious themes and the rhetoric of the sublime are especially prominent and affect the levels of representation. Framing Bishop's work and this chapter are two icons—the iceberg of *North & South,* the volcano of *Geography III*—which define the extremes of Bishop's meditation on the sublime: antivital idealism and the eruption of the void.

"The Imaginary Iceberg" (CP, 4) represents Bishop's strongest statement of desire to identify with an antivital ideal. From a poet famous for her later emphasis on questions of travel, it is striking for what it relinquishes: "We'd rather have the iceberg than the ship / although it meant the end of travel." Though she would in "Questions of Travel" indulge in catalogues of sights which it "would have been a pity / not to have seen," here, in the form of an imaginary iceberg, is "a scene a sailor'd give his eyes for." She holds the imaginary above the visible, eagerly relinquishing experience to a timeless symbolic vision. But careful readers of Bishop's poem will observe a characteristic ambivalence toward the ideal of mastery over life and self even in this apparent tribute. What the poem describes is the mind's attraction to, even need for, an idea of absolute autonomy, and a process of meditation by which this idea is approached and abandoned.

The first stanza of the poem insists on the choice of iceberg over ship as a choice of possessions, as though one might actually appropriate the infinite and absolute. "We'd rather have the iceberg than the ship; / we'd rather own this breathing plain of snow." Ownership is complicated here by a stance of subjection. The ship would become like the snow "undissolved upon the water," part of the "floating field" on which the iceberg "pastures." Experience, that is, would be drawn up onto the plain of imagination, on which the imaginary iceberg is erected and worshiped. Along with terms of ownership are terms of animation which permit an apostrophe to the imagination. The "plain of snow" is "breathing" because the water pulses under it. But this fact allows the poet a figure; she awaits a fuller revelation when the iceberg "wakes." Like the Romantic apostrophe, this iceberg-being is bound to elude the poet. Constructed on contradictions ("cloudy rock" and "moving marble"), it never achieves the presence the poet desires.

Like Yeats's "Sailing to Byzantium," "The Imaginary Iceberg" remains a poem of approach rather than realization. Each eleven-line stanza represents a phase of the meditation, closed off by couplets. The first stanza is hypothetical: it proposes a choice but absorbs what is lost into a paradoxical vision of the absolute. The next stanza shifts from the conditional mood of the ship to the declarative mood of the iceberg. Yet even as she tropes the iceberg into being, Bishop emphasizes the illusionary, rhetorical nature of this iceberg through metaphors of the theater. After exalting the iceberg for its "glassy pinnacles" which "correct elliptics in the sky," she writes:

> This is a scene where he who treads the boards
> is artlessly rhetorical. The curtain
> is light enough to rise on finest ropes
> that airy twists of snow provide.
> The wits of these white peaks
> spar with the sun. Its weight the iceberg dares
> upon a shifting stage and stands and stares.

"He who treads the boards" is an actor on a stage in theater lingo; thus the sailor has not actualized his desire. Yet the "scene" is now dramatic. The hypothetical "he" is "artlessly rhetorical." He has erased the belatedness of the figure and achieved a rhetorical mastery in which the fiction shows no sign of its invention. It is a stance of complete absorption in the world of the icon, its frozen eminence replacing nature. The "solemn, floating field" of the imagination in this sense "awakens" to the eternal symbol which "pastures there." The curtain goes up on the "airy twists" of the imagination. But the very emphasis on theatrical devices belies the illusion. The poem celebrates the sublime supremacy of the mind over the senses, over the material world: "The *wits* of these white peaks / spar with the sun" (italics mine). Yet having achieved this preeminence, the iceberg merely "stands and stares," without volition or consciousness. As the speaker turns from this visionary moment to consider the iceberg with more detachment in stanza three, the terms of praise are more ambiguous. The noncontingent iceberg which "cuts its facets from within" is "Like jewelry from a grave"—beautiful, but useless even as adornment and ready, like the stiff and idle thought in "The Weed," to break apart.

Perhaps it is not only by necessity but by will that in stanza three "the ship steers off / where waves give in to one another's waves / and clouds run in a warmer sky," that is, to the "warmth" of mutual surrender and change. These are the opposite of the iceberg—isolate, hierarchical, autonomous, permanent. This ship is not the Titanic; it survives its dream of whiteness. Yet the ideal does have a use, to "behoove the soul" with a symbol of the eternal within the temporal world. In later work Bishop drastically challenges this concept of the soul, "self-made from elements least visible," free of contingency and "fleshed, fair, erected indivisible." (Her more appropriate image will be the volcano.) But Bishop's attraction to the magisterial loftiness and aloofness of the iceberg ideal, even as it alienates her from her own temporal existence, is plain throughout *North & South.* Shelley's "Mont Blanc," "still, snowy and serene" and "piercing the infinite sky," is her prototype.[2] Taking the view of the sailor, she emphasizes the infatuation with the antivital ideal. Her beholder identifies with the powerful object even while the sensible, contingent, and individual self is threatened by it.

Yet within the poem is the memory of another iceberg, that of Melville's "The Berg," and with it another vision of the sublime as the treacherous magnetism of the void. Melville's poem, about the dream of a ship wrecking itself on an iceberg, speaks from outside the infatuation and looks on with horror. The poem begins and ends with sinister description:

I saw a ship of martial build
(Her standards set, her brave apparel on)

Directed as by madness mere
Against a stolid iceberg steer,
Nor budge it, though the infatuate ship went down.
The impact made huge ice-cubes fall
Sullen, in tons that crashed the deck;
But that one avalanche was all—
No other movement save the foundering wreck.
. . . . .

Hard Berg (methought), so cold, so vast,
With mortal damps self-overcast;
Exhaling still thy dankish breath—
Adrift dissolving, bound for death;
Though lumpish thou, a lumbering one—
A lumbering lubbard loitering slow,
Impingers rue thee and go down,

Sounding thy precipice below,
Nor stir the slimy slug that sprawls
Along thy dead indifference of walls.

Melville's poem presents the entity to which men are perilously attracted as a lifeless morass, a center of nonbeing. The heavy alliteration of his poem reinforces the weight and inertia of this magnetic, impassive presence which the brave and martial ship cannot resist. Melville's stolid iceberg nullifies the soul where Bishop's icy pinnacle behooves it. Yet Melville's disinfatuated vision, his horror of the abyss which the iceberg symbolizes, is not erased from Bishop's memory.

Closer to Melville's atheistic vision is that of Bishop's "The Unbeliever" (CP, 22). The figure for whom the poem is named aspires to no transcendent principle for which he'd "give his eyes" but instead "sleeps on the top of a mast / with his eyes fast closed." There is nothing up there to support him; his transport is without a foundation of belief. The Unbeliever remains suspended "in the air of the night," dreaming of a terrible fall into the natural abyss of the sea, "hard as diamonds" which "wants to destroy us all." But he trusts the power of his soul, trusts his fantasy, thus making his unbelief a kind of belief.

The poem offers two other vertical perspectives: the cloud imagines it stands on pillars; the gull thinks the air is like a marble tower on which his "marble wings" are set. Most readers identify Bishop with the unbeliever. But the structure of the poem—in which the unbeliever's remarks are in quotation, juxtaposed to those of the cloud and the gull similarly set in quotation—suggests the poet's distance from this hero. His unbelief, which is really a form of belief, is not the final thought of this agnostic. In a Blakean manner Bishop allows cloud and gull their relative perspectives. Bishop balances the stanzas, in which a series of short lines are closed off with a pentameter couplet. But the instability of the meter—ranging from dimeter to hexameter—heightens the precariousness of each stance. The cloud's illusion of a subjective absolute (he thinks himself "Secure . . . at the watery pillars of his reflection") is clearly undercut by the oxymoronic "watery." The gull seeks stability in a transcendent principle, founded on his illusion that the air is "like marble." But the unbeliever's trope should not be privileged, even if it is the one to which the poet is most susceptible.

Harold Bloom has read Bishop's "The Unbeliever" as an early commentary on the tradition of the sublime: "Think of the personae of Bishop's poem as exemplifying three rhetorical stances, and so as being three kinds of poet, or even three poets . . . The cloud is Wordsworth or Stevens. The gull is Shelley or Hart Crane. The unbeliever is Dickinson or Bishop . . . The cloud, powerful in introspection, regards not the sea but his own subjectivity. The gull, more visionary still, beholds neither sea nor air but his own aspiration. The unbeliever observes nothing, but the sea is truly observed in his dream."[3] The "unbeliever" does not experience the egotistical sublime, in which he might ascend to or become absorbed in a transcendent ideal. His negative sublime is a vision of powerful obliteration. But it is an illusion resulting from his height; closer up the sea is fluent (watery), not hard. The unbeliever gets to the top of the mast in sleep, "blindly" posting himself there on a golden bird (of Byzantium?) as though that alone might sustain him. It is only later, according to the gullible gull who "inquired into his dream," that the Unbeliever imagines his annihilation. Bunyan, following his biblical source (Proverbs 23:34: "yea, thou shalt be as he that lieth down in the midst of the sea, or as he that lieth upon the top of a mast"), criticizes all three stances, warning against Simple, Sloth, and Presumption.[4] They ignore Pilgrim and he continues on his travels, just as Bishop will return to inquiry and travel as the appropriate mode of consciousness.

The number of poems in *North & South* and *A Cold Spring* which invoke not only religious poets like Donne, Herbert, and Hopkins, but religious concepts and images, testifies to the importance of the divine in Bishop's early reflections. In most of these poems she expects revelation and finds instead a world abandoned of spiritual presence. But the expectation persists. Bishop's lifelong attraction to the poetry of George Herbert was not merely artistic; nor did she facilely translate his religious struggle into a modern, psychological struggle. To the Herbert scholar Joseph Summers, Bishop remarked on "how really concerned Herbert was with all these insoluble and endless and nagging problems of man's relationship to God . . . It is *real.*—It was real and it has kept on being and it always will be, and Herbert just happened to be a person who managed to put a great deal of it into magnificent poetry."[5] Bishop was another such person, though she faces "these insoluble and endless and nagging problems" quite differently from her perspective in a secular and skeptical age.

In modernizing the "problems of man's relationship to God," Bishop was most concerned with metaphor. The tradition she invoked based figurative language on the principle that nature was God's book. For Bishop, figurative language is no longer transparent but rather a condition in which we think and which determines our conceptions. Spiritual meaning recedes endlessly into this web of metaphors and is inseparable from it. "If we could only get through our own *figurativeness,*" she wrote in her notebook in 1934.

"God is for in, image within image, metaphor of metaphor—Even from day to day I think the levels I take my own *figures* on change, back & forth. So far I have probably only used four or five. (People less one sense—deaf, blind, etc.—how does it affect this general metaphor-life we all make use of?)"[6] Throughout the early poetry we find Bishop connecting the figurative power of the imagination with the search for an absolute, divine authority for that power. Her deictics vary—the divine is beyond, above, within—but a spiritual center remains the object of her tropes. She longs, as in "The Imaginary Iceberg," for a transparent, "artlessly rhetorical" image of the divine. But the poetry describes the elusiveness of this ideal in a world which seems to have been abandoned.

This sense of expectation and abandonment pervades "A Miracle for Breakfast" (CP, 18–19), Bishop's poem on the Depression which takes the Eucharist as its metaphor. The poem also invokes those antecedents to the sacrament, the Old Testament story of manna from Heaven and the New Testament story of the loaves and the fish. Herbert's poem "The World" provides the scene of Bishop's poem. Herbert describes the earth as God's palace defiled by human vanity and depravity, but which God generously rebuilds in Paradise. Bishop challenges these narratives of plenitude in poverty to express her contemporary situation. In this scene signs do not work wonders, the crumb is not transmuted to a holy presence nor the world, through grace, made a source of infinite supply. Where, the poem asks, is God's grace and plenty in this contemporary time of need?

The answer is not simply a negation of the divine principle. The beholder can experience delight in the grandeur of nature even while acknowledging her poverty. The crumb remains a crumb, though she may see a palace in it. "A Miracle for Breakfast," with its grumbling, matter-of-fact, commonsense voice, mocks and deflates the overly exalted voice of "The Imaginary Iceberg." But it also resists the panic of the Unbeliever, accepting a middle realm of an unpromising, but in its own right beautiful, land.

The sestina form of "A Miracle for Breakfast" is ideal for Bishop's purposes, to contrast the expectation of divine grace to the miracle of nature itself and to express the incongruity of poverty within the richness of the earth. As in "Anaphora" and "Love Lies Sleeping," Bishop uses the progress of morning light to describe a shift from high hopes to disappointment. Here, hungry souls await divine grace, which fails to come in the miraculous transmutation of nature they expect. But the poem does offer a qualified miracle: a new way of looking at nature, rather than a transmutation of it. The sestina form then also allows Bishop to explore figurative values and their relation to spiritual ideals—how we convert the finite to the infinite by metaphor. Her speaker does not find nature metamorphosed into infinite supply, but looks at the same nature (figured as a crumb) and sees it as a mansion, "made for me by a miracle." The miracle, that is, consists not in the transformation of nature but in the creation of nature itself, "through ages, by insects, birds, and the river / working the stone." In this revelation the speaker does not stand below, waiting for divine grace "from a certain balcony," but sits herself "on my balcony / with my feet up." This shift to an imaginative materialism anticipates Bishop's later value of sensory experience for itself. The end of the poem reminds us, though, that this perspective on nature does nothing to change the condition of poverty. The miracle is still at a distance: "A window across the river caught the sun / as if the miracle were working, on the wrong balcony."

Like Herbert, Bishop imagines the world as a stately house, from the balcony of which she looks out upon a river. Perhaps this is the river Jordan, across which lies the Promised Land. We might recall, however, that in Herbert's poem the balcony itself is built by Pleasure, unsatisfied with the fine dwelling it already owns. Bishop's world begins unsteadily. The personified sun on the river can barely get a footing, and the figures who behold this scene are going to be served a "charitable crumb" on a very cold morning, though they expect buttered loaves and "gallons of coffee." The ambiguous "man" who appears, an empty-handed, lofty God or Christ with "his head, so to speak, in the clouds," serves only "one rather hard crumb" which "some" (the disaffected atheists) "flicked scornfully into the river." The poet does not succumb to this cynicism, but looks out across the natural world from her grounded perspective and sees both its poverty, and its literal plenitude of "insects, birds and the river." She is able to call this actual world a mansion, but her vision is "not a miracle" because it does not provide her with consumable riches or end all want and suffering; "mansion" remains a trope, not a sacramentally realized presence of the divine in nature.

"A Miracle for Breakfast" resists the appeal to a higher power that can satisfy human hunger, turning instead to the beauty of nature, even in its poverty. Henceforth Bishop will focus less on those transcendent figures with their heads in the clouds and more on the immediate world, its richness and poverty. In place of sudden, divine intervention she stresses small details of the mutable world. Yet those "recurring thoughts" "in the back of my mind" nevertheless persist. Her emphasis in the descriptive poems is more on depths than on heights, but the vertical axis against the pull of the horizontal shapes her vision. The sense of figurativeness in everything remains, the sense of a ladder from the foul rag and bone shop. But the ladder leads to an absence. Only gradually and partially does the beholder recognize this absence as the force of her own mythopoetic imagination.

"Florida" (CP, 32–33) indeed concerns itself with "the detailed flatness of Key West" Bishop had mentioned in her notebook, rather than with loftiness. But the interest of the poem continually pulls us down, as if the ephemeral nature of the earth's surface might disclose some enduring principle beneath it. The beginning of "Florida" emphasizes the mutability of the natural world. Though tourists consider the state a haven of eternal youth, it turns out to be more lurid than florid, marked by decay rather than rejuvenation. "The state with the prettiest name" merely "floats" in brackish water; only loosely woven mangrove roots hold it together. Bishop describes nature's slow metamorphosis in figures that suggest sudden violence in the past; her vision of apocalyptic change contrasts with the facts of natural mutability. The oyster shells, made homeless by the death of the mangrove roots, become skeletons in the swamp, which is then "dotted as if bombarded, with green hummocks / like ancient cannon-balls sprouting grass." Many of

Bishop's descriptive poems repeat this contrast between apocalyptic vision and natural flux; it relates to her sense of how the imagination responds to temporality.

As if to check her own hysteria about invisible, apocalyptic forces, though, the poet introduces "unseen hysterical birds who rush up the scale / every time in a tantrum." The bird population includes the flashy and the clownish, making romantic Florida into a comic pageant. Yet the birds are impersonally beautiful, as well, "on sun-lit evenings," suggesting an appreciation of nature for itself, within temporal change. The turtles exaggerate the pathos of the scene, their "eye-sockets / twice the size of a man's"; but they belong to an endless metamorphic chain as they leave "their barnacled shells on the beaches." Again Bishop checks her sense of abrupt, vertical intervention with her sense of nature's gradual horizontal transformations.

But "Florida" never makes a final shift from one mode of apprehension to the other. A series of casual personifications, carried on in a list of shells' names (Job's Tear, Ladies' Ear), culminates at the end of the first verse paragraph in a focus on the mythic "buried Indian Princess." Again Bishop's vertical thoughts betray the flatness. Now the "monotonous, endless, sagging coast-line" is but the rotting skirt of this buried but spiritually abiding figure. The visual contrast of lovely shells along a monotonous beach is echoed in this long, stressed line, punctuated by the next, quick: "delicately ornamented." Bishop's attraction to surfaces is never overwhelmed by the lure of something beneath them.

Bishop uses personification (which the modernists eschewed along with many another useful trope) throughout her career with particular subtlety and self-consciousness. Here her self-consciousness intervenes to break the stanza and halt the movement away from descriptive surfaces toward mythic depths. The poet returns to description in the next stanza, but she replaces a detached, spatially vague enumeration of surface details with a newly focused downward perspective. That is, the description repeats in a naturalistic context the movement from surface details to underlying myth just enacted. The present tense of "Thirty or more buzzards are drifting down, down, down, / over something they have spotted in the swamp" makes the buzzards the surrogates of the beholder-poet, the "something" a more concrete substitute for the buried Indian Princess whom the poet projected. As we move from the shoreline inward, the mysterious swamp now becomes the focus. But the sky itself is swamplike, the birds like sediment, so that the "something" is both more immediate than anything in the previous stanza and also deeper, more mysterious, because nameless. No Whitmanian hermit thrush sings in this swamp; only the lovely, meditating voice of the poet playing along a range of internal rhymes and alliterations. The poem moves on to other ephemeral things. As the light changes from "sun-lit evening" to "After dark" the surface of nature becomes increasingly unreal, however: "the poorest / post-card of itself." Color, not only that of flashy birds but that of fading shells, is gone, replaced by the "fine blue solvents" and "black velvet" of decay. Out of this night darkness the poet imagines an ultimate darkness of a disappearing world, and the mythic voice ambiguously asserts itself through the ventriloquism of nature:

> The alligator, who has five distinct calls:
> friendliness, love, mating, war, and a warning—
> whimpers and speaks in the throat
> of the Indian Princess.

The status of this myth is as ambiguous as the message of the alligator. Bishop seems not to have determined what level of conviction will lie behind her trope of spiritual presence. Earlier in the poem, where "fireflies map the heavens in the marsh / until the moon rises," she introduces an image of transient, inventive order. Yet the poet longs to find a voice in nature, a buried spirit to predict the end of nature. Amidst the "detailed flatness" of Key West, then, even with her "eyes fixed on facts and minute details," Bishop's attention can be seen "sinking or sliding giddily off into the unknown,"[7] as she said of Darwin. The lure of background, of obscure heights and depths, of the sublime over the picturesque, continues in the descriptive poems of *A Cold Spring*, where Bishop associates it more explicitly with questions of origin and end. A Romantic poet might rest his interest in these obscurities and shift from visual to visionary awareness. Finding only abandoned meaning or (in the case of the Indian Princess) waning spirit, Bishop returns to the foreground, to the immediate, changing world.

Coleridge anticipates Bishop's objection to "all this loftiness" in a passage from *Biographia Literaria* which she recorded in her notebook:

> Something analogous to the materials and structure of modern poetry I seem to have noticed . . . in our common landscape painters. Their foregrounds and intermediate distances are comparatively unattractive: while the main interest of the landscape is thrown into the background, where mountains and torrents and castles forbid the eye to proceed, and nothing tempts it to trace its way back again. But in the works of the great Italian and Flemish masters, the front and middle objects of the landscape are the most obvious and determinate, the interest gradually dies away in the background, and the charm and peculiar worth of the picture consists . . . in the beauty and harmony of the colors, lines and expression, with which the objects are represented.[8]

Bishop renews the interest in foreground and middle, where the eye can find satisfaction, yet can acknowledge the lure of sublime background. This puts her between her contemporaries, concerned with luminous details and objects scrutinized with scientific precision (the roots and fern group), and her Romantic precursors, drawn to steep and lofty cliffs, to the misty regions of the landscape which invited their grand surmise.

In "Cape Breton" (CP, 67–68) Bishop's search for hidden meaning in the obscure regions of the landscape meets an impasse: "Whatever the landscape had of meaning appears to have been abandoned, / unless the road is holding it back, in the interior, / where we cannot see." The poet goes on to guess at what mystical signs might be written in nature's hidden regions. But we arrive at this center of interest only after twenty-nine lines of roaming description (exactly the same number of lines of description preceding the swamp focus in "Florida"). The poet seems to scan the landscape for a point of penetration, but satisfies herself, in the end, with an abstract image of flux.

Bishop's description of Cape Breton, while intensely visual and based on the pursuit of sight lines, defines no distinct perspective. Instead, it offers a general picture interspersed with several more immediate and more limited perspectives. At one moment our attention is taken to the outer islands, then onto the mainland; we look distantly at a road, follow a bus that comes along, then a passenger who gets off the bus; finally our attention is generalized to include the mist and the dark brooks. But as in the similarly structured "Florida," the apparently impersonal eye does reveal a participating consciousness which seems to be seeking out some place of entry or interiority from which it is repeatedly rebuffed.

The local fauna stand in, parodically, for the absent beholder. The "silly-looking puffins . . . with their backs to the mainland," standing "along the cliff's brown grass-frayed edge," gaze out at the sea's infinitude. As in many of Bishop's descriptions, though, the humor drops out quickly. This boundary becomes the edge of an abyss over which the sheep fall "into the sea or onto the rocks." The sea absorbs this shock and in turn is absorbed into the mist: "The silken water is weaving and weaving, / disappearing under the mist equally in all directions." As in "Florida," then, "Cape Breton" moves between the suggestion of apocalyptic change and gradual, natural mutability.

The pervading element in "Cape Breton" is the mist, traditional image of transience and mystery, of nature's fugitive quality. The presiding spirit of mutability, an "ancient chill" still touching the landscape, hints at its ultimate extinction. The mist is the penultimate phase in a metamorphic chain ending in this icy spirit : "like rotting snow-ice sucked away / almost to spirit; the ghosts of glaciers drift / among those folds and folds of fir." The sound of the line echoes its sense and recalls Frost's "Hyla Brook" in premature nostalgia and double ephemerality ("like ghosts of sleigh bells in a ghost of snow"). The language, like the mist, absorbs objects in the folds and folds of metaphor, where they become insubstantial and merely figurative. But punctuating this slow consumption of foreground are sudden, sharp, violent, and vital images—the stampede of sheep, the penetration of the "shag's dripping serpent neck," the pulse of the motorboat, the sawtooth edge of the firs. These maintain a balance in the description between the lulling, alliterative dream of the ancient chill and the sense of apocalyptic expectation, accented in harsher consonants.

The fugitive effect of the mist encourages the imagination to ground itself on something other than the senses. The pictorial tradition of the sublime has depended upon such effects to render the supersensuous nature of its objects. But Bishop thwarts the urge to find something behind the vanishing point or hidden within the mist. She contrasts the spiritual ghostliness to the positivism in the "dull, dead, deep peacock-colors / . . . certain as a stereoscopic view." A stereoscopic view avoids subjectivity by presenting two perspectives on a single object, thus checking the subjective flow of the poet's reflections.

Human agency is conspicuously absent from this scene. Frightening airplanes, pulsing motorboats, and bulldozers suggest technology transforming a landscape, but human beings do not emerge until the end of the poem. Traces of the human suggest a former presence and an illusion of some cataclysmic extinction. In a Romantic poet this would allow the free flow of the poet's meditation and invite the construction of an elegiac narrative (as in Wordsworth's "The Thorn" or "The Ruined Cottage"). Bishop's practical mind resists surmise. The road clambers along the "brink" of the coast (as though on the brink of falling over, like the sheep); the yellow bulldozers are "without their drivers" as though work were abruptly halted. But the obvious explanation comes in to check apocalyptic thinking: "because today is Sunday." Nevertheless, she imagines a present culture as though it were a former culture. In the third stanza Bishop describes the domesticated but abandoned landscape from the angle of an archaeologist contemplating ruins:

"The little white churches have been dropped [by some supernatural agency?] into the matted hills / like lost quartz arrowheads."

At this point in the poem (after the mention of Sunday and the little white churches) the speaker-beholder begins to search for meaning in scriptural terms. But the absences in the foreground of the description are not resolved by a presence in the background. While the bulldozers are supposedly abandoned in favor of spiritual pursuits "because today is Sunday," those higher purposes too "have been abandoned." In pursuit of a sublime, enduring meaning behind the abandoned foreground, the mind's eye moves into the "interior" beyond the visible, to "scriptures made on stones by stones." In imagining nature as a primordial holy book Bishop addresses a major tradition of sermons in stones, culminating in Wordsworth and Emerson. In American founding mythologies especially, the idea of the landscape as a revelation of God's truth had a strong hold. But the book of nature, for Bishop, is no longer readable or relevant in religious terms, only archaic and admirable and silent. Instead of a voice in nature Bishop finds a glyph, gray scratches made out of destroyed or decayed forests and scriptures written "on stones by stones," insular and unreadable signs which do not signify to the contemporary beholder.

Like Wallace Stevens in "Sunday Morning," Bishop turns from the religious sublime to a scene of natural mutability. She returns to the sensible world, to "thousands of light song-sparrow songs floating upward / freely, dispassionately, through the mist," just as Stevens returns, with more rhetorical flourish, to the casual flocks of pigeons with their "ambiguous undulations." Both poets displace timeless spiritual authority with beautiful, sensuous, but tentative, fleeting orders. Bishop accents the images with sounds, the hyphenated "brown-wet, fine, torn fish-nets" articulating the play of broken music against a pervasive silence. The synesthesia of the bird songs suggests the poet's shaping imagination, but it is of a different kind than the one seeking scripture in stones. The torn fish-nets suggest a humble attempt to capture some of the fleeting movement of life. But they are not instruments of mastery. For Bishop these are dispassionate, nonsignifying orders, part of the weave and mesh of nature, free of memory, passion, grief. Rising above the mist rather than hidden behind it, they suggest an alternative to the human impulse to permanent, apocalyptic myths: patterns without purpose, shaped and relinquished within time.

It is just at this point when the poet discovers an alternative order, a pattern without meaning or permanence, that the landscape ceases to appear abandoned and signs of human presence and vitality emerge. This is not an end-of-the world vision after all.

> A small bus comes along, in up-and-down rushes,
> packed with people, even to its step.
> (On weekdays with groceries, spare automobile parts,
> and pump parts,
> but today only two preachers extra, one carrying his
> frock coat on a hanger.)
> It passes the closed roadside stand, the closed
> schoolhouse,
> where today no flag is flying
> from the rough-adzed pole topped with a white china
> doorknob.
> It stops, and a man carrying a baby gets off,
> climbs over a stile, and goes down through a small
> steep meadow,
> which establishes its poverty in a snowfall of daisies,
> to the invisible house beside the water.
>
> The birds keep on singing, a calf bawls, the bus starts.

The poet, defeated in the search for transcendent agency or meaning, returns to a human scale and relative meanings. The symbols of sublime belief and of political and religious authority—the flag, the preacher's frock—become part of the quotidian. The school is closed, the flag is not flying, the priests are defrocked; the shelters and accommodations of culture are still denied. But the "poverty" is "established" gently, not apocalyptically. The man with the baby symbolizes vulnerability, but also a generational chain. He disappears behind a "snowfall of daisies," recalling but altering the glacial mist. His "invisible house," ephemeral as the water it stands beside, only mildly suggests a grave. In an earlier draft Bishop was more melancholy: "a gray house in front of the first that / looks as if it had been crying".[9] But there is no mourning here; disaster has been skirted at least for another day.

No apotheosis of loss weights this poem, no turning from loss to symbolic or metaphysical idealism. The consciousness of the poem follows out one last place of intimacy (the house) and surrenders it. Humanity does not control the point of view, though it remains a center of feeling in the poem. Bishop does not conclude, with Stevens, that "Divinity must live within herself." The various disappearances in the poem come together in a final image closed off to the interpreter.

> The thin mist follows
> the white mutations of its dream;
> an ancient chill is rippling the dark brooks.

The poem ceases its broad scanning of the landscape and its open, compiled clauses, turning instead to more general, abstract images and to a simpler syntax and rhythm. The tight weave of internal sounds in these lines ensures their decay in the mind. The parallel syntax echoes the mirroring in which the mist reads itself in the dark brooks. "Dream" and "ancient" cue the reader to prosopopoeia, to the invented, nonmimetic aspect of the reverie; but it is never strictly mythological, never wholly departs from particulars. Here the "vision" of the beholder takes on a new dimension. Both parts of the sentence include figures of reflection and correspondence repeatedly altered by time. Here at last are images of agency and communion, but which exclude the beholder. The dark brooks, reflective and profound, suggest a final focus of meaning and contemplation; but they also suggest the fluency of life and the force of mutability upon it. Their tense is continuous, not permanent. These are images of self-generating process: the mist is not the dream of some supersensible power but its own dream; the "ancient chill" is not a metaphysical principle acting upon the brooks but mutability itself, imagined mythopoetically. This alliterative and assonantal music sings no sermon.

These stages of meditation occur in many of Bishop's descriptive poems and define a characteristic movement. Repeatedly her eye is led from images of a disintegrating order or hierarchy (often vertically defined) to images of transience. That transience forms an attractive array of details; but the eye gravitates toward an obscure center in the landscape which the poet associates with profundities and mysteries of origin and destiny. Instead of providing a resting place, these dark centers rebuff the imagination. The poet returns to surface and to flux as the only reality in which the consciousness can act. Often Bishop relates this return to the emergence of a figure in the foreground—an animal or person—which becomes associated with ineffable, momentary coalescence of being rather than with an articulate order or wisdom. This structure parallels but revises the greater Romantic lyric, with its hierarchical movement from description to meditation, its pattern of crisis and resolution or fall and redemption. Bishop's structure of observation and reflection turns away from transcendent idealism toward the acceptance of change as absolute. "At the Fishhouses" (CP, 64–66) defines this structure of meditation most explicitly.

In "At the Fishhouses" Bishop explores the atmosphere of decline in an eschatological vision. She follows her usual pattern of loose description which builds up only gradually to thematic focus. Again we find the characteristic movement: horizontal images of transience and mutability dominating over vertical images of permanence and stasis lead to an obscure center of meaning, from which the beholder is excluded; the attention returns to the foreground and then moves off to an emblematic image of mutability.

"At the Fishhouses" is one of the earliest instances in which Bishop structures a relationship between observation and apocalyptic spirituality. From the beginning the poem's description prepares for a visionary leap. Indeed, "the surface of the sea" which appears "as if considering spilling over" in line 14 does spill over fifty-six lines later in an abrupt turn to vision from observation. The "dark deep" water, which she glimpses but evades several times, she finally touches and tastes in an imaginative baptism and deluge.

Bishop's concern with origins and endings emerges out of a competition in the levels of reference in the poem. This tension is focused in the middle of the poem with the encounter between the speaker (representing human, symbolic, vertical, and religious interpretation) and the seal (representing unmediated, immanent understanding of nature in flux). These two views converge, without resolving, at the end of the poem.

"At the Fishhouses" begins unassertively with a series of dependent clauses which seem to emphasize, through syntax, the difficulty of seeing:

> Although it is a cold evening,
> down by one of the fishhouses
> an old man sits netting,
> his net, in the gloaming almost invisible,
> a dark purple-brown,
> and his shuttle worn and polished.

The old man himself is "almost invisible" in this net of phrases. Fisherman, net, language, all such forms of mastery recede into the "gloaming," giving way to the strong, uncontrollable smell of rotting fish: "it makes one's nose run and one's eyes water" involuntarily. For Edmund Burke, such strong odors could produce an effect of the sublime. Here they are at least preparatory to such an effect, along with the dreamlike shroud created by the "gloaming."

As if in retreat from these powerful effects, Bishop's attention turns to the fishhouses highlighted in the title.

> The five fishhouses have steeply peaked roofs
> and narrow, cleated gangplanks slant up
> to storerooms in the gables
> for the wheelbarrows to be pushed up and down on.

Everything about her description of the fishhouses suggests their resistance to the fugitive effects of the first eight lines: their vertical thrust, the deliberateness of the wheelbarrows, the cleats which resist sliding. These literal "fortresses" anticipate the spiritual Fortress the speaker evokes later in the poem when she sings "A Mighty Fortress Is Our God." Against this image, however, Bishop sets the sea, which pulls the attention downward and threatens to spill over. Inverting mimetic norms in preparation for the visionary thrust of the poem, the poet describes the sea as "opaque." The land, by contrast, and even the fishhouses (now merely "small old buildings") are "of an apparent translucence" caused by a covering of fishscales and moss, signs of age and mortality. Where in Wordsworth's "Tintern Abbey" the scene is "green to the very door" and attests to nature's continuing vitality, here "all is silver." Helped by the assonantal *o*'s and alliterative *s*'s in the opening lines, the image marks the absorption of all things into nonbeing. The gaze moves upward again, "up on the little slope behind the houses" to "an ancient wooden capstan, / cracked, with two long bleached handles / and some melancholy stains, like dried blood." The capstan suggests a crucifix until we are reminded that the stains are not those of vertical incarnation but merely of mutability, "where the ironwork has rusted." This shift back and forth, from vertical to horizontal images, from symbolic to descriptive reference, initiates at the beginning of the poem a tension which will be central to its theme: the futility of human attempts to master flux.

The poem returns to the old man, who now takes on a more active role. As he "accepts a Lucky Strike" he becomes particular and emblematic at once, linked to the speaker in a specific ancestry ("He was a friend of my grandfather") and to the general erosion the poem describes, yet also a prophetic, even God-like figure, dispensing fate. Bishop's old man resembles, in his posture and role, Wordsworth's leechgatherer in "Resolution and Independence," as previous critics have observed; he shares the leechgatherer's representational ambiguity. Steven Knapp in *Personification and the Sublime* offers an excellent discussion of this problem in Wordsworth's

"Resolution and Independence," and his remarks apply well to Bishop's poem. Knapp explains the oddities and incongruities of the figure as Wordsworth's means of separating the leechgatherer's role as allegorical agent from his empirical status. Following Kant, Knapp stresses that the sublime depends upon this separation of concept and embodiment and its concurrent ambivalence.[10] In "At the Fishhouses" this division is more tentative and precarious. The fisherman is at once a symbol of destructive power and part of the world that is subject to destruction. Bishop treats her old man more metonymically than Wordsworth treats his, and only indirectly connects him with the powerful vision which follows their encounter. Yet he is almost comically symbolic of Fate as he "accepts a Lucky Strike." He is regally decorated with fishscale "sequins on his vest and on his thumb." While he scrapes off these "coats of mail" beside the "bloodied capstan" he is both divine and mortal, "his shuttle worn and polished," his blade "almost worn away," a receding image of mastery. Reinforcing the notion of the fisherman as divine agent, Bishop wrote to Anne Stevenson (March 20, 1964): "The last four lines of the first stanza . . . were a . . . donnée, as James would say, in a dream."[11] The poem will become more dreamlike later on, as the sea rises in her imagination. But just as the old man is rooted in empirical reality, so this vision of final deluge is based on something familiar: the tides in the Bay of Fundy which Bishop had undoubtedly witnessed.

The emphasis of the first half of the poem is upward: the fishhouses, the old man, the capstan. The poem shifts direction, however, turning to the sea and its correspondent figure, the seal. The middle stanza of the poem serves as a transitional space and a kind of physical and meditational ladder, up, across, down:

> Down at the water's edge, at the place
> where they haul up the boats, up the long ramp
> descending into the water, thin silver
> tree trunks are laid horizontally
> across the gray stones, down and down
> at intervals of four or five feet.

In a characteristic moment, Bishop turns her awareness to an impenetrable depth. All the previous images of mortality and mutability, the horizontal drift of surface pulling against the vertical fishhouses, seem to lead here, both visually and rhetorically. In "Cape Breton" this was the "interior where we cannot see." As the poet surrenders visual control she searches out a spiritual profundity. But Bishop has resisted this abyss from the beginning (like a disease she has acquired the susceptibility to), and she is not ready to confront it yet. In "Cape Breton" her attention shifted from the obscure scripture of nature to the birdsongs which rose out of the invisible depth. Here her attention turns to a seal who emerges out of the deep, dark space, a very secular prophet, antithesis to the old man.

Where the meeting between poet and old man reinforced a mythic habit of mind, that between poet and seal marks two contrastive understandings, one symbolic, the other literal, which the poem's imagery has developed. Indeed, the seal emerges to counter the symbolic fortress the mind builds against an unbearable elementality. Absorbing "sea" and "see," words repeated throughout the passage, the seal is the poet's messenger from the senses, the opposite of the obscure old fisherman (salt of the earth though he may be). The seal is immediate, highly visible and vital, particular and playfully anthropomorphic but not allegorical. If the old man is absence, the seal is presence. He serves as a foil to the meditative speaker and her culture, who respond to natural flux by invoking spiritual heights. While she sings "A Mighty Fortress Is Our God" (a God who, increasingly, seems hidden behind a fortress rather than serving to defend the world), he shrugs "as if it were against his better judgment." He embodies a kind of unmediated knowledge which challenges the prevailing interpretation of the beholder and helps to correct it. Their mutual but antithetical kinds of belief in "total immersion" (one figurative, one literal) mark distinct kinds of awareness.

The pragmatism of the seal does not undo the sublimity of the beholder's vision or banish the religious rhetoric of the poem. It only redirects it, back to the deep dark which has beckoned. The rhetorical and visionary mode of immersion of course dominates over the literal. First Bishop returns, as she predicted in her notebook, to the thoughts "in the back of my mind," the Christmas trees which "stand / waiting for Christmas." Ironically, they do not anticipate Christ's nativity but are, since they will be cut down, "associating with their shadows" in contemplation of their end. If the seal (serving as the poet's ally) lends a comic perspective to all this religious symbolism, he does not deem it irrelevant. The beholder moves rapidly from description to revelation as she turns back to the water, "suspended / above the rounded gray and blue-gray stones," and apocalyptic ice and fire consume her awareness. Bishop has used repetition (of sounds, colors, and words) throughout the poem as a major device for stimulating the shift from description to meditation. In this passage, in which the phrase "above the stones" is repeated four times, particulars are finally overwhelmed by a visionary flood.

The first two thirds of the poem have imagined the end of the world in terms of slow erosion. But the penultimate vision of the poem reimagines this process as an abrupt event. Finally the transmutation turns out to be more Heraclitean ("flowing, and flown") than Christian, a matter of process rather than cataclysmic intervention. The process is imagined in cataclysmic terms to give it sublime force. This Heraclitean (and, later in Bishop, Darwinian) sublimity is elemental, practical, and horizontal, not vertically transcendent. The qualifying devices of the poem—its empiricism and comic literalizations, its humor, its colloquialism—are temporarily suspended, and Bishop seems to have yielded her consciousness fully to this epiphany or imaginary baptism. "If you tasted it, it would first taste bitter, / then briny, then surely burn your tongue." But this revelation is communicated almost entirely in terms of the senses, synesthetically merged. "To see, hear, smell, taste, . . . feel with the sense of touch—hell" writes Ignatius Loyola in a passage that Bishop copied in her notebook from his *Spiritual Exercises*.[12] All the senses have been engaged in this poem and here converge in a Heraclitean consummation. Where Wordsworth departs into discursive wisdom, Bishop enters a sensuous trance. The revelation here "burns the tongue," silencing the beholder.

As the poem turns, at the end, to philosophical reflection, it remains tied to images, though they have become more explicitly figurative.

> It is like what we imagine knowledge to be:
> dark, salt, clear, moving, utterly free,
> drawn from the cold hard mouth
> of the world, derived from the rocky breasts
> forever, flowing and drawn, and since
> our knowledge is historical, flowing, and flown.

The poem seemed to be moving toward eschatological questions, but swerves to take up epistemological ones instead, asking not what fate is, or what God is, but what knowledge is. Even the definition of knowledge is figurative and speculative, a metaphor within metaphor, as Bishop wrote in her notebook about our idea of God. Here, we "imagine" knowledge to be "like" the burning brine. This is hardly the certain rhetoric of epiphany. Our knowledge of knowledge, like our knowledge of everything else, remains mediated. Yet "knowledge" here (not reason but understanding) resembles existence itself. Bishop's definition of knowledge indeed becomes a definition of transient life, not a defense against it. Against the "small, old" fishhouses and even the mighty fortress of religion, Bishop provides us with an image of mother earth, as an unprotective source and destiny. The figurative language here, like the "ancient chill" in "Cape Breton," makes no metaphysical claims; this is the freedom of, not from, necessity, the freedom of flux from the storehouses in which we attempt to master it.

The fragmented female anthropomorphism of the "cold hard mouth" and "rocky breasts" denies the gendered ascendancy of Mind as source over Nature. Bishop subordinates "knowledge" to nature, making it subject to flux and perhaps identical with it. This unnurturing image nevertheless resists the obsession with apocalyptic ending that informs the poem elsewhere. If knowledge and life are "flowing, and flown," they are also "derived . . . forever" from these unnurturing breasts, "drawn" from this unspeaking mouth. Bishop's conclusion is anti-Romantic, antimetaphysical. What is deep is not murky but moving and clear. What resolution and independence the poem offers hinge upon this consciousness.

In *A Cold Spring* Bishop ended her quest for a transcendental principle of meaning and value. Henceforth her vision would be insistently temporal, her sense of creative pattern and significance removed from any metaphysical basis and connected more with psychological and epistemological themes. But Bishop's turn away from idealism by no means resulted in a rejection of figurative values. If these values go underground in *Questions of Travel,* they reemerge in *Geography III,* where outer landscapes suggest and even allegorize inner landscapes. *Geography III* stresses iconography with its heraldic moose, its imaginary lion, its spiritual volcano. Bishop focuses on those moments within experience when the mind is made open, through the senses, to matters which are beyond its mastery. But while she gives mythopoetic shape to such moments, her imaginary heights and depths magnify forces and realities close at hand. Instead of standing over and against the contingent world, these iconic figures emerge from and express that world.

The geography lessons that introduce the volume tell us a good deal about what is to come. Bishop's very empirical-sounding epigraph (CP, 157) from *First Lessons in Geography* epitomizes a movement in the poetry from answered to unanswered questions, from mastery to perplexity. The questions in "Lesson VI" all have answers because they deal with generalities and abstractions. But when "Lesson X" (the true prelude to third-level geography) turns to particulars, the questions are no longer silenced by automatic answers, or even formed into complete sentences.

> *What is a Map?*
> A picture of the whole, or a part, of the
> Earth's surface.

What are the directions on a Map?
Toward the top, North; toward the
bottom, South; to the right, East; to the
left, West.
*In what direction from the center of the
picture is the Island?*
North.
*In what direction is the Volcano? The
Cape? The Bay? The Lake? The Strait?
The Mountains? The Isthmus?
What is in the East? In the West? In the
South? In the North? In the Northwest?
In the Southeast? In the Northeast?
In the Southwest?*

The items seem to spin off endlessly until all sense of defining order
and place dissolves; questions of where yield to questions of what.
Suspended from an answerable context, these words—island, cape,
bay, North, South—become available as tropes for an inner landscape as plural and proliferating as the earth, with a "center" equally
as arbitrary.

Like Auden in his sequence of landscape allegories ("Islands,"
"Lakes," and others), Bishop takes up various contours of the earth
as modes of consciousness. But at the same time those modes of
consciousness involve a fluent relationship to the earth, not just a
figurative relationship. Inside is continually permeated and shaped
by outside. We cannot but think of "Crusoe in England"—whose
island is a spatial rendering of accumulated memories, with fifty-two
volcanoes marking the weeks of a year—when we read *"In what
direction from the center of the / picture is the island?"* Crusoe's island is
indeed off-center, as he is, whether it represents the northerly
England (or Boston), or the southerly Brazil/Aruba/Galápagos. In
many ways, despite its higher degree of archetypal structure, *Geography III* is more spatial and visual in its conception than any other
volume of Bishop's poems. Loosed from the mastery of a system

or a metaphysical center, these archetypal meanings sustain the plurality and interdependence of a natural geography. At last, too, the topographer and the historian have ceased to compete and find a common mode of expression in spatial images that incorporate and express rather than deny flux. I will consider the archetypal rhetoric of *Geography III* throughout the rest of this book. In this chapter I will focus on its presence in one particular poem, "In the Waiting Room," in which the antimetaphysical icon of the volcano is especially potent.

The first question without an answer in *First Lessons in Geography* is *"In what direction is the Volcano?"* In the context of the geography lesson this is a straightforward matter. But in Bishop's figurative geography, where inside and outside flow into each other, the question is more complex. As the central icon of *Geography III*, the volcano is highly versatile, being both inside and outside, up and down, dead and alive, deep and high, solid and fluid, cold and hot. It provides Bishop with a metaimage of the world and her own emotional relationship to it. Perhaps most important here, the volcano is a static vertical icon which erupts into a horizontal flow. If the iceberg was the metaimage of control and autonomy, the volcano is the symbol of helpless volatility. Like the iceberg, the volcano is mostly invisible, not only geologically but in the sense that it is "imaginary," a symbol for the soul rather than an object in an actual landscape. Drafts of "In the Waiting Room" indicate the prominence the image of the volcano had for Bishop from the beginning of composition. Originally she had incorporated more details about the volcano from *The National Geographic:*

> The volcano,
> "the largest active crater
> in the world," Mount Katmai,
> "The valley of Ten Thousand
> Smokes." Thousands of upright
> plumes of steam, and called,
> I found out, fumeroles . . .

> There was a picture of
> Mount Katmai, with a line
> drawn in, in white, to show
> where it had blown its top off.[13]

Early on, too, Bishop had transposed the volcano onto the waiting room, the safe aesthetic distance of the sublime suddenly collapsing as the iconographic force of the image overwhelms the imagination: "Had a family voice misled me / into a crater of ashes / among Ten Thousand Smokes?"[14]

If icebergs behoove the soul with their suggestion of transcendence, volcanoes threaten immersion. The iceberg is supremely ordered as it "cuts its facets from within." The volcano erupts into amorphous flow which covers everything into one undifferentiated mass. To understand the iconographic importance of the volcano to "In the Waiting Room" (CP, 159–161), we need to consider what aspect of experience the poem relays. If the poems I have discussed so far emphasize a search for a meaningful, stabilizing center or absolute (yielding, as it may, to eschatological vision), "In the Waiting Room" describes the eruption of an abysmal vision into the controlling norms of consciousness. That eruption is connected with a sudden awareness of bodily contingency as a basis for connectedness to others, which in turn threatens the safe system of discrete entities which the speaker, and culture generally, rely on to order the world. The volcano is not a distant ideal or power, then, but something very close, inextricable from the perceiver rather than an object of aspiration or fear. The "something" which makes us all the same is also a "nothing," a void bursting the confines of language and culture.

Again Bishop moves from casual description to visionary reflection. The scene is a dentist's waiting room; the beholder is the author, three days before her seventh birthday. For thirty lines Bishop offers matters of fact from the point of view of a child most confident in their stability.

In Worcester, Massachusetts,
I went with Aunt Consuelo
to keep her dentist's appointment
and sat and waited for her
in the dentist's waiting room.
It was winter. It got dark
early. The waiting room
was full of grown-up people,
arctics and overcoats,
lamps and magazines.
My aunt was inside
what seemed like a long time
and while I waited I read
the *National Geographic*
(I could read) and carefully
studied the photographs:
the inside of the volcano,
black, and full of ashes;
then it was spilling over
in rivulets of fire.
Osa and Martin Johnson
dressed in riding breeches,
laced boots, and pith helmets.
A dead man slung on a pole
—"Long Pig," the caption said.
Babies with pointed heads
wound round and round with string;
black, naked women with necks
wound round and round with wire
like the necks of light bulbs.

The consciousness that initiates "In the Waiting Room" organizes experience in terms of stabilities of place, time, name. Bishop begins rather disinterestedly, lumping objects and people together. Her attention seems more absorbed by the images in the magazine, though she still presents them without much commentary, as unrelated to herself. Yet as the poem continues, it will be her sudden sense of resemblance to and association with everything named here so neutrally that generates the desperate questions and emotional unheaval at the center of the poem.

More specifically, the sudden revelation of the body, through the very alien images of the naked African women, paradoxically brings her to a disturbing personal/impersonal intimacy with herself and everyone around her. *National Geographic* was traditionally the medium through which readers could break the taboo of the body, but preserve cultural myths of distance and difference. It also reinforced a Western sense of superior mastery over "primitive" colonies. Bishop's poem shows how frail those hierarchical myths and distinctions are. Osa and Martin Johnson dressed in riding breeches and pith helmets may signify the brutal repression of the body (as does the strangulation of the African necks "wound round and round with wire"), but such images of repression are undercut by the universalism of "a dead man slung on a pole." We know nothing of the dead man's class or race—his state could be anyone's. (Drafts of the poem suggest that the dehumanizing "Long Pig" actually involved a misprint, but Bishop takes advantage of it to confront her reader with the boundaries of the human.) The child's consciousness is divided in these images. As reader of the magazine she shares cultural superiority, but this will give way to an identification, triggered by the figures of the naked women, with bodiliness and suffering. Her simultaneous repulsion and attraction are apparent:

> Their breasts were horrifying.
> I read it right straight through.
> I was too shy to stop.

The uncanny experience of something familiar in the strange pressures the fragile mastery of the world the child had maintained. She tries to avert her gaze by looking "at the cover: / the yellow margins, the date" as if to remind herself that what she sees has boundaries that separate her from it. To look up from the magazine would be now to make a connection, to see what it was I was in terms of the magazine's images, for the images have become iconic. The recognition of the body cannot remain contained in the imperial hold of the *National Geographic* but infects the room; the images on the page indeed become the room, no longer contained as mere pictures of faraway places.

Throughout the poem images, which promote resemblance, are more powerful than words, which designate differences. Looking at images initiates the trauma of identity in the poem; a "sidelong glance" is all the beholder can tolerate if the structures of difference are to be maintained. It is just at this juncture, where the powerful images in the magazine enthrall the beholder, that she hears the one sound of the poem, an *"oh"* of pain, accenting the middle of the steady trimeter lines. This sound is assigned to Aunt Consuelo and comes "from inside" the dentist's office. Yet "inside" itself has become a place without boundaries and thus difficult to distinguish from outside. Inside now includes, through an act of empathy or even introjection, the beholder's own mouth and later the entire waiting room, which becomes the inside of a volcano spilling over. The center is everywhere and nowhere, pressuring the steady beat of the trimeter lines.

Since the source of the cry becomes ambiguous, the cry itself becomes broadened in its meaning. "[An] *oh!* of pain" comes from the preverbal body, particularly (though not exclusively) the female body, which is inherently less differentiated than the male (detached from reproduction and nurture) and enduring more often than inflicting pain. The waiting room is a female space since waiting is what women do when they are maturing, preparing to give birth, and when the war is on. In the reproductive process the inside does indeed become the outside, so this may be figurative of a labor pain, or more abstractly, the pain of self-delivery into the world of relatedness. But the poem transcends gender in its exploration of "the family voice." This "unlikely" awakening to likeness does not lead to a reassuring sense of community but, since it is rooted in the shared abyss of bodily vulnerability, to the sense of "falling off the round, turning world / into cold, blue-black space" (like Emily Dickinson, "out upon Circumference"). If the wires round and round the necks of African women symbolize the strangulating force of culture, the round, turning world suggests a necessary force of gravity derived from the simple determinacy of objects and dates. This image of being outside of the world is paradoxically joined later in the poem to the sense of being inside a volcano, again dissolving distinctions of inside and outside, center and periphery. The room "was bright / and too hot. It was sliding / beneath a big black wave." And at the end of the poem "Outside, / in Worcester, Massachusetts" itself resembles the dormant volcano of the magazine, "black, and full of ashes." The symbolic eruption of objects into icons recedes in the last stanza of the poem as the beholder returns to places and dates. But we are obviously meant to see a change in the consciousness it records. The perceptual reality the beholder returns to after the metaphoric abyss has none of the categorical confidence with which the poem began. Worcester is now "night and slush and cold," and it is a time of "War." Indeed, war is a crisis of difference on a national scale. From the narrow sphere of the child's awareness, we have moved out over continents and across history. We are now not only emotionally but politically inside a volcano.

In "In the Waiting Room" Bishop remembers an experience of oneness:

> What similarities—
> boots, hands, the family voice
> I felt in my throat, or even
> the *National Geographic*
> and those awful hanging breasts—
> held us all together
> or made us all just one?

But the sense of oneness, without the metaphysical reference, is abysmal rather than blissful; it derives less from transcendent unity than from a fragmented vision of human contingency. Here Bishop clearly separates herself from Wordsworth, whose "Ode: Intimations of Immortality" decries the fall into difference and social definition and takes comfort in the promise of spiritual oneness derived from recollections of childhood. While a "timely utterance" restores Wordsworth's hope, the *"oh"* of pain marks for Bishop the abyss over which the body tilts. But throughout Wordsworth's poem are hints of another sublime which he resists but which becomes the focus of Bishop's poem. Wordsworth's insight into the condition of homelessness "In darkness lost, the darkness of the grave" begins (until the revision of 1820) in the lines "the grave / is but a lonely bed . . . A place of thought where we in waiting lie." That waiting place becomes, for Bishop, a "blue black space" from which there is no heavenly deliverance. Wordsworth again suggests a sublime of the void in which "custom" (like the bindings of culture Bishop depicts) becomes an abyss "Heavy as frost, and deep almost as life!" But Wordsworth rebounds with "O joy !" in a faith renewed through memory.

Coleridge precedes Bishop in doubts about this rebound. Indeed, there is much that aligns the two writers. Bishop's gothic and grotesque qualities, her moods of anxiety and dejection, her sense of otherness, all identify her as a modern Coleridge. Her notebooks and letters testify to the hold this poet had over her imagination. Writing to Robert Lowell (December 2, 1956) about the experience of reading Coleridge's letters, Bishop remarked:

> I read Coleridge, and read him, & read him—just couldn't stop—until he and the waterfall *roaring* under the window, and ten times its usual size, were indistinguishable to my ears. By the time he'd had "flying irregular gout," got himself drenched once more, was in debt, hating his wife, etc.—I couldn't believe that I really existed, or not what you'd call *life,* compared to that:—dry, no symptoms of any sort, fairly solvent, on good terms with all my friends (as far as I know).—I want very much to write some sort of piece, mostly about C, but bringing in Fitzgerald's "The Crack-Up," Dylan T., H. Crane, etc.—but don't know whether I know enough or have enough material at hand.[15]

These remarks in themselves contain aspects of the sublime. The natural iconography of the roaring waterfall blends with an intense reading experience (just as the volcano image merges with the immediate scene in "In the Waiting Room"). The little girl in Bishop's poem reads the magazine "right straight through" just as Bishop "couldn't stop" reading Coleridge. And her view of the world in this poem is similar to Coleridge's, who responded to Wordsworth's Immortality Ode with "Dejection: An Ode." Certainly Bishop would have been moved in a personal way by these lines in which the Wind speaks of human fears and agonies:

> What tell'st thou now about?
>   'Tis of the rushing of an host in rout,
> With groans, of trampling men, with smarting
>   wounds—
> At once they groan with pain, and shudder with the
>   cold!
> But hush! there is a pause of deepest silence!
>   And all that noise, as of a rushing crowd,
> With groans, and tremulous shudderings—all is over—
>   It tells another tale, with sounds less deep and
>   loud!
> A tale of less affright,
>   And tempered with delight,
> As Otway's self had framed the tender lay—
>   'Tis of a little child
>   Upon a lonesome wild,
> Not far from home, but she hath lost her way:
> And now moans low in bitter grief and fear,
> And now screams loud, and hopes to make her mother
>   hear.

This child recalls Bishop's youth more accurately than Wordsworth's happy shepherd boy. We hear its voice most poignantly in "In the Waiting Room."

While "In the Waiting Room" can be read as a glimpse into an abyss, then, it is also a poem of baptism, into the unsheltering truth of human connection and contingency. Volcanoes, too, "behoove the soul," for they signify the disruption of complacent difference and detachment, the encounter of the isolate self with the "similarities" that "make us all just one," even if the basis of that oneness is not a transcendent identity but a shared contingency.

Most of Bishop's poems return from their pursuit of heights and depths, as "In the Waiting Room" does, to the historical reality. She does not fall off into a timeless blue-black void. But Bishop returns to an uncertain world and often to the experience of travel. If the child in "In the Waiting Room" must project her imagination out to Africa in order to discover the contingency of her own existence, travel itself becomes a metaphor for that contingency.

Excursive Sight

This book asks how the questions of mastery—political, psychological, epistemological—which Bishop raises determine the shape of her poems and their way of seeing. Bishop's emphasis on travel throughout her career, as subject and theme, involves all these questions and has important consequences for her poetics. She developed a poetry of excursive vision.

It is not surprising that Bishop would find in travel a metaphor for consciousness. Her father, who died in Bishop's infancy, was connected with the shipping industry. She told Anne Stevenson: "My family seems to have been fond of wandering like myself—two, perhaps three, of the sea-captain's sons, my great-uncles, were Baptist missionaries in India."[1] Of course the experience of travel was, in her youth, as much a matter of exile as of quest. After the death of her father she moved to Great Village, Nova Scotia, to the home of her maternal grandparents, who cared for her after her mother's breakdown when Bishop was five. Her asthma, along with other problems, took her back to the Boston area for secondary schooling, to the home of her paternal grandparents and an aunt, in Worcester. After college at Vassar Bishop traveled in Europe, living in Paris for a year, then returned to New York City. Asthma sent her to Key West, Florida, though she lived in a hotel in New

York intermittently. A trip planned for around the world ended with an allergic reaction to a cashew in Brazil, where she was nursed to health by Lota de Macedo Soares, with whom she made a home in the mountains near Rio de Janeiro. Lota's suicide, precipitated, perhaps, by Bishop's excursion to Seattle, caused Bishop to flee Brazil and return to Boston, where she died in 1979. These are familiar facts to lovers of Bishop's poetry, despite the poet's reticence about her personal life. They form the condition of her existence and thus the basis of her vision. To Elizabeth Spires she commented: "I was always a sort of a guest, and I think I've always felt like that."[2] But Bishop found, out of this personal exile, not only a universal metaphor of homelessness but an opportunity for invigorating vision. If travel is an inevitable condition of mind and experience, it can be a means to free ourselves from a parochial view of the world, to heighten sensation and invention.

Travel is not merely a topos, occasion, or metaphor in Bishop's poetry, but a genre in the broadest sense—an attitude and meaning which find expression in a particular set of representational strategies. Travel is the spatial equivalent of her temporal vision. Bishop's travelers are driven by contradictory impulses. They want change, renewal, orginality, but also mastery (whether aesthetic, intellectual, or political) over the world they approach, in terms of the world they left behind. Bishop sees this double impulse of nostalgia and novelty as inescapable; she also sees both aims as illusory. Yet by emphasizing travel as a condition rather than merely a quest she defines a way of seeing that mediates between thought and experience, between the mind's laws and the test of those laws in experience and representation. Without a confidence in permanent archetypes, she asks, how can I order sensation? What sort of knowledge, pattern, meaning, is possible within excursive vision? If consciousness is always traveling, what orders can it nevertheless perceive and what sorts of truths might it hope to grasp?

These questions of travel, the subject of this chapter, run throughout Bishop's career. "Over 2,000 Illustrations and a Complete Concordance" introduces her ambivalence between the mastery and orderliness of the archetypal book (and the cultural hegemony it symbolizes) and the unruliness of travel. "Arrival at Santos" and "Brazil, January 1, 1502" examine the persistence and self-defeat of the colonial mentality. "Questions of Travel" examines the ironies of excursive vision, the failure to master different worlds with imported attitudes, and the discovery of value in the imagined particular. In "The Moose" and "The End of March" Bishop integrates the fragmented particulars of excursive vision with archetypal thinking, as a means of coming to terms with nature and one's own mortality. "Santarém"relates excursive vision to memory and portrays with sympathy an idealizing but restless mind.

When Elizabeth Bishop set sail for Europe after college she had already begun to meditate upon the relationship between imagination and travel that would become the subject of "Questions of Travel." Nearly thirty years before that poem was published, Bishop took up her notebook and wrote:

> If I stretch my thought to Egypt, to India, downtown, it is in my thought I see them and they are not, at the time, reality for me. If I go to these places it is a different matter. Reality, then is something like a huge circus tent, folding, adjustable, which we carry around with us and set up wherever we are. It possesses the magical property of being able to take on characteristics of whatever place we are in, in fact it can become identical with it.[3]

This simple opposition between the world merely contemplated in the mind and the world seen does not reduce, however, to a dichotomy between imagination and reality. The traveler does not abandon thought and take up substance. If "thought" is insufficient to know reality, it nevertheless remains a mechanism of perception, giving shape to what is seen. Reality, as something we "carry around with us and set up wherever we are," is a construct, yet, like any circus tent, it becomes an arena for illusions, "able to take on the characteristics of whatever place we are in." The young poet's enthusiasm reveals her preference for this versatile traveler's reality over armchair speculation. On another day during this passage to Europe she continued:

> I twirl like a button on a string, stretched between N.Y. & somewhere in Europe—
>
> As we get nearer, the actuality of the places we are going to see increases. Of course reality goes with one— but it is as if these cities, paintings, highways, churches were being built now, rising up, taking on color & dimension & perspective—[4]

Travel again makes reality, here in the more conceptual form of "actuality," appear fresh for the beholder, even original. Yet again it contrives reality rather than encountering a preexistent substance. Bishop sees the new scene "taking on color & dimension & perspective" very much like a work of art, with the difference that the beholder's position changes and reconstructs the scene.

These two passages express Bishop's very complex feelings about cognition, about how the mind represents the world to itself. It asserts the value of the mind voyaging out from ideas toward their objects and adjusting those ideas according to a new environment. The new representations, on the other hand, arise not from the objects themselves but from the beholder who brings "reality" with her, yet reconstructs it with each fresh apprehension. This "sense of constant readjustment" becomes a generative principle in Bishop's art, determining her narratives of beholding, her collapse of static, hierarchical orders and her tentative shaping of particulars. The complement to the traveler's constant reconstruction of reality is what Bishop called, in a letter to Marianne Moore, "that uneasy heightening of sensation that I think is really essential to travel."[5] To Anne Stevenson she wrote: "Lack of observation seems to me one of the cardinal sins."[6] Travel heightens sensation by dismantling old ideas; close observation becomes a source of renewal and reinvention. Bishop must surely have been attracted to Henry James's idea in *The Art of Travel* that "one's visions, on the whole, gain more than they lose by being transmuted into fact." Facts, he argued, and she would agree, "give more to the imagination than they receive from it."[7]

But this fresh and flexible sense of reality derived from travel can produce a certain uneasiness in the beholder as she misses a defining stability, a "home" where she masters her reality. Like a button spinning on a stretched string, the beholder's position between the familiar and the approached reality can be dizzying. The mind retains an idea (and inspires a desire) for what is original, unmediated, unchanging. There are times in the course of all the folding and adjusting when one fails to construct a habitable world and experiences what Bishop describes in "In the Waiting Room" as "the sensation of falling off / the round, turning world / into cold, blue-black space." The poet experienced something very like that sensation during this same, generally optimistic passage to Europe. She called the sensation "homesickness."

> Twice now, both times at the table, (which is natural enough) I have been overtaken by an awful, awful feeling of deathly physical and mental *illness*—something that seems "after" me. It is as if one were whirled off from all the world & the interests of the world in a sort of cloud-dark, sulphurous grey, of melancholia. When this feeling comes I can't speak, swallow, scarcely breathe. I knew I had it once before, years ago, & last night, on its 2nd occurance I placed it as "*homesickness.*" I was homesick for 2 days once when I was nine years old; I wanted one of my Aunts. Now I really have no right to homesickness at all. I suppose it is caused actually by the motion of the ship away from N. Y.—it may affect one's center of balance some way; the feeling seems to center in the middle of the chest.[8]

Bishop seems to dismiss the feeling when she says it is "caused actually by the motion of the ship," but that motion may itself be the literal equivalent to an existential condition, a constant transition that threatens all sense of attachment and belonging. If Bishop has "no right to homesickness" it may be because she has no home; yet she will go on to take that condition as at least figuratively true of everyone. Homesickness, in her poetry, does not depend upon a prior sense of being at home. It depends upon an idea of home as place of origin and innocence, where there is no stretch between the mind's ideas and experience, between desire and representation. Bishop sets this idea against the feeling of disequilibrium and the sense of the void so frequent in her poetry. One of the great virtues of her poetry is the honest ambivalence with which she faces both travel and home, both the pressure of constant adjustment and the nostalgia for an alternative, for a habitation of the mind's ideas and aspirations.

Bishop's poem "Over 2,000 Illustrations and a Complete Concordance" (CP, 57–59) confronts this ambivalence directly in a contrast between archetypal images in a book and glimpses from travel held in memory. The poet peruses an old illustrated Bible and concordance (it had belonged to her grandfather) and compares its orderly world with her memories of travel—fragmented and profane. Within this simple opposition, however, the poem allows both an integration of text and travel and an understanding of what each has to offer the imagination.

Bishop begins the poem by carefully describing the concordance as a static visual text: ahistorical, diagrammatic, perspectiveless. Such scenes are seen "in thought," to recall her notebook entry, and are not "reality" for her.

> Often the squatting Arab,
> or group of Arabs, plotting, probably,
> against our Christian Empire,
> while one apart, with outstretched arm and hand
> points to the Tomb, the Pit, the Sepulcher.
> The branches of the date-palms look like files.
> The cobbled courtyard, where the Well is dry,
> is like a diagram, the brickwork conduits
> are vast and obvious, the human figure
> far gone in history or theology,

gone with its camel or its faithful horse.
Always the silence, the gesture, the specks of birds
suspended on invisible threads above the Site,
or the smoke rising solemnly, pulled by threads.

Bishop organizes the images in a noncontiguous, geometric fashion equivalent to the arbitrary verbal order implied by a concordance (as opposed to the narrative of the Bible itself, as we shall see). Each image is a tableau with figures gesturing toward an unseen center of significance. Smoke and birds seem controlled by some invisible thread. While these images bespeak an ideal order (the cobbled courtyard is "like a diagram"), that order seems arid and hostile to human sympathies and passions. Bishop clearly identifies this order as her cultural inheritance, but the tone with which she refers to the contending Arab culture betrays her doubts about its hegemony. The "Christian Empire," represented here in drawings or photographs of the Holy Land, appears to exist in a wide, eternal space indifferent to humanity (its hegemony threatened by a diverse world, figured in the squatting Arabs, which does not participate in its rituals). "The brickwork conduits / are vast and obvious, the human figure / far gone in history or theology, / gone with its camel and its faithful horse." These timeless, sacred places, void now of the human stories (Bishop leaves open whether they are "historical or theological") which gave them ritual significance, appear simply foreign. These relics are "granted a grim lunette" through which we can peer and try to conjure the holy spirit, but Bishop has already questioned its presence. These images wrenched from life and set "in cattycornered rectangles" "resolve themselves" into a hierotactic order, but "caught in the toils of an initial letter," a typographical emblem of the divine "Word" that "grants" them their place, they seem in need of escape (perhaps by means of the "date-palms" that "look like files"). By the end of the passage she has revealed her cultural inheritance as desperately out of touch with contemporary reality.

Bishop finds that escape through a metaphor of penetration. The "eye drops, weighted" (by too intense a gaze on these sacred sites) "through the lines / the burin made," drop, that is, from text to world. The page becomes the shore, a prelude to the figurative crossing of representation (from text to world) and the memory of the poet's actual crossing to foreign lands. The static lines begin to "move apart"

> like ripples above sand,
> dispersing storms, God's spreading fingerprint,
> and painfully, finally, that ignite
> in watery prismatic white-and-blue.

The Word begins to release its tight hold over the imagination and its objects. Bishop describes this release of textual order as a Heraclitean crossing of fire and water, painful and delightful. From the world of the biblical concordance with its rigid, arid orders, she moves to the world of flux and vitality held in memory. These memories undermine the authority of religious symbols. She loses, in this venture, the solemn coherence of eternal, archetypal space, but as it burns and liquidates she recalls the raucous vitality of the actual worlds she has glimpsed in travel. From the textual mastery of archetypal space she returns to history.

A stanza break marks the figurative and literal ocean she crosses. At the beginning of the second stanza the ship enters "the Narrows of St. Johns." Characteristically, Bishop's change in orientation in-volves a change in scale, these "Narrows" immediately contrasting the "vast and obvious" ritual spaces. The images of memory, unlike those of the text, involve scattered details rather than grand designs. Where the Book was characterized by reverential silence and sacred monuments, travel impressions are marked by profane noise (high-lighted with the alliterative *g*'s) of people and animals. The bleating goats, the jukebox songs, the giggling prostitutes, the goggling guides express a pervasive sexual energy and exuberance that will not conform to a Christian paradigm. But where there is life there is also death. In contrast to the sacred Tomb with its ritualized spirit she finds a dead body littering the arcade; later she encounters the grave of a "poor prophet paynim" whose spirit has long since been blown away by desert winds. Bishop reencounters the ancient ambivalence: life is curtailed by death; the book escapes death, but also life. Bishop's doubt about the authority of Christian archetypes pervades the first two stanzas of her poem.

But the opposition between the two stanzas is not absolute, and the very forms that were undermined reenter in a new way. Each scene from memory is a parodic reflection of some biblical episode; the old schematic meanings are comically released into a life heartily indifferent to them. There are no holy revelations at St. John's (the place is entirely careless of its namesake), only glimpses of goats leaping up cliffs. The poppies irreverently split the mosaics; the dead volcanoes (anticipating Crusoe's) "glistened like Easter lilies," and the golden length of evening proffers for epiphany a dripping plush. The annunciation is an English woman pouring tea and observing that the Duchess is going to have a baby; Magdalenes appear as "little pockmarked prostitutes" who fling themselves naked and giggling against the speaker's knees.

One reading of these allusions is ironic: against the myth of invisible power amidst ancient and sacred spaces, actual memory offers a vision of anarchic and profane life. Thus religious ritual and tradition are diminished: "the Collegians marched in lines, / crisscrossing the great square with black, like ants." The memories test the myths of eternal significance and find them archaic and merely textual representations. But the allusions to biblical myth are not simply parodic or nostalgic; they disperse myth into life, the sacred into the profane. The humans "far gone in history or theology" have returned to continue the oldest story. The traveler orders experience in imagination and memory, but does not engrave or entomb it. Bishop's paratactic style and excursive vision do not relinquish symbolic patterns and values but merge them with the haphazard and the vital, where their hold is precarious. Everything may be only connected by "and" and "and," but parataxis (the scheme of enumeration and sequence as opposed to hierotaxis or subordination) is, of course, the major syntax of the Bible itself. The Bible narrates the story of continually deviant and propagating generations, though its commentators, systematizers, and illustrators may emphasize the hierarchical structures within this endless story.

There is something "awful but cheerful" about these scattered snapshots until the end of the stanza with its *memento mori*. The "pockmarked prostitutes" offering their wares for cigarettes remind the poet that the underside of all this vitality is death. "It was somewhere near there / I saw what frightened me most of all." The Tomb in the biblical concordance suggests a center of immortal significance around which the images are organized; but the engravings on the grave of "the poor prophet paynim" have eroded, to leave only the ironic exhortations "yellowed / as scattered cattle-teeth." The exuberant, prismatic surface of life here leads to a "keyhole-arched stone baldaquin" in which no spiritual presence is locked. "Open to every wind from the pink desert," this tomb is "half-filled with dust, not even the dust / of the poor prophet paynim who once lay there." Like one of the Arabs "plotting . . . / against our Christian Empire," the guide Khadour "looked on amused" at the Christian tourists, finding their holy land abandoned of spiritual meaning. This characteristic moment in Bishop's travel vision marks the dark sequel to her images of prismatic flux. Here Bishop locates the fundamental opposition between text and world. This encounter with the empty tomb forms the motive for her retreat from observation and memory into representation and art. It is the source, as well, of the "homesickness" she described on her passage to Europe.

The traveling imagination, seeking shelter from such annihilations and from the general fatigue of too much stimulation, turns back to the "heavy" book, weighted with the significance of engraved images. Bishop again breaks the stanza, but the white space is not absolute. As "The gilt rubs off the edges / of the pages and pollinates the fingertips" the book mingles with life, turning to dust, dispersing itself into the guilty world, yet also disseminating into that world its abiding mythic values. Returning to the book, her eye settles on an "old Nativity" significantly different, in its visual and linguistic representation, from the diagrammatic images of sacred sites that introduce the poem. A spiritual presence emanates from this homely site:

—the dark ajar, the rocks breaking with light,
an undisturbed, unbreathing flame,
colorless, sparkless, freely fed on straw,
and, lulled within, a family with pets,
—and looked and looked our infant sight away.

Here the real discontinuity of the book and the world becomes clear, and thus the tone of desire seems strongest. Unlike the earlier hieratic version of the book, this image is presymbolic and elemental. It represents itself, as the Word made flesh, rather than pointing to a higher force of the Word, in whose "toils" it is caught. Yet the plain language does not mask the fictionality of this ideal. "Why couldn't we have seen / this old Nativity while we were at it?" she asks, rhetorically. She could not have seen this old Nativity during her travels because its colorless, sparkless, unbreathing flame burns only in the imagination, unlike the "prismatic white-and-blue," that Heraclitean, watery fire of life, which earlier broke in under God's spreading fingerprint to dissolve the textual gaze. The passage is full of admiration for the power of art to inspire belief in its vision of innocence and originality. Unlike the grim lunette that holds the theological relic, this simple picture combines the virtues of immediacy and familiarity with those of abiding significance. The poet describes it in the most ordinary terms: "a family with pets." In contrast to the haughtiness of the Christian Empire and the Seven Wonders of the World, its modesty is eloquent. Bishop longs for a condition of awareness equivalent to the scene, an "infant sight" to match the scene of infancy. She seems, indeed, to identify herself, through illusion, with the infant in the image. But to have "looked and looked our infant sight away" may not be to sustain it. "Away," as in Keats, signals the end of illusion. The antithetical pun in "away" suggests the wish that one may forever gaze into the scene of innocence, forgetting time; yet it also reminds us that looking, observation, itself exists in time. One may in fact cause the departure of innocence, may use up one's infant sight (which after all is fresh only at first glance) in the act of looking. The beholder seems to feel no ambivalence toward this image. But the poet is wiser and reminds us that this representation, though "undisturbed," is also "unbreathing." This eternal flame, "freely fed on straw," is "colorless, sparkless" in contrast to the ignited life she recalled from her travels. Our representations express the mind's desires and ideals. They pry open the dark, light up the rock of necessity until they lull us into belief. In a sense this final vision reintroduces the Christian appeal which the middle of the poem eroded. The poet admits a nostalgia for the kind of epiphany she knows the world defies. But Bishop will always test such representations against what she knows of life from experience and memory.

"Over 2,000 Illustrations" presents, in three separate stanzas, three kinds of vision: monumental (in which the mind's forms preside over particulars), excursive (in which particulars challenge and assault the mind's forms), and domestic (in which the mind outdistances the monumental with its idea of home). In each stanza Bishop examines questions of mastery in terms of the relation between desire and representation, between cultural order and deviant reality, and between imagination and experience. Bishop reflects on various approaches to rhetoric: one dominated by pattern and archetype, one by allusive but elusive particulars, and another by symbols of the ideal. That middle state of excursive vision becomes her focus in *Questions of Travel,* which is about the "folding, adjustable" traveler's reality and the problems and questions that arise in that condition. The sense of an "engravable" pattern is repeatedly challenged as the beholder encounters unfamiliar worlds and struggles to shape them in relation to memory and expectation.

In *Questions of Travel* Bishop explores tensions between the desire for what is new or strange and the inclination to see it in terms of what we have known. Bishop goes further than a political and psychological reading of this ambivalence; she represents it as a conflict inherent in our awareness. Reality, as a construct in which we live and perceive, "goes with one" even as one attempts to escape it. The traveler is caught, then, in an ironic desire for both difference and mastery. In both "Brazil, January 1, 1502" and "Arrival at Santos" Bishop portrays beholders troubled by the resistance of the worlds they encounter to the versions of reality that they have inherited or contrived. The poet orders her images to expose the irony of her situation. In "Questions of Travel" she seeks a more viable relationship between imagination and experience. But it is in two great poems from *Geography III*, "The Moose" and "The End of March," that she discovers a way to release the imagination within excursive vision rather than restraining it.

Bishop's questions of travel are not only psychological and epistemological but political, especially for the North American. The poems in the Brazil section of *Questions of Travel* all deal with the ironic quest for a new Eden by forms of culture and consciousness that inherently defeat that ideal. The ideal itself, she shows us, denies the separate identity of the worlds encountered, and founders when confronted with it. Excursive vision attempts, then, to adjust the inherited constructions of reality ("circus tents") to the differences of the sensible world. Excursive sight is "stretched" between past and present, between home (as it is constructed in memory) and foreign lands. If "2,000 Illustrations" distinguished between the timeless patterns of the book and the scattered details of memory, these poems distinguish between the memory of cultural constructs and a reality which defies expectation.

"Arrival at Santos" (CP, 89–90) opens *Questions of Travel* in the voice of a tourist from a northern-industrial region, in search of paradisal innocence in the primitive south. Her colonialist view is thwarted, however. Her disappointment and irritation upon arrival at contemporary Santos can be heard in her parody of the finger rhyme "here is a church, here is a steeple" in which everything is placed and predictable.

> Here is a coast; here is a harbor;
> here, after meager diet of horizon, is some scenery:
> impractically shaped and—who knows?—self-pitying
>   mountains,
> sad and harsh beneath their frivolous greenery,

with a little church on top of one. And warehouses,
some of them painted a feeble pink, or blue,
and some tall, uncertain palms.

The alternate rhymes echo the poet's sense of decorum and mastery,
but the lines increasingly spill over in extra syllables and enjambments as the poem goes on. The prim syntax which opens the poem
quickly gives way to its elusive material. She is not only affronted
but deeply confused and more than a little threatened by the unwelcoming, uncertain order she finds, in contrast to the exotic but
transparent landscape she expected.

The tourist who had expected "a different world, / and a better
life, and complete comprehension / of both at last, and immediately"
finds instead a humdrum port, vaguely resembling what she had
imagined, yet elusive. "Meager," "impractical," "self-pitying,"
"frivolous," and "uncertain," this landscape affronts the traveler's
egoistic dream. More important, it presents a scene not fully present
or prominent, not imbued with meaning lovingly bestowed upon
the beholder, but obscure, uncooperative. These faint colors ("feeble
pink, or blue" warehouses as well as "frivolous greenery") present
a distinctly unromantic nature. "Finish your breakfast," the poet
reminds herself, voicing an imperative to return to the present and
immediate life, to break the nostalgic dream. Indeed, the arrival at
Santos becomes almost perilous as a boat hook (perhaps another
symbol of specifically sexual peril) catches Miss Breen's dress. The
appropriative traveler finds herself vulnerable to a world that refuses
to fit her preconceptions. She has not found the southerly land of
innocence to substitute for her post-lapserian northern home "in
Glens Fall / s, New York." The "fall" here rhymes with the "six
feet tall" Miss Breen, making her fall a hard one indeed. Miss Breen's
untypical stature and profession ("a retired police lieutenant") remind us to what extent she herself may be an exile in her own
"home, when she is at home." She and her companion, the poet,
seem, indeed, to be looking for home as much as fleeing one. They
nevertheless cling, like the colonialists before them, to the comforts

of home: "The customs officials will speak English, we hope, / and leave us our bourbon and cigarettes." While on the one hand they rely on familiar stimulants in the face of a landscape which proves less than stimulating, on the other hand they are astonished to find not primitive nature awaiting civilized mastery, but signs of an alternative culture to their own. This culture hails its own set of conventions, even its own flag (the only "brilliant" color in the place, obstructing the tourists' imperialist advance).

The tourists reassure themselves that this place is not their destination. "Ports are necessities," transitional spaces through which we pass to an ultimate horizon, they presume, in which they will experience "complete comprehension / . . . at last, and immediately." Yet Bishop's poetry gives us little besides transitional spaces. Her "homes" tend to be constructed out of old buses or railroad ties. The traveler must accept the constant slippage of reality, the sense of each "arrival" marking a point of departure toward an elusive destination. Ports (and bights, waiting rooms, islands) cannot be fixed in representation. Excursive vision forms transitional patterns of understanding as it sets up its circus tent. The ending of "Arrival at Santos" rises above its parodic speaker to reflect on the nature of representation itself in the condition of travel.

> Ports are necessities, like postage stamps, or soap,
>
> but they seldom seem to care what impression they
>   make,
> or, like this, only attempt, since it does not matter,
> the unassertive colors of soap, or postage stamps—
> wasting away like the former, slipping the way the
>   latter
>
> do when we mail the letters we wrote on the boat,
> either because the glue here is very inferior
> or because of the heat. We leave Santos at once;
> we are driving to the interior.

Bishop draws from the familiar traveler's baggage (of ports, postage stamps, and soap) to characterize the essential problem of the traveler's awareness. The representations she is able to form of the world she encounters have none of the desired boldness of color or definition, nor any ability to fix a reality for her or anyone else. The syntax here "slips" along the sound play just like the postage stamps on their inferior glue, shifting the focus of the sentence as the mind travels on. Bishop here turns her theme toward the act of writing itself, ungluing her similes. The wasting and slipping under the similes of soap and postage stamps mark the condition of all representation in contrast to the mind's desire for final thought. If the postage stamps slip, the letters do not reach home; the place cannot be conveyed because the vocabulary of home is obsolete. Ten lines after they "are settled" they "leave Santos at once; / we are driving to the interior" in ironic pursuit of that ideal which exists not in the interior of Brazil but in the elusive interior of their minds.

The passengers of the ironically titled "Arrival at Santos" are exiles from a dominant culture who nevertheless bring with them that culture's archaic values and preconceptions. The contradictions and disappointments they meet as they try to construct a vision of reality along these lines do little to defeat their ideal. In an early draft of an unfinished poem called "Bloody Boulevards" Bishop describes the horizon as a concept which we mistake for a reality, a point on the horizontal, determined by the limits of vision, which we misread as the beginning of a vertical, an ultimate destination. "We all need the horizon, so it hardens / in its definition: the horizon . . ."[9] For the traveler the horizon exists in a dynamic relation to immediate sensations which, as they fail to meet the terms of expectation, push the horizon back. "Other things that you & I imagined / were not often so obliging. / Still the horizon is unbroken."[10] Bishop does not imagine a mode of awareness free of the fiction of a horizon. But her deluded travelers view "the horizon" not as a relative construct, like "reality" itself, but as an object of their pleasure and conquest. In this they echo sentiments indigenous to American literature.

Henry David Thoreau, perhaps the greatest American excursive writer, turns a casual saunter into a crusade. His essay "Walking" presumes that the imperial traveler, leaving his home, may be at home anywhere. Indeed, in American frontier ideology the concepts of home and horizon are closely intertwined, the one defining and defined by the other.

> I have met with but one or two persons in the course of my life who understood the art of Walking, that is, of taking walks—who had a genius, so to speak, for *sauntering,* which word is beautifully derived "from idle people who roved about the country, in the Middle Ages, and asked charity, under pretense of going à la Sainte Terre," to the Holy Land . . . Some, however, would derive the word sans terre, without land or home, which, therefore, in the good sense, will mean, having no particular home, but equally at home everywhere. For this is the secret of successful sauntering . . . But I prefer the first . . . for every walk is a sort of crusade . . . to go forth and reconquer this Holy Land from the hands of the Infidels.[11]

Bishop addresses this presumption of conquest in "Brazil, January 1, 1502" (CP, 91–92), in which the poet, her companion, and perhaps all of us, delighting in a nature decked out for our pleasure, find ourselves implicated and indeed trapped in an ancient cycle of lust. For Bishop it does not at all follow that, "having no particular home," one is "at home everywhere" or may take dominion. The beholders in "Brazil, January 1, 1502" immediately attempt to domesticate what they see, converting nature to tapestry, as Bishop tells us through her epigraph from Kenneth Clark: ". . . embroidered nature . . . tapestried landscape." Clark is describing landscape painting that gives the effect of needlework. But Bishop describes a scene in nature, apprehended as if it were "just finished and taken off the frame." The baroque syntax of the long first sentence, kept under control by the line endings, reinforces the effect of the intricate detail woven into an overall visual pattern. But what appears at first to be mere aesthetic shaping becomes linked, later in the poem, to a suspect moral and political shaping.

> Januaries, Nature greets our eyes
> exactly as she must have greeted theirs:
> every square inch filling in with foliage—
> big leaves, little leaves, and giant leaves,
> blue, blue-green, and olive,
> with occasional lighter veins and edges,
> or a satin underleaf turned over;
> monster ferns
> in silver-gray relief,
> and flowers, too, like giant water lilies
> up in the air—up, rather, in the leaves—
> purple, yellow, two yellows, pink,
> rust red and greenish white;
> solid but airy; fresh as if just finished
> and taken off the frame.

Reading nature as tapestry, we assume several things: that it is designed for our pleasure, edification, and consumption; that it is a unified and symmetrical object; and that it is two-dimensional, vertical, and static yet, since it suggests depth, also penetrable. More than presumption, this reflects the structure of the mind. We apprehend "nature" as "landscape," as something intelligibly ordered. Here the ordering is a benign gradation of size and color, dominated, as tapestry tends to be, by foreground. But the very emphasis on foreground implies that all of nature has come forward to "greet" the beholders. The poem's beginning echoes Coleridge's "Lines Composed While Climbing the Left Ascent of Brockley Coomb": "Ah, what a luxury of landscape / meets My gaze!" Bishop withholds until later in the poem the ironic implications of this presumptuous mastery. Here her identification as a contemporary beholder with the beholders of 1502 (and, by the ambiguity of "theirs," with the original beholders, Adam and Eve) seems entirely positive.

But Bishop quickly begins to turn her description against the easy mastery of "embroidered nature" by drawing out the sexual and political undertones of the experience. The tourists' wish for specular possession of Brazil is likened to a wish for sexual possession, and both are finally compared to colonial aggression. Bishop's description, though primarily spatial, reenacts in its visual development a narrative of the Fall. Her speaker indeed recognizes "Sin" in the foreground of this "tapestry," thus ironically identifying the scene with Eden. Bishop makes fun of her speaker's allegorical ordering of nature, treating it as a form of imposition, a conceptual mastery of nature by ideas. But she also appropriates the allusion to the Fall in order to make a point of her own: our rapacious gaze defeats the very yearning for an apprehension of original nature, which in any case is merely a mirage.

If the landscape appears as art, art and nature are both approached in terms of a prior construction of the feminine as specular and erotic object. At first the construct is Edenic; the virgin freshness of the new year and new land suggests a paradise on earth. But this ideal feminine garden soon becomes a bower of bliss, a Spenserian Court of Sin in which the female Nature is no longer innocent hostess but maddening viper, particularized as a "red hot" female lizard.

The shift expressing the beholder's ambivalence toward nature occurs gradually in the description. At first the picture is entirely frontal; description presents foreground. But the rest of the poem both reverses the initial impression and unfolds as a logical consequence of it. As our pleasure in foreground becomes satiated we pursue an illusion of depth, of something within or behind the surface which we might possess. This visual move to background and depth thus finds an equivalence in the beholder's erotic desire. But the visitors, wanting to penetrate and possess this lovely scene they have constructed, become caught in its web. The charming foreplay of description excites the desire for meaning:

> A blue-white sky, a simple web,
> backing for feathery detail:
> brief arcs, a pale-green broken wheel,
> a few palms, swarthy, squat, but delicate;

and perching there in profile, beaks agape,
the big symbolic birds keep quiet,
each showing only half his puffed and padded,
pure-colored or spotted breast.
Still in the foreground there is Sin:
five sooty dragons near some massy rocks.
The rocks are worked with lichens, gray moonbursts
splattered and overlapping,
threatened from underneath by moss
in lively hell-green flames,
attacked above
by scaling-ladder vines, oblique and neat,
"one leaf yes and one leaf no" (in Portuguese).
The lizards scarcely breathe; all eyes
are on the smaller, female one, back-to,
her wicked tail straight up and over,
red as a red-hot wire.

As the "fabric" becomes a "web" the orientation of the picture moves downward; more *"r"* sounds are introduced and the scene becomes oblique, dark, violent, without disrupting the charmed tone of the description. Having converted nature to art, the visitors proceed to look for its significance. Bishop's irony works doubly here, mocking the lofty symbolic narrative we impose on nature ("big symbolic birds") yet revealing how we unwittingly reenact the narrative in our own rapacious will to possess nature as symbolic meaning. As we associate "meaning" with "depth" the "big symbolic birds" stand in profile, unlike those initial images which "greet" the beholder in full-face. Their "beaks agape" in shock, they make a gesture we must interpret. "Sin" refers not only to the erotic images in the scene but to our "sin," the erotic element of interpretation which wishes to possess nature. "Still . . . there is Sin" may at one level delight the beholders as another proof that they have discovered a timeless Eden; for the poet this "still" marks the crux of the beholder's self-entrapment, her *et in arcadia ego.*

As if to keep the chase going, the poet reparticularizes the scene and returns to the descriptive level. "Sin" turns out to be "five sooty dragons near some massy rocks." After the gradually cloying decoration of the first stanza, nature is now in siege; the rocks are "worked" by lichens, "threatened" by moss, "attacked" by scaling-ladder vines. The baroque curves reveal their serpentine aspect. Obliquity replaces transparence, and desire is deferred by inference and translation: "'One leaf yes and one leaf no' (in Portuguese)." The full enticement of the beholder comes when the scene turns away from her entirely, when "all eyes / are on the smaller, female [lizard], back-to, / her wicked tail straight up and over, / red as a red-hot wire." Of course this version of nature as a dangerous enticement is no less a construction than the original virginal one. It expresses the unwitting logic of the beholder's rapacious vision, which requires a metaphor of pursuit and penetration.

The landscape, which originally greeted the beholders, turns its back on them, inviting pursuit into its illusory depths. Here the poem breaks, shifting in the next stanza to 1502 and the perspective of the Conquistadors, with whom the modern visitors ironically identify.

> Just so the Christians, hard as nails,
> tiny as nails, and glinting,
> in creaking armor, came and found it all,
> not unfamiliar:
> no lovers' walks, no bowers,
> no cherries to be picked, no lute music,
> but corresponding, nevertheless,
> to an old dream of wealth and luxury
> already out of style when they left home—
> wealth, plus a brand-new pleasure.
> Directly after Mass, humming perhaps
> *L'Homme armé* or some such tune,
> they ripped away into the hanging fabric,
> each out to catch an Indian for himself—

those maddening little women who kept calling,
calling to each other (or had the birds waked up?)
and retreating, always retreating, behind it.

The "Just so" at first implies that the landscape is an unchanging
tapestry, always "fresh" for the cultured traveler seeking the delights of primitive nature. But the full ironic force of the description
weighs the history of rapine upon this "just so" and is further
developed by what follows it. Bishop reduces the phallic brutality
of the Conquistadors ("hard as nails") to a diminutive pomposity,
"tiny as nails, and glinting, / in creaking armor." She makes the very
object of their pursuit, the genii loci in the form of Indian maidens,
a fiction based on a lack of observation: they mistake the immediate,
diverse, unpossessable surface of nature (the birds waking up) for
a quasi-human depth. The tapestry does not veil nature (imagined
as heathen female to be pursued and subjugated) but absorbs its
invaders. The framed scene becomes an infinite regress of beholders.
To the Edenic myth is now added the story of the Crucifixion, which
Bishop treats in a similarly ironic way. These "Christians" "hard as
nails" repeat the brutal sacrifice in the name of which they march.

The ultimate master in this poem is history, which the travelers,
both contemporary and sixteenth-century, attempt to deny and
thereby ironically repeat. The scene is "not unfamiliar" to the
beholders of any age because they impose the constructs of the past
upon what they encounter in the present, a past "already out of
style when they left home." We enter the layers of history as we
tear away at the hanging fabric, though we sustain the illusion that
they are penetrating a maiden depth. Thoreau imagined that he
could undo history, could "go forth and reconquer this Holy Land
from the hands of the Infidels" (such as the lusty Conquistadors
who ironically fail to worship nature as God's image). Bishop's
modern view is more humble. She implicates herself in the lust,
catches herself in the erotic spectacle she has constructed from
nature. The mind continues to play its old tricks on the eyes,
promising us a paradise of yielding yet mysterious nature. The

desire for perceptual and cognitive mastery over the particulars of nature persists in the contemporary beholder.

For the nineteenth-century travel writer the assumption of timeless authority stabilized the traversal of space. The distinctions between the wandering, nature-loving Thoreau and the greedy, rapacious Conquistadors may seem vast, but the imperial rhetoric of their excursions brings them closer together. Quoting Alexander Selkirk, Thoreau exclaims in *Walden:* "I bathe my head in atmospheres unknown to my feet." The earth is his "Olympus," so he can claim: "I am monarch of all I survey / My right there is none to dispute."[12] Even as a "saunterer," then, Thoreau assumes the stationary prospect of the mastering gaze. The basis of his monarchy may be more ideal than that of the Conquistadors, but the impact on how details in a landscape are drawn into a pattern of significance remains the same: nature is a text and the beholder feels united with its author. Emerson's description of Thoreau's writing emphasizes the power of the imperial mind over all nature's plurality. "His power of observation seemed to indicate additional senses. He saw as with a microscope, heard as with ear-trumpet, and his memory was a photographic register of all he saw and heard. And yet none knew better than he that it is not the fact that imports, but the impression or effect of the fact on your mind. Every fact lay in glory in his mind, a type of the order and beauty of the whole."[13] Such remarks provide a model of awareness which is, being essentially atemporal and unitary, the very antithesis of travel. Fact, in the transcendentalist's treatment, is but a register of the divine; experience leads to apotheosis.

All but the last sentence of Emerson's commentary could apply to Bishop as well as to Thoreau. While Bishop unifies her poems thematically and formally, they do not propose a cosmic unity of which facts are the type. Rather, patterning in Bishop's poetry of travel tends to be tentative and local, driven more by the imaginative (not strictly psychological) needs of the beholder than by some divine order of which the poet is interpreter and participant. Bishop's consciousness is travel-bound, temporal, and particular. Where it does allow for cognitive shaping her imagery suggests ideas of mutability and history rather than timeless totality. Thus Bishop's patterns, rather than emerging in epiphanic moments, tend to be gradual, contingent, and nonapocalyptic. Bishop is interested in the experience of beholding available to the ordinary person, not just the visionary, transcending poet. Hers is the perspective of the tourist, the passenger, the stroller on the beach, or some other distinctly unheroic, often collective identity, slow to catch on but often granted insight through careful attention to the world. The world is pieced together without benefit of revelation, from glimpses in time that give something back to the imagination. Bishop's confidence in the cumulative force of these glimpses varies. Her grotesque style is not always aspirational; it can be decreative and anxious. But she offers an alternative to apocalyptic vision that sustains the moral and imaginative value of observation. She replaces transcendence and mastery with pleasure in discovery and surprise, in variety and particularity, and in the way the world invites but eludes the interpreting mind. Excursive sight, in Bishop's poetry, defines a dynamic, open relation between fact and interpretation, in which the poet's cognitive reality is repeatedly folded and adjusted. The knowledge gained in these poems pertains less to things in their relation to the "order and beauty of the whole" than to history and to the beholder's desires.

Several stylistic and rhetorical qualities follow from the choice of travel as a major figure of consciousness. As we saw in "2,000 Illustrations," the choice is not one of an inchoate stream of particulars over against the diagram, but rather between a static, declarative shaping of the world in thought and an experimental shaping of the world observed. Visual and conceptual order in Bishop's poems of travel is exploratory, gradual, and transient. Images are fragmented and perspective is uneasy; imaginative shaping yields to the discoveries of the eye. Indeed, the traveler's experience repeatedly defeats her desire for visionary mastery. Unfamiliar reality assaults her sense of proportion and scale. But the particular, spun out from the flux of images, remains a source of delight and a stimulus to the interpreting, mythopoetic imagination. Bishop does not ask her reader to chose between a unified and a particularized view of the world. Her poems entertain many unities, aesthetic and conceptual. But she constantly adjusts these to change and to the uniqueness of all she beholds. Similarly, her poems often present particular, sensible objects as sources of self-forgetful pleasure, which nevertheless arouse the shaping imagination.

The representation of discursive sight leads Bishop, most often, to a paratactic rather than a logical or associative structure. The postcard, the travel notebook, dashed-off first impressions provide the contexts for even her most meditative poems. Her lists have the desultory and formless appearance of random observations culled from memory. But the catalogue with its rhetoric of democratic enthusiasm, its sense of the continent's diversity, is basic to American literature. As Lawrence Buell argues in *Literary Transcendentalism*, "The catalogue is prized chiefly by Transcendentalists as the closest verbal approximation they were able to achieve to the boundless vitality of nature."[14] Bishop's travel writings, like Thoreau's, are "catalogues extended through time and space," with the difference that they are no longer indexed to a divine principle. She arranges and sorts according to questions of history and self-location.

The choice of the catalogue form implies a certain relinquishing of overt control over the whole, a heightening of the particular over the general. The catalogue records glimpses and reflections but does not allow these to become stable; it moves on to other first impressions. Transcendentalists dealt with this apparent formlessness by constant reference to the law of organic form and the revelation of unity in all things. Bishop's catalogues tend to submerge their conceptual principles. Her traveler is more likely to register puzzlement or complaint in nature's endless flora and fauna than ecstasy in the evidence of God's infinite book. Her poems sound more like postcards than literary journals; they represent first impressions sketched before a scene becomes too schematized or reflection too deep, and sent home to those living an old way of life.

But if the journal, catalogue, and postcard in Bishop reduce poetic authority over observation, they do not entirely erase it. She creates circus tent constructions, transported to the strange locale and taking on the color and quality of their new surroundings. The interpretive mind accompanies the quest for new images and sensations. "All thinking is analogizing, and it is the use of life to learn metonymy," wrote Emerson, and Bishop would agree, though with the qualification that no supreme fiction, no ultimate metaphor, overrides the local force of metonymy.[15] Bishop represents consciousness struggling to establish meaningful order in the moving plethora of facts, struggling to read fact before it slips away from its names. Simply bearing witness to the world's variety remains a positive value within the poems as significance advances and retreats. That shaping will always be "historical"—both a reading of history and historically contingent.

"Questions of Travel" (CP, 93–94) marks a shift away from the critical irony of "Arrival at Santos" and "Brazil, January 1, 1502," in which the observer's will to shape the world according to archaic or ethnocentric desires is punished with disillusionment or frustration. In "Questions of Travel" the observer's openness to the inscrutable world of particulars results in compensations for the weariness the poem first expresses. These compensations—of heightened sensation, imaginative play, historical and personal awareness—constitute a positive alternative to the dreams of originality and novelty, transparence and mastery, that motivate the traveler. The speaker recalls her travels, not now from the point of view of someone at home with a book, but of someone still amidst strange surroundings. The sense of "home" as an alternative to travel no longer seems valid. Though the present scene bewilders her with its rate of change, its obscure fragments of history, she is able to construct, in memory, a perceptible reality and to interpret it, partially, and for herself.

Excursive vision is dynamic and plural; thus Bishop organizes the images and concepts of "Questions of Travel" to emphasize particulars and ad hoc reflections over mastering patterns of image and theme. Here are "questions" that have occurred and images that have stayed in the process of folding and adjusting the circus tent of reality to new surroundings. The poem begins in complaint about all the flux and first reflects negatively on the motives for travel. But as the speaker begins to itemize what has been seen along the way, the poem takes on a more balanced, even delighted tone. The act of travel itself is portrayed not as a quest but as a questioning, an interrogative and interpretive rather than an appropriative or purposive stance. As such, the poem orders its images as invitations to questions and interpretations, some more conclusive than others.

Like "Over 2,000 Illustrations" and "Arrival at Santos," "Questions of Travel" begins in complaint: the world encountered in travel cannot be mastered and seems indifferent to the aesthetic and cultural expectations of the beholder. Instead, its own metaphoric power overwhelms her. Instead of expressing discomfort at the meager quality of the landscape (as in "Arrival at Santos"), Bishop here protests its plenitude, of a monotonous, Heraclitean variety: "There are too many waterfalls here." Too many for whom? For the human perceiver, whose tolerance for change and loss is more limited than nature's. The tourist prefers change in the landscape to be circumscribed by permanence. But this reality causes her imagination to work against desire, to speed up rather than halt the flux. Her tropes emphasize temporality rather than spatial stabilities, project her forward in time rather than evoking primal scenes. Bishop marks the movement in several extended, enjambed lines and repeated words:

> There are too many waterfalls here; the crowded
>   streams
> hurry too rapidly down to the sea,
> and the pressure of so many clouds on the
>   mountaintops
> makes them spill over the sides in soft slow-motion,
> turning to waterfalls under our very eyes.
> —For if those streaks, those mile-long, shiny, tearstains,
> aren't waterfalls yet,
> in a quick age or so, as ages go here,
> they probably will be.

But if the streams and clouds keep travelling, travelling,
the mountains look like the hulls of capsized ships,
slime-hung and barnacled.

Bishop's imagination accelerates flux far beyond normal visual apprehension, leaping from streams to the sea, from the present to a
future age when "streaks" will become "waterfalls." Causal links
speed up as clouds become waterfalls "under our very eyes." Where
Wordsworth sees "stationary blasts of waterfalls," Bishop sees them
"travelling, travelling." Space compresses time and expresses it but
does not fix it. The "tearstain" waterfalls suggest not only her own
lament but a universe of loss. The mountains, which ought to
provide an antithesis to this flux of the streams and falls, become
metaphorically absorbed into the flux as "the hulls of capsized ships,
/ slime-hung and barnacled"—abandoned to mutability. The patterning and figuring impulses of the beholder work against her
desires; she seems desperate for some anchor in this flow.

The poet finds a staying influence in two sources which resist the
broad sweep of the first stanza. The first is self-reflection, which
situates her in personal history as opposed to the vast geologic
history she imagines herself witness to. The second is attention to
unique particulars, which steady the pace of her meditation, in
contrast to the initial, generalized images of change and catastrophe.
These "anchors" do not offer the possibility of "a better life, a
different world and complete comprehension of both," do not, that
is, offer transparence or mastery. But self-location and attention to
individual facts promote her engagement with an alien world.

The poet first turns from the dizzying force of change around her
to an analysis of her motives for travel. "Should we have stayed at
home and thought of here?" But this very quesiton presupposes
fixed points which the poem undermines as it continues. "Home"
turns out to be nowhere, and "here" has been defined by flux. The
poem goes on to consider skeptically, but finally to choose, what it
reveals as a necessary condition of travel. But this does not render
the moral quandary meaningless, for in choosing and thus affirming
travel she redefines it, against mastery and toward inquiry.

The second stanza of "Questions of Travel" names several quests impelling the traveler: the quest for the exotic ("strangest of theatres"), for the new perspective ("the sun the other way around"), for the unique ("the tiniest green hummingbird"), and for the mysterious ("inexplicable old stonework"). These objects do not offer any structure or pattern. They are presymbolic or postsymbolic, but empty of significance for the beholder. They mark the traveler's quest for novelty and variety, reduced in "one more folded sunset" to a form of repetition. The epistemic value of this collection of empirical phenomena is small; but even while questioning her motives the beholder remains susceptible to the "childish" pleasures of pure sensation and discovery. Indeed, she implies an affirmation of things "instantly seen and always, always delightful" as they are to a child. The childish motive, the infant sight, is valued for itself. The traveler's baggage has, always, "room / for one more folded sunset." As the poet reflects upon what, from her travels, might have been dispensed with, her attitude changes. We must "dream our dreams / and have them too" because the imagination with its broad outlines needs the constant counterpoint of worldly particulars, needs even to enter history (with all its repetition). Imagination, defined as "dream" at the beginning of the poem, now becomes the interpreting and ordering mind. The catalogue rhetoric of the poem reduces the authority of mental arrangements, but does not belittle it.

> But surely it would have been a pity
> not to have seen the trees along this road,
> really exaggerated in their beauty,
> not to have seen them gesturing
> like noble pantomimists, robed in pink.
> —Not to have had to stop for gas and heard
> the sad, two-noted, wooden tune
> of disparate wooden clogs
> carelessly clacking over
> a grease-stained filling-station floor.
> (In another country the clogs would all be tested.

Each pair there would have identical pitch.)
—A pity not to have heard
the other, less primitive music of the fat brown bird
who sings above the broken gasoline pump
in a bamboo church of Jesuit baroque:
three towers, five silver crosses.
—Yes, a pity not to have pondered,
blurr'dly and inconclusively,
on what connection can exist for centuries
between the crudest wooden footwear
and, careful and finicky,
the whittled fantasies of wooden cages.
—Never to have studied history in
the weak calligraphy of songbirds' cages.

Once again we find Bishop's spatial arrangements forming a "calligraphy" of historical import. This wonderful catalogue of souvenirs appears random, but the artist's memory has shaped it to reveal a way of looking at, even of tentatively interpreting, the world. This is the world of humans and domesticated nature, though, not the inscrutable world of elemental nature, or of ruins lost to historical understanding, which the first stanza depicted. What the poet recalls from her travels are images of home—not her own, of course, but coloring it by association. These scenes are marked by a very precarious effort at order.

An expressive silence frames this second list, first the silence of the trees along the road, "like noble pantomimists," and finally the "golden silence / in which the traveller takes a notebook, writes." Between these silences are sounds, not voices, yet significant for the listener. The objects of memory are not the empirical validation of "imagined places." Rather, the observed world becomes the stimulus to the interpreting imagination. The order the beholder forms does not represent an alternative to the vision of continuous, rapid flux at the beginning of the poem. The focus on particulars here, however, and the relation of those particulars to one another do modify the feeling of futility at the outset. Things observed are far from mastered, but they are "pondered," however "blurr'dly and inconclusively," for what they reveal of human history. Where the "old stonework" and its setting had formerly seemed "inexplicable and impenetrable," the "strangest of theatres" also contains gesturing pantomimists. The force of fate that earlier seemed to propel the streams into waterfalls is here (the travelers having had to stop for gas) the happy accident which occasions insight. The singular detail from nature in the first stanza ("the tiniest green hummingbird in the world") signified nothing but itself. Here, a human detail, the wooden clogs, suggests a story that generalizations cannot discover: that within the careless, makeshift world of travel and flux (the road, the gas station with broken pumps, the plebeian footwear) men have aspired to higher and more perfect things. The birdcage in the form of a "bamboo church of Jesuit baroque: / three towers, five silver crosses" is an ideal of shelter, a symbol to stand against the feeling of "too many waterfalls." The images of songbird and cage, which appear so frequently in Bishop's poetry, and often together, suggest the "less primitive music" of the lyric impulse in the midst of historical consciousness (with its own "sad, two-noted, wooden tune"). This "centuries"-old connection between historical reality and "fantasy," between travel and dream, is precisely what the beholder reenacts in her questions of travel. It is the general law which embodies all the others.

For this reason the poem turns inward from studies of history to self-study, not as a final solution but as an inevitable step.

> —And never to have had to listen to rain
> so much like politicians' speeches:
> two hours of unrelenting oratory
> and then a sudden golden silence
> in which the traveller takes a notebook, writes:

These lines flow directly from the catalogue, as if they were a natural part of it. What is the traveler's place in this endless catalogue? The outer world again becomes a deluge, one of rain like "two hours of unrelenting oratory." Nature finally has a voice, a relentless one, but it is in "golden silence" that the beholder is stimulated to write. The deluge is perhaps also, through the simile, the deluge of platitude—especially about who we are, what we owe our allegiances to, where our home and future are—the platitudes that fill up "politicians' speeches." The traveler goes beyond these platitudes to a sense of freedom within necessity, a yielding to travel. But the stimuli of travel—the heightened sensations, hieroglyphs, and ritual pantomimes—must also be quieted for self-reflection to occur. Bishop echoes Thoreau, who at the end of *A Week on the Concord and Merrimack Rivers* writes:

> Silence is the universal refuge, the sequel to all dull discourses and foolish acts, a balm to our every chagrin, as welcome after satiety as after disappointment; that background which the painter may not daub, be he master or bungler, and which, however awkward a figure we may have made in the foreground, remains ever our inviolable asylum, where no indignity can assail, no personality disturb us.
>
> The orator puts off his individuality, and is then most eloquent when most silent. He listens while he speaks, and is a hearer along with his audience.[16]

Bishop's oracle of silence remains cryptic. The general law is not one that can escape the interrogative of travel. It is the law of travel.

> ". . . *Continent, city, country, society:*
> *the choice is never wide and never free.*
> *And here, or there. . . No. Should we have stayed at home,*
> *wherever that may be?*"

The poet begins here like a politician or an orator. Against the self-doubt at the beginning of the poem she offers a theory of determinism: there are few real choices anyway. For Thoreau "walking" was a liberation from social and cultural constraints into the infinity of the world over which God reigns and the poet presides. For Bishop "freedom" is a condition of inanimate nature figured in the flux ("dark, salt, clear, moving, utterly free") rather than a condition of the self. But she checks herself. The *"No"* concludes the poem in uncertainty, or rather, in change, and makes the end a reflective image of travel, not its apotheosis. In this sense it offers the only just reply to Pascal's remark, which Bishop paraphrases in the beginning of her poem, "I have discovered that all the unhappiness of men arises from one single fact, that they cannot stay quietly in their own chamber."[17] Pascal presumes a concept of home which Bishop dissolves. The question "Should we have stayed at home" is preempted by another question, "wherever that may be," which perpetuates the quest.

Bishop's travel poems, dominated by catalogues of things seen, include moments of reflection and retrospection, acts of tentative summing up and taking stock, assessments of the relation between process and goal. These end-of-the-line moments arise when the tolerance for plurality and particularity wears down; they do not mark a mastery over the world's variety. Bishop's questers remain questioners, not politicians or orators. The interrogative mood shapes her reality as well as her syntax. As the world resists her efforts to master it as knowledge, the questions turn inward and abstract. It is in this manner that *Geography III* can be read as more self-reflective than Bishop's earlier work, not because the self is its primary subject or the significant center of all visual experience. If the self is more prominent in *Geography III* than in other volumes, it is less integrated and less located than before.

The other major difference between the travel poems of earlier volumes and those of *Geography III* is that the latter are more overtly figurative and even archetypal within a descriptive norm. In the course of excursive vision Bishop develops central moments of coalescence and plenitude which she often figures in vertical images. But these are not epiphanic in the sense that they might foreshadow a transcendent destiny. Nor are they mythological. They remain within a horizontal, evolutionary view of the world and the self in the world. They represent a momentary integration of imagination and elemental being in time. While these images do not accumulate as a mythic system, they arise at characteristic, compensatory moments, after the fear of death has gripped the traveler's consciousness or the dream of home has proved illusory. "The Moose" and "The End of March" are strikingly similar in pursuing this structure of anxiety, dream, and compensatory vision in time. Without overriding the plurality and particularity of the traveler's observations, the intense, figurative moments in these poems give them a thematic and formal resolution that some earlier poems lacked.

I have defined excursive vision in Bishop's poetry as a gradual and tentative constructing of reality from the immediate material of observation. Within her folding and adjustable "circus tent" the world appears fragmented and unresolved. In *Geography III* Bishop allows for a new kind of shaping that preserves the sense of the road and is not overarching or teleological. To the catalogue she adds a stronger accent of trope, becoming less hesitant about designing memories of travel to express emotional problems and resolutions. *Geography III* continues the nostalgic dream of home but provides alternative satisfactions: moments of plenitude in flux, of imaginative habitation in the wilderness.

In "The Moose" and "The End of March" Bishop's excursive vision ceases to be a form of restraint against imagination (against the imposition of desires upon the experiential world) and instead becomes a satisfying integration of imagination with experience. The imagination is allowed to do more than merely "ponder" "blurr'dly and inconclusively." She allows, instead, moments of completeness through figurative power which are not merely a return to self-reflection. These are not optimistic poems. They offer no shelter from mortality, insisting on our inability to master fate or nature. But as they yield to flux they discover profound satisfaction in imaginative responses to the elemental world.

"The Moose" (CP, 169–173) describes a bus trip from Nova Scotia on the way to Boston, during which the vehicle passes through small towns, enters an "impenetrable wood," and is forced to stop because of a moose on the road. The poem builds in anxiety as it moves from a domesticated landscape, but the encounter with the moose, which halts the travelers, brings "the sweet / sensation of joy." Excursive vision, with its fragments and conjectures, replaces the mastering structures of domestic vision. But excursive vision is rewarded, not with epiphany but with a moment of coalescence that no other structure could provide. The accumulative, as opposed to apocalyptic, vision of Bishop's travelers in these poems becomes the equivalent of the process by which experience becomes poetry. A plurality of fragments gradually become ordered and distilled into an assertive form. By basing poetic invention on experience, however transformed through language and imagination, Bishop unites herself with ordinary beholders.[18] The travelers no more see objective truth in the form of the moose than the poet transparently tells a literal event. The travelers are predisposed to value the encounter with the moose by the series of interpretive acts that precede it.

"It was all true," Bishop told Elizabeth Spires about "The Moose," going on to mention minor alterations and compositional arrangements. "It was written in bits and pieces over a number of years and, finally, it all came together."[19] The poet is portrayed, like her travelers, as a slow absorber of reality rather than a visionary. The most complete record of the event retold in "The Moose" is a letter to Marianne Moore dated August 29, 1946, a full thirty years before the publication of the poem.

> I came back by bus—a dreadful trip, but it seemed most convenient at the time—we hailed it with a flashlight and a lantern as it went by the farm late at night. Early the next morning, just as it was getting light, the driver had to stop suddenly for a big cow moose who was wandering down the road. She walked away very slowly into the woods, looking at us over her shoulder. The driver said that one foggy night he had to stop while a huge bull moose came right up and smelled the engine. "Very curious beasts," he said.[20]

The details are reordered and reappropriated in the poem, but they are nevertheless the same. A later letter to Anne Stevenson dated

March 6, 1964—still twelve years before the poem's publication—fills in the earlier part of the poem: "Great Village is very small and well-preserved . . . dark red soil, blue fir trees—birches, a pretty river running into the Bay through 'salt marshes.'"[21] Out of this "material" base Bishop developed her spiritual narrative.

> From narrow provinces
> of fish and bread and tea,
> home of the long tides
> where the bay leaves the sea
> twice a day and takes
> the herrings long rides,
>
> where if the river
> enters or retreats
> in a wall of brown foam
> depends on if it meets
> the bay coming in,
> the bay not at home;

Bishop returns in this poem to some of the imagery of "Cape Breton," a scene of closed shelters, ubiquitous mist, meandering road and bus. Both poems start from a broad, detached prospect and move in to the human scale of the bus. Each pursues a dreamy, contemplative mood but punctuates it with peripheral glimpses of catastrophe. What most distinguishes "The Moose" is the focusing, restorative moment in which the animal appears. Where "Cape Breton" loses direction and dissipates in an abstract figure of mist, the feelings arising from the troubled enumerations of "The Moose" are absorbed in a final, satisfying image which is not simply a shift away from reality, but rather an integration of imagination with reality coalescing in a single image, an integration of excursive and symbolic vision.

At the beginning of "The Moose" Bishop works for a grammar and syntax that embody the condition of consciousness in which travel predominates. As in "Questions of Travel," the poem eventually slows its syntactic arrangements to a pace of meditation. But the first impression is one of flow. The streamlined arrangement of words on the page (twenty-eight stanzas of six short lines each) and the apparently endless first sentence of the poem prepare us for the horizontal consciousness of "The Moose." ("Cape Breton," by contrast, pursues a more relaxed, meandering line appropriate to a detached speaker.) Line breaks, mostly end-stopped, define a processional, trimeter rhythm. They emphasize the shortest grammatical units, especially prepositional phrases, which push the main, controlling clause farther and farther from the reader's grasp. A series of fragmented glimpses anticipate but never identify a centering or unifying object. The prepositions drive the description, emphasizing horizontal movement (in contrast to the ups and downs of "At the Fishhouses"): "from," "where," "on," "past," "through." Even "down" intersects the vertical: "down rows of sugar maples." The verticals—sugar maples, clapboard churches, twin silver birches, hollows and rises—merely accent the traversal. The first two stanzas describe "home" as a "narrow," literally provincial place, thus stimulating the urge for movement, just as the opening "From" is no grammatical resting place (as a subject in this position would be), but only a mark of departure. But a chain of images and a clear rhythm do emerge in the opening stanzas. The "home of the long tides" in the first stanza transforms the meaning of "home" to a transitional space and initiates a flow that effects the "river" in stanza two; the river in turn determines the "silted red" look of the sun which reddens the sea or "veins the flats' / lavender, rich mud / in burning rivulets." The river, extended to the sky, transforms that celestial permanence into a lava flow.

The sense of fragmentation basic to excursive sight intensifies in the next section of the poem, a catalogue extended in space and time. The poet says "good bye" to the comforts of home—"the farm," "the elms," "the dog." The fog encloses them all so that they are lost not only to the traveler but to the world. The spatial departure of the poet thus becomes parallel to the temporal departure of day and, by extension, of living things. Bishop similarly coordinates the westward movement of the bus with the advance of evening, allowing metonymic associations without disrupting the descriptive purpose of the stanzas. The bus itself is a kind of battered body, a mutable thing, its "dented flank" of blue enamel set against the "pink" flesh-tones of the sky reflected on the windshield. But these associations are left as gestures only.

In stanza eleven the nature of the fragmentary images changes. In place of a domesticated world closing down or bypassed, we find an obscure world riddled with danger signs.

> A pale flickering. Gone.
> The Tantramar marshes
> and the smell of salt hay.
> An iron bridge trembles
> and a loose plank rattles
> but doesn't give way.
>
> On the left, a red light
> swims through the dark:
> a ship's port lantern.
> Two rubber boots show,
> illuminated, solemn,
> A dog gives one bark.

The syntax of this passage reinforces the panic building in the images as the darkness overtakes the flickering world, punctuated by red lights, rattles, and barks. Bishop checks the accelerating anxiety of the poem, however, with the entrance of the "freckled woman" into the bus. Real and particular against the ghostly signals outside the bus, she predicts the moose, calling the night "grand," clearly enjoying something greater than her own domestic world. Her cheery presence cannot dispel the gloomy, gothic atmosphere, however.

Though anticipated in the mystical fog and the anthropomorphic "lupins like apostles," the mythic orientation of the poem really begins with the entrance into the New Brunswick woods in moonlight. In this light the darkness becomes an allegorical predator. (She will have to move away from allegory to integrated myth.) The impenetrable woods have preternatural agency, "hairy, scratchy, splintery," wolflike in relation to the ephemera of mist "caught in them like lamb's wool." But Bishop does not yield to the temptation of allegory. She naturalizes the image again, softening the effect of the animation with "on bushes in a pasture." The allegorical potential of "hairy" is resisted; once again Bishop checks her apocalyptic thinking. Excursive vision remains gradual, tentative, accumulative.

The fantasy of the predatory woods causes the poet to seek shelter in the reverie of a safe home—the "Grandparents . . . in Eternity." Thus the poet removes herself entirely from the surroundings rather than allegorizing them. This "dreamy divagation / . . . slow hallucination" arises within the collective unconscious of the passengers rather than in a superior poetic awareness. The dream imagines an alternative to the predatory darkness, a state of affirmation or acceptance rather than fear of life and death.[22] This comprehensive and consoling vision (rendered in the most homely terms of grandparents in an old featherbed) responds from outside experience to the vision of disaster that the poet pursued from the bus window. The grandparents represent the end of the line, a nonexcursive view in which things are "cleared up finally" (no longer misty or dark); everything that was going to happen has happened. The dream is also a memory of Bishop's childhood in Nova Scotia (a return, in reverie, to the place from which she has just departed). These are her own grandparents she remembers, talking of people in her family or village, though now their overheard conversation is projected into a domestic concept of "Eternity." "Eternity" for Bishop is the end of the line, a retrospective rather than a transcendent point of view in which anxiety, regret, anticipation have no place. It is not a place of mastery (as the night as predator is) but of acceptance.

But the traveler cannot dwell in this dream of domestic Eternity any more than in the allegorical paralysis before the void. Its point of view lies outside experience. While the dream relieves the tension from prior stanzas, the beholders must reenter experience from this restorative reverie and integrate the divided consciousness of the poem which excursive vision and reverie have created. The moose provides this integration.

The affective power of the moose is due in part to her full representational presence in the poem, after a long sequence of glimpses, gestures, premonitions, and dreams. She is not on the peripheries but "in the middle of the road." Whatever figurative value accrues to her is reckoned with her unmistakable reality. The moose is distinctly not part of a dream—the bus jolts to a stop—yet she retains a preternatural, otherworldly character within her elemental reality. She emerges from "the impenetrable wood" and remains associated with its dangers and mysteries, yet "'it's a she'" and thus gentler, less "hairy, scratchy" than the woods. She is "high as a church" and hieratic in her presence, yet she is also "homely as a house," familiar, domestic. The "homely" may suggest an uncanniness in the moose, that combination of the domestic and the otherworldy, the familiar and the strange which Helen Vendler so eloquently described.[23] With that uncanniness comes ambivalence. The moose is "safe as houses," that is, not securely safe and perhaps even dangerous. Yet there is no impulse to turn away from her. She is "Towering" yet "antlerless." She "looms" yet her feet are planted firmly on the ground. She does not recede but rather approaches the travelers, "comes out" to express the unknown. They deliberately "look" now; they do not merely glimpse.

The travelers respond with words conspicuously inadequate to the presence. The "man's voice" that "assures us / 'Perfectly harmless'. . . ." would diminish the grandeur of the female moose; the "quiet driver" finds the moose "Curious" but is himself peculiar in "rolling his r's." But if their speech does little to master the presence they have encountered, the poet clearly respects her "childish" fellow travelers in their capacity to experience, collectively, an intense feeling.

The encounter with the moose, as representative of elemental nature, allows a communal response unavailable within the provincial world of "fish and bread and tea," which is organized for comfortable survival. But it is connected to the dream which immediately precedes it, in which the realities of death, sickness, even madness that erode domestic security are recognized and accepted. Before the dream the world was seen by an isolated excursive viewer as a series of disparate, fragmented particulars ominously hinting at some vague apocalyptic threat. The passengers awake from this dream to the sensible world momentarily coalescing in the figure of the moose, which can be viewed with curiosity rather than dread. She is "homely" not because she represents a return to the illusion of protection left behind but, conversely, because the earth itself in its very elementality is a kind of home. Bishop viewed this idea more negatively in "Squatter's Children" (CP, 95), where she was challenging Wordsworth's notion in the Immortality Ode that nature is God's mansion:

> Children, the threshold of the storm
> has slid beneath your muddy shoes;
> wet and beguiled, you stand among
> the mansions you may choose
> out of a bigger house than yours,
> whose lawfulness endures.
> Its soggy documents retain
> your rights in rooms of falling rain.

But in "The Moose" this momentary yielding to nature as home produces "this sweet / sensation of joy" both physical and spiritual at once, because the beholders have passed through the dream in which loss and pain have been accepted.

In her notes for the poem Bishop recorded this aphorism: "our nature consists in motion; complete rest is death."[24] The poem emphasizes the transience of the moment and the bitterness of its passing. Bishop's figure-in-the-road is traditional. Wordsworth is often halted in his travels, but the figures that loom out from his excursions are generated by and quickly absorbed into his visionary autobiography. They prefigure an apocalyptic vision and usually prepare for abstract meditation. The clarity of the moose's presence, and the absence of commentary by the poet on her symbolic import, add to her affecting power. Far less allegorical, she belongs to her environment and to time, not to any teleology. Bishop and her fellow travelers can crane their necks backward and see an image in the moonlight. But that image is also temporal: "then there's a dim / smell of moose, an acrid / smell of gasoline." "The Moose" reminds us that excursive vision does not "fix" an image into a grim lunette or tapestry, but enters it as a temporary focus for imagination that needs coalescence. The moose satisfies the desire for spiritual meaning (high as a church) and for familiar order (safe as a house) without losing its primary impact as a physical presence. In this sense, the moose is the integration of the symbolic imagination with excursive vision.

"The End of March" (CP, 179–180), a poem about a walk along the beach at Duxbury toward an abandoned house, moves through representational stances in a way that parallels "The Moose." From a fragmented, transient view of the world it gravitates toward a desolate allegory, from which it recovers first through a dream of home but finally through an immediate if temporary reconciliation to nature in a moment of imaginative and sensual delight. The dream of home in this poem is rather different in the stance toward experience it posits. Both are end-of-the-line spaces. But instead of "Eternity," where everything is cleared up, the "proto-dream house" of "The End of March" presents a representational ideal in which the facts of the world no longer intrude at all. Autonomy and completeness are achieved by closing the world out. As attracted as Bishop is to this dream, she awakens from it, as in "The Moose," to the reality of travel. But again she finds compensation in an imaginative response to the physical world.

The characteristics of excursive vision—grotesque fragmentation of images and their signification, reduction of poetic authority, progressive and accumulative rather than instantaneous and totalizing vision, surprise and discovery rather than apotheosis—are all present in "The End of March." Yet Bishop finds a larger role for the imagination than in other excursive poems. She develops an antimythological myth, a pattern of relatedness for her observations which is at once creative and grounded in equinoctial realities.

As in "The Moose," we enter a landscape that withdraws from

rather than greets the beholder: "withdrawn as far as possible, /
indrawn: the tide far out, the ocean shrunken, / seabirds in ones and
twos." The growing sense of exposure, this time to "The rackety,
icy, offshore wind," drives the imagination toward desolate allegory
and retreat from experience, before it becomes reconciled to reality.

> The sky was darker than the water
> —*it* was the color of mutton-fat jade.
> Along the wet sand, in rubber boots, we followed
> a track of big dog-prints (so big
> they were more like lion-prints). Then we came on
> lengths and lengths, endless, of wet white string,
> looping up to the tide-line, down to the water,
> over and over. Finally, they did end:
> a thick white snarl, man-size, awash,
> rising on every wave, a sodden ghost,
> falling back, sodden, giving up the ghost. . . .
> A kite string?—But no kite.
>
> I wanted to get as far as my proto-dream-house,
> my crypto-dream-house, that crooked box
> set up on pilings, shingled green

Bishop organizes the poem by introducing a number of image
fragments which she reimagines and assembles into a fabulous plot
which binds the imagination to experience. At this point the symbolic meanings she reads in the detritus on the beach (like Walt
Whitman "seeking types" in "As I Ebb'd with the Ocean of Life")
are not reconciled to reality but rather drive the beholder away from
reality. The "lion-prints" on the sand, like the hairy, scratchy woods
in "The Moose," suggest the barest outlines of an allegorical
agency. But even here we may infer an element of humor in the
poet's attitude toward this allegory, arising as it does from the
homely proverb that March comes in like a lion. The excursive
vision leaves the lion figure as a gesture only; it is simply enumerated and suggestively juxtaposed to another fragment: the "kite

string . . . but no kite." This image of disconnection marks the shift to fantasy. As if frustrated by the fragmentation of excursive vision, which turns up a "sodden ghost," the poet seeks its opposite, an entirely autonomous state in the "proto-" "crypto-" dream house. The monument, too, was a "crooked box / set up on pilings." Artichoke-like, the dream house has interiority but no core. But the ghost or spirit "given up" by the kite will be reimagined in the house as a new continuity: "electricity, possibly / —at least at the back another wire / limply leashes the whole affair / to something off behind the dunes." The house replaces the kite she couldn't find on the beach, Benjamin Franklin's transmitter of electricity and thus "A light to read by," against the darkness that pervades the poem.

The end-of-the-road quality of the house is indicated by its "palisade / of . . . railroad ties" protecting it from the spring tides. Yet "Many things about this place are dubious." The house is hypothetical and obscure, but perhaps dubious as well as an object of desire. Indeed, it reminds one of a grave, a crypt, as well as a work of art. The hypothetical ideal "within" means complete removal from the world known to the excursive beholder.

> I'd like to retire there and do *nothing,*
> or nothing much, forever, in two bare rooms:
> look through binoculars, read boring books,
> old, long, long books, and write down useless notes,
> talk to myself, and, foggy days,
> watch the droplets slipping, heavy with light.
> At night, a *grog à l 'américaine.*
> I'd blaze it with a kitchen match
> and lovely diaphanous blue flame
> would waver, doubled in the window.

Here is an image of total self-illumination and self-reflection (with a hint of intoxication), very different from the parallel retreat from excursive vision, the dream of grandparents in Eternity in "The Moose." What they have in common is a sense of completeness, but here the completeness is solipsistic. If the traveler cannot fully represent what she sees but is reduced to glimpses and gestures, in this dream house she achieves a perfectly insular form of representation in which the outer world becomes indifferent. Reading and writing become circular acts; inner illumination swells because of outer obscurity; and imagination doubles itself instead of seeking an engagement with the objects of experience. Here is a complete mastery over the material of consciousness, no longer fragmented but comprehensive, whole. But Bishop is not the poet of such "pure poetry." The house is boarded up, and she returns to excursive vision.

Bishop's attention shifts to the immediate scene and the present, but her outlook has changed. As she turns her gaze toward nature and its equinox, the sun comes down to illuminate the world "for just a minute."

> The sun came out for just a minute.
> For just a minute, set in their bezels of sand,
> the drab, damp, scattered stones
> were multi-colored,
> and all those high enough threw out long shadows,
> individual shadows, then pulled them in again.

This vision in the last stanza of the poem can only come after that affirmation of imaginative power. This is an excursive vision—fragmented figures, particular and natural imagery, of a particular and suggestive world. But the world is animated and framed (in bezels of sand) to give it regal value; the "long shadows" suggest not only the season and hour but imaginative extension of the finite physical world. The illuminated stones on the beach offer a better object for the imagination than do the dream house (autonomous, solipsistic imagination) or the kite (transcendent aspiration) because they stand within life, not above or beyond it. The lion returns, however, to engage the imagination beyond the physical world of "multi-colored" and "individual" reality. Instead of a figurative fragment he is now a fully realized, unifying fiction. But he is not a myth of fate; he is a figure of imagination. The power of the imagination is such that all the troubling fragments are "cleared up" in this fable; a sense of completeness is allowed within excursive vision through self-conscious fiction. Bishop is not satisfied merely to behold the stones and enjoy their "long shadows" of associative possibility. She will relate them to the other details of observation, giving unity to her experience.

> They could have been teasing the lion sun,
> except that now he was behind them
> —a sun who'd walked the beach the last low tide,
> making those big, majestic paw-prints,
> who perhaps had batted a kite out of the sky to play with.

If "The End of March" suggests we are subject to the whims of fate, depicted as sublime power, that power is also seen to have its benevolent side.[25] We are reminded that March comes in like a lion but goes out like a lamb. Bishop's quiet, amused style marks her integration of the sublime with the ordinary. Similarly, she integrates the natural with the fictional.

The lion-sun as a figure for both Fate and Imagination, considered as one in their effect on phenomena, brings Bishop close to Stevens (a poet she once memorized, though later found too abstract). Her final fable of the lion offers a tentative shift from the broken orders of transcendent aspiration marked at the beginning of the poem in the formation of the geese and the battered kite. Surely Bishop would have remembered Stevens' "The Sun This March" as she sought a resolution to "The End of March." For Stevens, the March sun "Makes me conceive how dark I have become." Stevens' sun "re-illumines things"; it follows winter's "voices as of lions coming down" with its own "hallucinations." Stevens, who believed that the imagination, like a lion, "can kill a man" ("Poetry Is a Destructive Force") with its power, appears weary of the equinoctial rhythms of the imagination; yet "The Sun This March" broke a long silence for Stevens. Bishop, similarly, preempts the power of Fate and its threat to poetic authority by identifying with that power through the image of the playful lion, converting Fate to an image of Imagination and asserting imaginative pattern, tentatively and playfully, over the fragments of excursive vision.

From her initial ironic portraits of complacent travelers, Bishop moved toward an affirmation of excursive vision in these late poems. This is not a consistent tone even in *Geography III*, but it is a dominant one. "Santarém" (CP, 185–187), one of Bishop's last poems, makes perhaps the strongest contrast to the critical ironies of earlier work, especially "Arrival at Santos." But it presents a contrast as well to the mythopoetic structures that inform "The Moose" and "The End of March." Instead of grumbling at her failure to set up her circus-tent reality in new surroundings, Bishop relishes the collapse and convergence of orders and boundaries. She shows pleasure in the confusion and irreverence of the place, its very chaotic, faulty details, which resist all efforts at conceptual mastery.

> Even if one were tempted
> to literary interpretations
> such as: life/death, right/wrong, male/female
> —such notions would have resolved, dissolved, straight off
> in that watery, dazzling dialectic.

This is pastoral of a kind, ending dualisms and annihilating all that's made not to a green thought but to sheer gold. But the scene offers none of the escape which characterizes Marvell's garden. Bishop insists this is *not* Eden, even as she makes the comparison.[26] The place is "mongrel," resisting racial and political as well as conceptual mastery. The scintillant beauty of "everything gilded" suggests that the poet has achieved, in memory, a kind of aesthetic mastery over the scene. But she attaches no idealized permanence to this "gold" look of things. Everything is emerging, decaying, and converging in an elemental unity without structure. Promenades fall into the river, flowers overtake buildings. The world is ground down into the *shush, shush, shush* of golden sands. Hierarchies dissolve as people and zebus merge in the earth. Punctuating the golden surface is a somber blue, necessary antidote to the heat of desire. Though at the beginning the poet recalls that she "really wanted to go no farther," the place is so much defined by flux and crossing that we are not surprised when the ship's whistle blows at the end.

What distinguishes "Santarém" from "Arrival" is the tense. "Santarém" is a memory—"Of course I may be remembering it all wrong / after, after—how many years?" As such it can be ordered as form and meaning beyond the terms of excursive sight. In "Santarém" Bishop sets this inevitable fictionalizing quality of memory against the highly qualified idealism of the town. She entertains a certain nostalgia, that is, while remaining self-conscious about the difference between a memory and a reality, about memory's power to transform what might affront one on arrival or what might be troubling or threatening realities. A lightning storm survived ("*Graças a deus*—he'd been in Belém") becomes part of a picturesque landscape. What were once facts of oppression are absorbed into charming oddities and local color: "(After the Civil War some Southern families / came here; here they could still own slaves. / They left occasional blue eyes, English names . . .)."

Before she departs the poet takes a souvenir from "the blue pharmacy" (place where hurts are soothed). She finds an emblem for her ambivalence, an "empty wasps' nest from a shelf: / small, exquisite, clean matte white, / and hard as stucco," which her fellow traveler, Mr. Swan, finds ugly. A miniature of the stucco houses in Santarém, it suggests some of the complexity of all the homes she entertains in her poetry. Once the dwelling of pests, a source of stings, a motive for travel, it becomes, as a souvenir, not just innocuous but beautiful, a treasure, a kind of poem.

Memory's Eye

The muse of poetry, like her sisters, was born of Mnemosyne, goddess of memory. Bishop might even agree with Baudelaire, who wrote in "The Painter of Modern Life": "Genius is nothing more than childhood recovered at will."[1] But if she sees memory, with Wordsworth, Yeats, Proust, Baudelaire, and others, as her primary creative resource, it is not a means of transcendence. As she developed away from these influences, she resisted idealizations of the past. Bishop's childhood is not free from spatial and temporal constraints; memory is not recuperation. Instead, Bishop views memory as a thread of life, a dynamic principle of limited continuity in a world of discontinuities.

While Bishop eschewed confessional poetry, she frequently made the particular scenes, pleasures, and troubles of her childhood the focus and thematic center of her writing. Readers familiar with the facts of Bishop's biography—loss of parents, her mother's madness, the poet's own illness, romantic crises and confusions, uprootedness and travel—easily make connections between the life and the writing. But my aim here is not to discover what specific events and places from the past determined Bishop's vision, or how these events were transformed to poetry and narrative. Rather, I wish to trace Bishop's interest in the faculty of memory and its relationship to imagination. Even her most personal or particular poems have, in this regard, a theoretical import, though always experimental. And as Bishop's ideas about poetry changed, so did her ideas about memory and its relation to the life of the imagination. Bishop's early symbolist poetry ("Paris, 7 A.M.," "Quai d'Orléans," and others) presents memory abstractly, as a faculty that denies the plenitude of the present and leads to stony feelings of loss and nostalgia. In "The Bight" and a story, "The Sea and Its Shore," Bishop struggles with the "litter of old correspondences," but sees the mind as active; she replaces the past as fossilized symbol with the past as an amorphous mass of significant fragments. But in poems of mid-career, "First Death in Nova Scotia" and "Sestina," for instance, she brings specific memories into intense visual focus, where they become iconic and bear an active, continuous relation, as iconic events, to the perceptions of the present. In late poems such as "Crusoe in England," "Five Flights Up," and "North Haven," the sense of the present and the force of iconic memory come into a tense but dynamic relationship which enriches experience even when it is painful.

In an early notebook entry made about the time she wrote "The Weed" (with its image of the river holding "shut in its waters" all the scenes it once reflected), Bishop tried to imagine some control over the stream of consciousness: "mechanical devices it would be useful for the mind to possess: 1. A motion-picture camera for taking 'stills.' 2. A gadget rolling the mind to turn back to the 'identical spot,' make the necessary connections, & turn ahead—as with the typewriter."[2] But the mind possesses no such exact device. Memory is, rather, involuntary, transforming and disruptive.

During her final year in college Bishop wrote an essay for an English course in which she attempted to explain the nature of memory and its effect on experience and, further, attempted to prescribe a time sense for narrative fiction which would be based on this theory of "experience-time." Bishop quotes Eliot's "Tradition and the Individual Talent" in order to apply his broad notion of literary history to a prescription for the novel. But she shifts almost immediately to an analogy with experience. "This is Sunday.

If I try to think of Friday I cannot recreate Friday pure and simple, exactly as it was. It has been changed for me by the intervening Saturday . . . A constant process of adjustment is going on about the past—every ingredient dropped into it from the present must affect the whole."[3] While Bishop's example refers only to personal history, her attention to Eliot's theory suggests a wider context for the time sense she is defining. Returning to her discussion of the novel, Bishop complains that almost no work of fiction "deliberately makes use of this constant readjustment" which her experience demonstrates. Proust, she argues, has made some attempt, in that he "picks one moment of observation and shows the whole past in the terminology of that particular moment." But this is not dynamic enough for Bishop. "This method achieves, perhaps, the 'conformity between the old and the new' . . . but since the conformity itself must be ever-changing, the truth of it, the thing I should like to get at, is the ever-changing expression for it." Virginia Woolf in *The Waves* relies too much on static thoughts and symbols. Experience, for Bishop, is not constituted that way: "We live in great whispering galleries, constantly vibrating and humming, or we walk through salons lined with mirrors where the reflections between the narrow walls are limitless, and each present moment reaches immediately and directly the past moments, changing them both."[4]

Bishop has taken Eliot's ideas (and perhaps those of Henri Bergson) in a new direction. The essay reveals her impatience with the static, repetitious quality of art and interpretation, her sense that experience is far more dynamic. For her, neither past nor present are·stable points on a line. She subordinates Eliot's teleology almost entirely to the "constant readjustment" that occurs through the faculty of memory. Memory is never merely repetition for Bishop. It affects and is affected by present events, like the circus-tent reality she described in her travel notes. The mind is no more free of temporality than nature is, nor is either bound by a strictly linear time.

Bishop's year in Paris after college reinforced her attraction to symbolist and surrealist art. Two major themes pervade this art and find their way into Bishop's early poetry: childhood is a romantic time of imaginative freedom, and modern life is characterized by dull repetition and repression. The aim of the artist is to recuperate, through reverie toward childhood, that condition of liberation from time and space. Bishop's "Paris, 7 A.M." (CP, 26–27) describes the disoriented state of early-morning consciousness, which shifts the mind out of the temporal present and into memory. The poet addresses these preoccupations with childhood and loss, but resists the notion of the artist's transcendence. In this poem time becomes calcified as one of the dimensions of space, where it is aesthetically and conceptually controlled, but not mastered or transcended.

In Baudelaire or Hart Crane the temporal disorientation at the beginning of "Paris, 7 A.M." might trigger a shift toward the visionary infinite. But in Bishop the confusion about where she is in time (she knows, of course, and tells us so in the title) becomes a symptom of ennui. Retrospection at first merely exposes the accumulation of repetitious moments.

> I make a trip to each clock in the apartment:
> some hands point histrionically one way
> and some point others, from the ignorant faces.
> Time is an Etoile; the hours diverge
> so much that days are journeys round the suburbs,
> circles surrounding stars, overlapping circles.
> The short, half-tone scale of winter weathers
> is a spread pigeon's wing.
> Winter lives under a pigeon's wing, a dead wing with
>   damp feathers.

In order to collapse distinctions of time and space, the poet imagines many clock faces designating different times superimposed upon one another to create an image she can call "Time." The particulars of the scene, mastered by this conceptual symbol, lose their experiential force but do not become vehicles of transcendence. Time, not eternity, is an "Etoile." Bishop evokes a pun in order to emphasize a difference: the French word *étoile* refers both to celestial stars and to those starlike convergences of streets in Paris (such as Etoile de

Gaulle). The spatialization of time is not liberating, then (as it can be in Baudelaire or Wordsworth); it merely shifts the imagination to another finite dimension. But even the Paris streets in this poem are evoked only as a metaphor, derived from the superimposed positions of the clock hands surrounded by circles (the circumference of the clock, the cycle of a day). The outer world, as memory or as present surrounding, has no compelling reality for the speaker. The "hands point histrionically" not in high drama but because they record history and because they gesture to time itself, to the irrecoverable past, without focusing any moment in the present. The clock faces are ignorant because each points differently and because their gestures contain no meaningful, timeless reference. The star-clock expands to become a map of Paris (the city's streets as a whole were also organized as spokes) and symbolizes the ennui of days as "journeys round the suburbs," pointlessly repetitive.

Bishop extends this ennui in another spatialized change, another "overlapping" pattern which suggests the poet's aesthetic and conceptual mastery as distinct from experiential mastery or transcendence of time: "The short, half-tone scale of winter weathers / is a spread pigeon's wing." The pigeon, like the star, inverts tradition; where the dove symbolizes spirit as flight and purity, this urban pigeon is a spatial figure of passing time as dull repetition; this "dead wing with damp feathers" can achieve no ascendency.

The second stanza introduces yet another spatial image of temporal awareness, the winglike overlapping of the rooftop slate, which is integrated with the pigeons by their literal presence on the rooftops.

> Look down into the courtyard. All the houses
> are built that way, with ornamental urns
> set on the mansard roof-tops where the pigeons
> take their walks. It is like introspection
> to stare inside, or retrospection,
> a star inside a rectangle, a recollection:
> this hollow square could easily have been there.
> —The childish snow-forts, built in flashier winters,

could have reached these proportions and been houses;
the mighty snow-forts, four, five, stories high,
withstanding spring as sand-forts do the tide,
their walls, their shape, could not dissolve and die,
only be overlapping in a strong chain, turned to stone,
and grayed and yellowed now like these.

The courtyard is integrated with the first images of the clock as "a star inside a rectangle." The starlike pattern of the courtyard stones suggests an introspection which is also a retrospection, reinvoking the clock faces. This pattern of overlapping and repeated correspondences does not, however, imply any satisfying unity. Like the rhymes which shape the stanzas ("weathers"/"feathers" in the first stanza, the involuted "introspection"/"retrospection"/"recollection" and then the terrible "high"/"die" in the second), these patterns achieve constant echo and overlap without redeeming pattern.

The poem explicitly laments the lost cosmos of childhood, the morning *étoile,* which has fallen into time. Into the retrospective space the poet introduces childhood memories, "the childish snow-forts, built in flashier winters." But these forts (built against time, perhaps) have no ammunition; there are no stars inside the ice. Thus the snow-forts have become cemeteries with burial urns to decorate them. It may be within the power of the child to defy limits, to square the circle, but the squares around these circles mark their limit.[5] Bishop had not yet found, for poetry, an equivalent to the dynamic "experience-time" she called for in the novel. Perhaps it had not yet occurred to her that such an aesthetic was appropriate to lyric.

Like "Paris, 7 A.M.," "Quai d'Orléans" (CP, 28) makes a link between the process of memory and the symbolizing process of the mind. Again the poet views memory as stony retention. In this poem, however, the contrastive ideal is not a child's state of timeless wonder but nature's state of forgetful flux, as figured in the Seine river and the leaves that float on its currents.

The particular setting of "Quai d'Orléans" may have prompted Bishop's reflections on memory because of its prominence in

Proust's novel *Swann's Way*, but the relationship she describes between memory and flux is quite different from his. In Proust memories become projected onto objects and are awakened by a beholder's chance encounter with them. These happy moments release the beholder into timeless reverie which the work of art preserves. But in Bishop's "Quai d'Orléans" the past is neither invested in enduring objects nor revivified; it merely remains, a negative trace, a static fossil in the flux, which impedes the beholder.

"Quai d'Orléans" describes the formation of a memory out of experience, but also the formation of a trope out of particulars. In both moves, the vertical resemblance of metaphor is contrasted to the horizontal connection of things in nature. Memory becomes an instance, perhaps the model, of the figurative habit of mind, which takes the imprint of nature and repeats it as pattern and significance. The first two-thirds of the poem delights in this process of resemblance in which the momentary particulars of nature are subsumed. But as the poet turns from the objects of beholding to her own state of mind, she discovers her isolation from the grand drift of things she has imaginatively ordered. She is left with the image as a memory trace.

> Each barge on the river easily tows
>   a mighty wake,
> a giant oak-leaf of gray lights
>   on duller gray;
> and behind it real leaves are floating by,
>   down to the sea.
> Mercury-veins on the giant leaves,
>   the ripples, make
> for the sides of the quai, to extinguish themselves
>   against the walls
> as softly as falling-stars come to their ends
>   at a point in the sky.
> And throngs of small leaves, real leaves, trailing them,
>   go drifting by
> to disappear as modestly, down the sea's

    dissolving halls.
We stand as still as stones to watch
    the leaves and ripples
while light and nervous water hold
    their interview.
"If what we see could forget us half as easily,"
    I want to tell you,
"as it does itself—but for life we'll not be rid
    of the leaves' fossils."

Bishop's rhyme scheme is elegant: abba if one counts the shorter lines as part of the first lines, or abcdedfb. The alternation of long and short lines perhaps mimics the lapping of waves. The images at first reinforce the impression of flux. Within this aesthetic logic one might expect the mighty wake behind the barge to be the image of memory: the powerful impact of an event in one's life or unconscious. But when the wake is figured as a giant oak leaf, it symbolizes transience. The river prevails as the metaphoric oak leaf is trailed by "real leaves" "floating by." Bishop returns the image to nature's flux where resemblances dissolve. The giant leaves as tropes have "mercury veins" and "extinguish themselves." This graceful dissolve reaches to the stars, which join in the flux and, falling, "come to their ends / at a point in the sky." The imagination seems to join the universal drift, but the very insistence on the unifying metaphor of the leaves resists it. A return to the beholders breaks the trance.

The beholders "stand as still as stones" in contrast to the drift of leaves and water. Now the "leaves" become "leavings" in memory, fossils that separate the consciousness from nature's "interview" of "light and nervous water." The river's reflective nature (its interview) contrasts with the mind's reflections, which remain isolated (indeed, the two beholders do not actually speak). The natural order of dissolve opposes the order of resemblance. The mind takes the part of sediment in this watery scene, accepting the insubstantial fossil imprint, becoming a helpless receptacle of memory traces.[6]

Bishop returned to this contrast between nature's forgetful

fluency and the stony weight of memory in "Five Flights Up" (CP, 181) the last poem in *Geography III*. The structure, theme, and even certain images of the poem recall "Quai d'Orléans." The poet, standing once more above an active scene, details the graceful forgetfulness of nature only to conclude by contrasting her own paralysis in memory. "Yesterday brought to today so lightly! / (A yesterday I find almost impossible to lift.)" But by the time of *Geography III* Bishop had developed a rhetoric that allowed the poetry to engage in the immediacy and flux it described, rather than simply symbolizing it in abstract patterns and repetitions. The representational style of "Five Flights Up" resists the final weight of the speaker's memory, where the abstract images of "Quai d'Orléans" predict it. The poet, looking down from a window, watches the emerging day. Where "Quai" immediately begins to weave the images into a symbolic pattern, "Five Flights" imitates the simple iteration of life that it celebrates. The present tense here is immediate and particular, not the abstract continuous present of "Quai."

> Still dark.
> The unknown bird sits on his usual branch.
> The little dog next door barks in his sleep
> inquiringly, just once.
> Perhaps in his sleep, too, the bird inquires
> once or twice, quavering.
> Questions—if that is what they are—
> answered directly, simply,
> by day itself.

Consciousness moves as simply as light. Bishop presents objects without troping on them. The present tense posits a mode of awareness that could be "answered . . . by day itself," without reference to anything beyond or before it. Identity is not an issue; the bird is happy enough to be unknown, not as Keats's mystical bird in the dark garden but as mere anonymity. The human perspective is introduced in the third stanza as an intrusive third person

("His owner's voice arises, stern, / 'You ought to be ashamed!'"). We remain focused on the life of the dog, who "Obviously . . . has no sense of shame," for whom black is not a moral color. "He rushes in circles in the fallen leaves," and the observing consciousness resists punning on them. The word "obviously," which begins the final stanza, suspends the authority in the poem, for if it sounds contemptuous as an echo of the owner's attitude, it sounds wonderfully relaxed as an echo of all the obvious vision that precedes and follows it, where "everything is answered." The sense of shame is here associated with self-consciousness and memory, states the beholder suspends as she describes pure animal being. The last line (the fifth flight after four stanzas), in which the beholder finally speaks in the first person, marks the end of the trance, the return of memory, that identifying human faculty.

"Quai d'Orléans," while meditating on nature's grand dissolve, betrayed it with fossilized symbols. "Five Flights Up" follows a similar shift from nature's flux to beholder's memory, but its engagement with particulars defines a sharp contrast between early and late Bishop. The change from a symbolic to a descriptive style implies changes in Bishop's sense of memory, from something static and regressive to something dynamic and creative. Bishop experimented, in between these phases of her career, with various, more fluent relations between things as metaphoric counters and things as natural material. In "The Bight" (CP, 60–61) Bishop specifically explored this problem of "correspondences" in relation to memory.

While retaining the image of the mind as sediment, "The Bight" offers a different and more enabling theory of memory than do the poems of *North & South*. The poet dredges no fossils but "a dripping jawful" of disorganized debris, resisting definite symbolic pattern, but perhaps for this reason more malleable for the present beholder.

"The Bight" describes a scene in Key West: the quality of the water and marl, the sundry shipping that enters her prospect, the animal life. Instead of ordering the scene into a metaphoric pattern Bishop allows a psychic symbolism to emerge suggestively within the immediate description. Indeed, the permeability of surface becomes important to both descriptive and symbolic meanings in the poem. The epigraph to the poem, "On my birthday," sets the reader's expectation that this watery scene will be a locus of introspection and retrospection. Such self-reflection, however, turns out to involve a complex flow between inner and outer correspondences and between past and present, rather than a dichotomy (as in the previous poems). The low tide's sheer, gaslike surface suggests the transparency and insubstantiality of the immediate scene and the mind's susceptibility to memory.

> At low tide like this how sheer the water is.
> White, crumbling ribs of marl protrude and glare
> and the boats are dry, the pilings dry as matches.
> Absorbing, rather than being absorbed,
> the water in the bight doesn't wet anything,
> the color of the gas flame turned as low as possible.
> One can smell it turning to gas; if one were Baudelaire
> one could probably hear it turning to marimba music.

The synesthetic correspondences give way to psychic correspondences. Natural fact, word, and feeling become absorbed into each other indeterminately. As in "The Weed," Bishop imagines the body not only as landscape but as psyche. Thus the exposed "ribs of marl" suggest that the beholder's feelings have become prominent. The water, as psyche, is a sponge which draws up external reality.

This exposure brings the poet close to panic, ready to ignite. But that inner life which has become prominent in low tide is not an essential, unified foundation of awareness but itself a "litter" of "correspondences." These correspondences emerge from personal as well as symbolic debris: "torn-open, unanswered letters," things "not yet salvaged . . . from the last bad storm." Bishop evokes Baudelaire in her poem in part to distinguish herself from him. Her synesthesia does not lead to Baudelaire's dark, mystical unity of "long resounding echoes from afar." Baudelaire's "Correspondences" employs memory to gain access to ideal truths, of which nature is the temple. For Bishop, nature is not a temple but an amorphous sea, which in the partly enclosed area of the mind (as bight) may yield some shapeless mass of old correspondences. She discovers no mystical unity but the unidealized sediment of memory, a depth consisting of dead material (Key West's marl being that black sediment of dead coral which Milton used to construct Hell). Yet she turns in her poem from infernal images to self-parody, balancing the "awful" with the "cheerful." The crashing pelicans, frowsy sponge boats (with the air of "retrievers") and soaring man-o'-war birds all become figures for the mind's inquisitive, introspective, and retrospective activity. The mind is overzealous to the point of violence with its pickaxes and scissors, making everything rhetorical, interpreting everything for itself. But it does, if only rarely, come up with something.

In a letter to Robert Lowell (January 1, 1948) describing the bight in Key West, Bishop wrote, "It reminds me a little of my desk."[7] The same analogy between writing and landscape, based on the "litter of old correspondences," informs "The Sea & Its Shore," (CPR, 171–180). The main character of the fable, Boomer, represents Bishop's own struggle to construct meaning out of the fragments of a cultural past, just as "The Bight" concerned her personal past.

The fable represents a protagonist employed to keep the sand free of papers, though he reads and attempts to order the scraps before he burns them. There is so much writing that the sand itself has begun to appear inscribed, the sandpiper's tracks like punctuation marks. The sense of place and of the present disintegrates under the plethora of words. Scraps of paper have replaced primary experience, and yet their writing is not ordered or meaningful in the present. "The whole world he saw, came before many years to seem printed, too" (CPR, 178). Boomer tries to relate the messages on these papers to his own life, but he can never complete the process of decoding, and his identity seems to yield to their flux and authority: "In a sense he depended on 'their imagination' and was its slave, but at the same time he thought of it as a kind of disease" (CPR, 177–178). He struggles for individual mastery—for personal relevance and authority over the scraps of the past. Eliot's "individual talent" has become overburdened by a tradition on its way to ablution rather than posterity. The more Boomer reads the less he retains, as one scrap (which Bishop herself copied in her notebook and credited to Coleridge) reminds him: "The habit of perusing periodical works may properly be added to Averrhoe's catalogue of ANTI-MNEMONICS, or weakeners of the memory" (CPR, 176).[8]

If the visual surface of the world has become, for Boomer, a myriad of enigmatic inscriptions, his own identity, within the story, is absorbed into a visual image. "A picturesque sight, in some ways like a Rembrandt," Boomer eludes the reader just as the written fragments elude him. Yet in contrast to the flitting papers this portrait, which begins and ends the story, has a unifying, absorptive force. He is "picturesque" rather than textual, an icon rather than an inscription, not transparent but cogent. In later work Bishop would make more thorough use of the visual as a unifying principle against the fragments of a world of signs.

The poems of memory in *Questions of Travel* continue to tell a story of confusion and struggle in a world of significant fragments. But Bishop treats specific scenes from childhood as iconic events, providing these poems with a cogency and plenitude the others lack. In a letter to Anne Stevenson Bishop remarked: "Like most poets—I have a really morbid total recall of certain periods."[9] And to Elizabeth Spires she commented about childhood: "You are fearfully observant then."[10] The two remarks are congruent, linking past and present. It is such a link that Bishop began to attempt in her writing, years after she had proposed it as a theory of memory in "Dimensions of a Novel":

> We have all had the experience of apparently escaping the emotional results of an event, of feeling no joy or sorrow where joy or sorrow was to be expected, and then suddenly having the proper emotion appear several hours or even days later. The experience could not really have been counted chronologically as having taken place, surely, until this emotion belonging to it had been felt. The crises of our lives do not come, I think, accurately dated; they

crop up unexpected and out of turn, and somehow or other arrange themselves according to a calendar we cannot control . . . If I suffer a terrible loss and do not realize it till several years later among different surroundings, then the important fact is not the original loss so much as the circumstance of the new surroundings which succeeded it letting the loss through to my consciousness.[11]

What Bishop most often remembers is a childhood world fractured by symbolic awareness. The experience of loss becomes associated with a discovery of discontinuity between real and symbolic presences. But the experience of memory provides, outside of any single moment of the present that it may disrupt, a thread of life, a rhetorical structure around which identity forms.

Bishop might well agree with Wordsworth, then, that the child is a parent to the adult. But this is not because the child is a "seer blest." Probably inspired by the *Lyrical Ballads* as well as Blake's *Songs of Innocence,* Bishop adopts the language of the primer in conveying the child's eye, but like Wordsworth she is interested in that awareness for which the primer has no catechism. Unlike Wordsworth, Bishop does not endow the child with transcendental intuitions. Childhood is not an immersion in the present or a time without time. Because of asthma and eczema as much as inclination, she spent most of her childhood reading, living vicariously in stories and pictures and in the world of memories her elders imposed on her. Almost every memory in Bishop is secreted around some kind of representation: a book, a map, a drawing, a postcard, a photograph. The child exists in a social world full of signs, and if she is superior to the adults in her sensitivity, she is not happier or more secure than they, despite their efforts to suppress the awareness of loss and discontinuity. Memory revives the scene of questions which sustain their importance in adult life. Indeed, it is because such questions are never answered that they persist.

In "In the Village" (CPR, 251–271), about her mother's breakdown, Bishop recalls her aunt and grandmother unpacking the mother's trunks from Boston and finding signs of an alternative life, particularly "A bundle of postcards. The curdled elastic around them breaks. I gather them together on the floor" (CPR, 225). Some of these cards are decorated with metallic crystals as if to assert their luminosity against her gray life: "The crystals outline the buildings on the cards . . . Some . . . have words written in their skies with the same stuff, crumbling, dazzling and crumbling, raining down a little on little people who sometimes stand below . . . What are the messages? I cannot tell, but they are falling on those specks of hands, on the hats, on the toes of their shoes, in their paths—wherever it is they are" (CPR, 255). Typically, these images produce the sense of foregrounding and of discontinuity at once. The imagination enters the illusion, but at the same time confronts distance. Representations are in the present but not of it. The postcards have also become dislodged from the spaces they were made to represent, suspending their beholders in a state of incomplete illusion. Again the discontinuity between reality and representation destroys the coherence of spatial experience. These postcards themselves contain messages, and on it goes.

"In the Village" also concerns how such memories are carried and experienced. The figure of memory in this story is synesthetic—a visual stain that releases some other sensation, a sound, a smell. "A scream, the echo of a scream, . . . a slight stain in those pure blue skies, . . . The scream hangs like that, unheard, in memory . . . Flick the lightning rod on top of the church steeple with your fingernail and you will hear it" (CPR, 251). The scale of this image suggests that the narrator is looking at a picture. The hand of the present looms over the tiny memory, and the story will gradually move in to the scene, first in the third person, then in the first, until the beholder is no longer the distant adult but the remembered child. The stain recurs in the memory proper as the child (in first person) watches her aunt and grandmother unpack the mother's suitcase from Boston, a Pandora's box of memories. "A bottle of perfume has leaked and made awful brown stains. Oh, marvelous scent, from somewhere else!" The "stain" as memory trace in the narrator's consciousness is hardly "marvelous," but the word explicitly links the two moments.

Since representations repeatedly trigger emotional upheavals in Bishop's writing, it is not surprising that her central memory of the world's uncontrollability should occur in a story called "Primer Class," about a child's encounters with numbers, writing, maps, and other signs. Growing up means coming to terms with signs. "Primer Class" (CPR, 3–12) is in part a series of childhood anecdotes about the relationship between personal and public signification and about the very indeterminate relationship between those signs and the world. These are not only the themes of her memory but find their corollary in the experience of memory itself. In the child's private system, in which signs resemble what they represent, the equivalent size of the Canadian and world maps has a parallel equivalence in reality. Her literal-mindedness associates the shapes of letters with their meanings. She fashions a very economical alphabet ending in G, until she learns that the world's alphabet is more complex. But numbers are the most disturbing signs. They preserve the memory trace, perhaps because they are what she has "never solved," but also because their abstraction, their nonreferential nature, makes them perfect repositories for association. On the other hand, to master numbers also might allow her to be free of necessity, free of time and space. In the child's as in the primitive's, the mathematician's, the gambler's imagination, to master numbers is to be truly powerful. Bishop as a child was particularly fond of the number eight, the number that looks like the sign of infinity, which she would struggle to master "against the desire of one's painfully cramped fingers" (CPR, 5). She was equally fond of her power to wash her slate, as though she could erase the world, and the past. "It dried like clouds, and then the very last wet streak would grow tinier and tinier, and thinner and thinner; then suddenly it was gone and the slate was pale gray again and dry, dry, dry" (CPR, 5–6), a literally clean slate, a pristine forgetfulness in contrast to the world of history and consequence.

Bishop's poems and stories usually lie within the frame of

memory, leaving the adult rememberer implied, or outside it. But several stories and a few poems frame the experience they describe within the later experience of the adult, drawing attention to the rhetorical nature of memory itself. "Primer Class" begins by describing a recurrent experience of involuntary memory, explicitly linking an iconic object and an iconic mental state and recalling, now in entirely metaphoric terms, the imagery of "The Fish":

> Every time I see long columns of numbers, handwritten in a certain way, a strange sensation or shudder, partly aesthetic, partly painful, goes through my diaphragm. It is like seeing the dorsal fin of a large fish suddenly cut through the surface of the water—not a frightening fish like a shark, more like a sailfish. The numbers have to be only up to but under a hundred, rather large and clumsily written, and the columns squeezed together, with long vertical lines between them, drawn by hand, long and crooked. They are usually in pencil, these numbers that affect me so, but I've seen them in blue crayon or blurred ink, and they produce the same effect . . .
>
> The real name of this sensation is memory. It is a memory I do not even have to try to remember, or reconstruct; it is always right there, clear and complete. The mysterious numbers, the columns, that impressed me so much—a mystery I never solved when I went to Primer Class in Nova Scotia! (CPR, 5, 6)

An involuntary memory is the clearest example of how the iconicity of the past disrupts the coherent surface of the present. It is a swift contribution of the unconscious mind, the validity of which is recognized immediately, though the conscious mind must take pains to understand it. The figure of the fish recalls Bishop's metaphors of mind as water and the sudden breaking through to the surface of unconscious trophies. Without a notion of iconic force we could not explain the disproportion between these sensations and Bishop's reaction to them. What could be more familiar than a delivery boy's account book, a lottery-ticket seller's notebook, a barkeeper's homestitched pad? Numbers have no iconic force of their own, but crudely rendered numbers suggest the beholder's own earlier struggle to master their symbolic system. The effect is painful in that it dredges up and reproduces the feelings accompanying a painful experience. But the sensation is aesthetic first, in that the memory takes place outside the context of vulnerability, and second, simply in the recognition of the structural and figurative form of the image.

In discussing the layers of iconicity in Bishop's poems—the frames within frames—one cannot avoid the psychoanalytic concept of screen memory. Screen memory is that process by which the psychic force of an event is displaced iconically onto another which the subject thus remembers with a particular intensity having no obvious cause. Screen memory is another example of the figurative operations of memory. Such displacement might well account for a number of Bishop's poems in which apparently unimportant objects or scenes are singled out for attention. In the case of "Primer Class," all the universal childhood anxieties about learning the alphabet and multiplication tables may have been intensified by absorbing the personal disaster of the mother's insanity. It was in this year of primer class that Bishop's mother was committed to the asylum.

While the sign-fractured scenes of childhood are disorienting to the child, memory provides a schematization. This schematization is not a mastery of the child's chaotic experience, but an ordering of it for the present. Within the frame of childhood the problems of representation are already inscribed, but have a disintegrative force. The later schematization of the past transforms these problems to an integrative force. The inner iconicity of memory provides a thread, an inward coherence, against the discontinuities of experience. Thus the activities of memory and poetry are analogous as well as causally connected for Bishop; both promote a principle of unity moving through time which connects the consciousness to its past, even if the past may be fictionalized. The connection is between the originating fiction (the fearful observance which becomes iconic) and the force of that fiction in adult life (through its many transformations.)

In the preceding discussion I have begun to show how Bishop developed a means of representing "experience-time" and moved away from the idea of memory as dull repetition or nostalgia. I have suggested that this "experience-time" is visually based, that it depends, at least in part, on iconic representations, as opposed to the more verbally based semiotics of the early work.

Two poems from *Questions of Travel,* "First Death in Nova Scotia" and "Sestina," demonstrate Bishop's move toward visualizing, as opposed to symbolizing or illustrating, the past. These two poems are best understood not as portraits of childhood awareness or simplified versions of adult problems, but as literary depictions of memories, inherently iconic in their mode of representation. These poems imitate the scanning of a mental image from an early period in life.

Richard Wollheim, a philosopher of art influenced by Freud, has begun to describe the state of memory in relation to the sense of a unified life. His ideas are especially useful in appreciating nondiscursive, nonnarrative, visually based poetry such as Bishop's because he insists that event-memory is inherently iconic. Memories are not, he argues, like sentences, which must be decoded in order to function. While they are representational, they are not conventional; they arise in the mind interpreted, carrying psychic force and determining our dispositions—our knowledge, our desires, our feelings, our behavior. Unlike our dispositions, our iconic mental states have phenomenology—we experience these thoughts. Thus while a strictly linguistic model is inappropriate, a theatrical model allows for the active-receptive aspect of these scenic thoughts. The theatrical analogy allows Wollheim to stress the plenitude and intentionality of the iconic mental state; the actor analogy allows for point of view; the audience analogy allows for its cogency. All are internalized and simultaneous. Wollheim's model provides a structure for understanding the phenomenon Bishop calls "experience-time." It also helps us understand the rhetorical nature of her memory poems.

Bishop's poems are never detached reflections on the human condition. We can better read them with an inscribed imaginer in mind whose disposition is altered by the meditation. Memory presents a special case of iconicity, for it is dependent on an earlier event which it keeps causally alive. But this anterior reference makes it all the more significant as a thread of life. While origin-bound, it is also forward-directed, a criterion of identity, indicative and creative. Bishop's memories are seldom reassuring—the past is shadowed by feelings of exile, inadequacy, vulnerability, crisis. But as memories they establish a continuity beyond the disunity of experience.

The theatrical model is particularly helpful in appreciating Bishop's memory poems, for it allows us to accept the child's point of view while recognizing the adult audience inscribed in the poem. Without such an inscribed personal audience, the subjective vocabulary of dolls, frosted cakes, and royal couples in "First Death" (and the naive relation to signs) would be merely coy. Bishop does not, that is, endow the child's perception with special authority, only special sensitivity, particularly to objects of iconic power or potential. Bishop remembers in order to complete experience; she recognizes the meaning that she has invested in objects during an earlier perception. The medium of the influence is visual, not verbal, because the child and adult share a visual vocabulary, but also because the iconic event-memory has phenomenological reality for the adult. Child and rememberer participate in an experiential as well as a rhetorical continuity that becomes, for Bishop, a ground of identity.

The notion of an event-memory with theatrical force in the imagination applies well to "First Death in Nova Scotia" (CP, 125–126). The poem describes in the first person a child's experience at a wake. It demonstrates both the force of iconic objects in the child's consciousness and the power of a childhood event to become an iconic memory.

Iconic density in the world's appearances affects the child's no less than the adult's experience. As an unsophisticated reader of signs, making little distinction between the actual and the represented, the child is most susceptible to the influence of iconic objects, most open to fantasy, and most literal-minded. The child is also an active producer of icons, projecting anxieties and desires onto the objects of her environment. Like the adult's, the child's iconic world is fragmented and elusive. It does not satisfy the desire for coherence and immortality which it awakens. The child-beholders in Bishop's poems experience ontological uncertainty expressed by, if not caused by, their sensitivity to iconic objects. The child in Bishop's work is particularly attracted to representational objects as sharing an aura of indeterminacy; they are framed and aloof from their setting, immune to its dangers, yet they spread their influence into it. But the child discovers the problem inherent in all iconic objects—that they are present to us, but we are not present to them. This fact leads, in part, to the child's sense of helplessness before iconic objects. She cannot gain access to the knowledge or power she imagines they hoard; she cannot defend herself against the force with which her desire or anxiety has invested them.

"First Death in Nova Scotia" recounts just such an experience of ontological confusion in the presence of iconic objects. The icon arises to fill the space left by death and absence, but it does not adequately fit that space. The child in this poem struggles to comprehend a surface in which some objects are iconic and framed while others are not, a single surface containing varying levels of determinacy. The poem begins by matter-of-factly listing the objects in the room as though they existed (as indeed they do as objects) on the same plane. The trimeter adds a dirgelike weight to the lines, but it also isolates the objects of perception to suggest the slow absorption of the beholder:

> In the cold, cold parlor
> my mother laid out Arthur
> beneath the chromographs:
> Edward, Prince of Wales,
> with Princess Alexandra,
> and King George with Queen Mary.
> Below them on the table

stood a stuffed loon
shot and stuffed by Uncle
Arthur, Arthur's father.

But these enumerated objects quickly take on iconic power in the poem, a process which leads to the child's confusion and the disruption of her tangible world. Their silence confirms their iconic power; their lack of speech to affirm or deny her speculations extends their indeterminacy. A stuffed loon, chromographs, a corpse—what sort of being do these objects have, and how does it relate to her own being and that of her surroundings? Do they have agency? Is a corpse like a doll? Yet this is a doll that has not yet been painted, whereas the figures in the chromographs are complete in themselves. Arthur is somewhere between the real and the iconic.

Jack Frost had started to paint him
the way he always painted
the Maple Leaf (Forever).
He had just begun on his hair,
a few red strokes, and then
Jack Frost had dropped the brush
and left him white, forever.

An uncanny, demonic quality pervades the poem, invested most vividly in the sightless eyes of the loon. They seem to harbor a special knowledge, connected with Uncle Arthur's mysterious power to kill, a power looming ambiguously in the beholder's mind over Arthur and over herself.

While the child's conception of death is naive and confused here, the reader has no access to a wider concept. The discontinuity between reality and representation, between living things and the images that dead things leave behind, continues to infect the adult beholder's eye as it surveys the landscape. Indeed, against the myth of child ineptitude and adult mastery Bishop writes scenes in which the child's crises are in direct consequence of some adult failure of authority—a grandmother's reticence, a mother's breakdown, a foolish aunt's scream of pain. Yet this oxymoronic "first death" marks a point of origin for the adult who is remembering. The poem is written in the first person and thus identifies itself as a memory. Arthur, the loon, the chromographs are in turn icons of a past whose influence is carried into the child's present but only completed in the present of the adult. Their effect is to dissolve the unity of self in relation to the present. But as a memory the poem also implies a unity which the earlier experience of iconicity had broken. The question asked at the end of the poem—"how could Arthur go?"— is not answered, but its echo in the narrator's present establishes her identity with the child.

The success of the memory, as of the poem, lies in its schematization of a previously chaotic experience. While the child's verbal understanding has confused the "forever" of Canada's emblematic maple leaf and national anthem with the "forever" of death, the color scheme of the poem, framed in iconic memory, does make a distinction. The child's eye is drawn to red as signifying the indeterminate realm of the icon, and is blocked by white, the color of cessation, signifying the frozen realm of death. The maple leaf, the red eyes of the loon (the artificial, truly representational part of him), the red costumes of the royal couples, stand out in the poem against Arthur's white skin, the frozen lake, the snow. The simultaneity of the iconic and the dead leads the child to imagine an ontological continuity between them. The loon eyes Arthur, the royal couples invite Arthur to be the smallest page at court. Yet that continuity is broken as the child perceives a gap which the adult expresses in the color scheme:

> But how could Arthur go,
> clutching his tiny lily,
> with his eyes shut up so tight
> and the roads deep in snow?

As representational objects, Arthur and the loon join the royal couples in rhetorical power over the beholder, but they lose agency. It is here that the beholder discovers the discontinuity between the iconic and the real. The mild tone (kept from becoming laconic by the processional ten-line stanza) suggests the distance of the adult in this case more than the understatement of the uncanny.

We may clarify our sense of how Bishop imitates the experience of memory when we compare "First Death" to Lowell's "My Last Afternoon with Uncle Devereux Winslow," on which Bishop may have modeled her poem. Lowell's poem has none of the force of reified memory. On the contrary, the adult narrator constantly intrudes with comments, so that the event recorded does not have its own iconic force but is part of a narration in which the past self is the mythic hero. Bishop, by contrast, reduces the externalized voice and schematizes from within the event-memory so that the narrator's and reader's identification with the child-beholder is complete.

"Sestina" (CP, 123–124) is far more stylized and impersonal than "First Death in Nova Scotia." This difference makes it no less an imitation of an event-memory, however. The scene is that of a child and grandmother at home amidst domestic objects, uncannily animated to suggest not only a child's fantasy but a psychically charged situation. The poem presents objects which, along with a child's crayon drawing, demonically express a repressed awareness of change and loss.

If we consider "Sestina" as representing the work of memory, we might understand the speech ascribed to objects not simply as a child's animation but also as a poet's trope. Based on the iconicity of memory itself, the description offers a verbal equivalent of memory's visual influence. Between the third-person narration and the childish form of the perception it is impossible to fix a single subject who is seeing this scene, unless we understand it as a memory in which an adult removed from the scene recalls a more immediate point of view. This is why the child's drawing, which appears in the fifth stanza, is called "inscrutable" in the last line while still implicitly interpreted within the vision of the poem.

> *It was to be,* says the Marvel Stove.
> *I know what I know,* says the almanac.
> With crayons the child draws a rigid house

and a winding pathway. Then the child
puts in a man with buttons like tears
and shows it proudly to the grandmother.

But secretly, while the grandmother
busies herself about the stove,
the little moons fall down like tears
from between the pages of the almanac
into the flower bed the child
has carefully placed in the front of the house.

Time to plant tears, says the almanac.
The grandmother sings to the marvellous stove
and the child draws another inscrutable house.

Again the rhetoric of the poem is based on the rhetoric of memory itself. Its influence on the reader is connected with an implied influence on the internal audience, the remembering adult. Indeed, the scene of child and grandmother in country house is autobiographical. Here, as in so many poems, Bishop reminds us that a house is no shelter from pain and loss, that it may in fact be the scene of anguish, even for the child. The poem tells a story of domestic rituals aimed at resisting the "equinoctial tears" which nevertheless force their way in. But Bishop performs in the poem the operation of memory in which adult schemata bring forward the unschematized awareness of the child in a consciousness freer of guilt, shame, or fear.

The mnemonic sestina form serves several functions in the poem. Its emphasis on nouns heightens the iconicity of the poem and intensifies the image by repetition so that it appears obsessive. The form also suggests the primer language of the child, which does not distinguish orders of being or tenses and thus permits the projections which the memory poem recalls. Bishop uses the form inventively, allowing considerable rhythmic variation ("dance like mad on the hot black stove") and loosened order within the sequence of nouns to express a fluent relation of objects within the frame of the scene.

The poem does not, then, simply exploit iconic strategies for rhetorical purposes; it evokes an early use of such strategies. The simple present of the child cannot accommodate what is hidden or past or to come, so these become mystically invested in the objects: the annunciatory, birdlike almanac, the marvel stove. The poem does not so much discriminate kinds of knowledge as disperse a single knowledge possessed by the child who cannot accommodate it (but who expressed it in her drawing): the knowledge of a generational gap, a missing mother, as well as a broader knowledge of loss.

What are these poems of childhood doing in a volume called *Questions of Travel?* Bishop may want to make an analogy between the condition of the traveler and that of the child. Both find themselves in situations where the codes and frames of reference which have given them security break down. Both experience, as a result, a heightening of sensation as they struggle to reconstitute reality for themselves. We have already seen how Bishop links the concept of home to the concept of travel, and how memory is a constant informing one's experience of the present. We can see, further, that Bishop's idea of "experience-time" involves a radical displacement and disorientation through memory which is akin to the experience of travel.

Bishop more explicitly links her themes of travel and memory, geography and history, in *Geography III.* Among these poems, "Crusoe in England" is the most expansive (CP, 162–166). This ambitious poem examines a number of themes, among them the contemporary feeling of exile from inherited orders and values, the breakdown of a positivist view of the world, the arbitrariness of language and systems of meaning, the limits of Romantic solipsism, the need for invention and companionship to offset the loneliness of the void. These and other themes all involve questions of mastery, particularly in relation to memory. The lyric matrix of personal memory and experience intersects with a wider matrix of cultural memory and tradition. The poet of "The Bight," finding personal correspondences, and Boomer of "The Sea & Its Shore," seeking present order and meaning out of the litter of culture, meet in the archetypal figure of the shipwrecked traveler, trying to construct his circus tent in the most alien surroundings. Crusoe is shipwrecked in time as much as in space; indeed, the poem challenges the stability of both means of self-location. Time and space become figuratively intertwined in the poem's theme of exile. Employing the freedom of the archetype from temporal and spatial constraints, Bishop nonetheless particularizes her speaker so that contradictions and conflicts arise in his representation. Within the rhetoric of personal reflection, she explores the limits of past orders in approaching the reality of the present, and the disorientation which cultural and personal memory creates.

"Crusoe in England" explores memory in a number of different ways. As a poem of travel, it takes up the problem of the beholder whose cultural inheritance no longer fits the modern and alien world he confronts. The Christian faith in God's wisdom and Enlightenment confidence in reason, which bolstered Defoe's Crusoe, fail Bishop's Crusoe. Not even the later, Romantic faith in solitude and imagination serves his situation. Yet memory, and the desire it excites, do inspire creativity in this barren place. It is only in England, where desire and creativity have "petered out," that memory becomes a force of repetition and stagnation. Bishop's Crusoe discovers memory as a constant of human consciousness. There is no unmediated experience against which memory is set. But Bishop contrasts two modes of memory, one that establishes a thread of life, one that merely petrifies life in the past.

Geography III, as its title suggests, pursues questions of knowledge, finding old, inherited convictions inadequate to order experience. Defoe's Crusoe was already a latter-day Adam, but he found his Christian belief strengthened in experience. Bishop told George Starbuck that she wanted to "re-see" Crusoe "with all that [Christianity] left out."[12] Crusoe finds himself in an untenable, barren garden (where there is "one kind of everything"). His power of naming is reduced to "play"; he has no dominion over the animals but instead tends to distance nature by his efforts to claim it.

In harmony with Defoe's Christian faith is his faith in Enlightenment principles of reason and empirical knowledge. His Crusoe is sustained by the memory of his culture, reaffirming not only spiritual laws but scientific methods. Since knowledge is conveyed in the form of sensible images, so empirical philosophy argued, the increase of sensible experience would lead to an increase in knowledge. But empirical knowledge is faulty for Bishop's Crusoe, and sensory experience heightens the sense of unreality. The scientific gaze depends, he discovers, on memories of scale, proportion, resemblance which do not fit the reality he confronts.

> Well, I had fifty-two
> miserable, small volcanoes I could climb
> with a few slithery strides—
> volcanoes dead as ash heaps.
> I used to sit on the edge of the highest one
> and count the others standing up,
> naked and leaden, with their heads blown off.
> I'd think that if they were the size
> I thought volcanoes should be, then I had
> become a giant;
> and if I had become a giant,
> I couldn't bear to think what size
> the goats and turtles were

Bishop's Crusoe has a scientific mind (he knows, for instance, that the island is probably basalt), but his rationality provides little help in this irrational world. The experience has made him skeptical, so that when he reads of a new island he treats the discovery as an illusion, a trompe l'oeil: "caught on the horizon like a fly." Crusoe on the island makes several efforts at empirical inquiry—he counts the volcanoes, tries to account for the rain, notes the waterspouts, and registers the flora and fauna. But such observation does not amount to useful knowledge. On the contrary, it becomes nightmarish:

                                    I'd have
        nightmares of other islands
        stretching away from mine, infinities
        of islands, islands spawning islands,
        like frogs' eggs turning into polliwogs
        of islands, knowing that I had to live
        on each and every one, eventually,
        for ages, registering their flora,
        their fauna, their geography.

No increase in knowledge accompanies this accumulation of data; no teleology underlies this endless archipelago. Crusoe is a desperate Darwin, trailing off into the unknown. Perhaps the ultimate breakdown of empiricism and its legacy of logical positivism occurs in Crusoe's temporal displacement. If he is displaced geographically, he is also displaced temporally, for if we stay with the fiction of Defoe's Crusoe, this eighteenth-century man can "remember" lines of poetry written a century after his invention. Bishop's playful exposure of fictional surfaces and her play with the atemporal archetype has a specific point to make about the relativity of chronological time, not only within the bounds of personal experience, but out into cultural memory.

Of course it was Wordsworth who made the most of the atemporal force of memory within temporal experience. The Romantics returned to explore emotional, personal, and spiritual experiences and desires which Enlightenment thought had neglected. But this memory of a Romantic, subjective tradition supports the exile no better than the Enlightenment tradition. Romanticism's version of nature as a secular paradise is clearly rebuked in this antipastoral poem. But Romanticism's view of memory itself as a form of transcendence and compensation makes it especially suspect. Crusoe finds no real consolations in memory. Romantic memory depends upon the power of metaphor, which Crusoe finds extremely limited. Failing to penetrate the substance or impose meaning upon the island, he thinks about an ideal England and begins to transform the objects of the barren landscape into figures of the past. The turtles hiss like teakettles,

> Snail shells lay under [trees] in drifts
> and, at a distance,
> you'd swear that they were beds of irises.

But only at a distance, or with his eyes shut, can he invoke the idealized image of the past. The reality of the island continually disrupts his reverie.

These failed reveries precede and follow an allusion to Wordsworth's "I wandered lonely as a cloud" and constitute a challenge to the process described in that poem.

> I tried
> reciting to my iris-beds,
> "They flash upon that inward eye,
> which is the bliss . . ." The bliss of what?
> One of the first things that I did
> when I got back was look it up.

The anachronism, in which the Enlightenment Crusoe remembers (with gaps) the Romantic Wordsworth, reinforces Bishop's challenge to chronological time. But such inversions of chronology affect Crusoe differently from Wordsworth, for whom they trigger the transcending power of imagination. Wordsworth, feeling "lonely as a cloud," saw "a crowd, / A host, of golden daffodils" that drew him out of his abstraction. In later solitude he would recall them (not as they actually were but as they were transformed in his imagination) and be transported.

> For oft, when on my couch I lie
> In vacant or in pensive mood,
> They flash upon that inward eye
> Which is the bliss of solitude;

And then my heart with pleasure fills,
And dances with the daffodils.

In Wordsworth, experience is typically fulfilled in memory's after-image. "I gazed—and gazed—but little thought / What wealth the show to me had brought." Loneliness is a site where powerful memories form to provide the later time-transcending bliss of solitude. Time is confused, but not transcended, in "Crusoe in England." Crusoe remains "lonely as a cloud" on this cloud-dump of an island. His loneliness is never converted to ideal solitude, which has the power of metaphor to make an absence present. Memory erases more than it fills in. The afterimage leads one into a labyrinth where life and memory become confused and the future looks like the past.

If Crusoe remembers his experience on the island as a time of disorientation and deprivation, however, it was also, he recalls, a time of creativity and passion. Crusoe celebrates his "home-made" world and "home-made" identity—his construction of orders and values ("island industries") based on memories but created out of and for the present circumstance. Crusoe nostalgically remembers this struggle to create a viable reality for the present out of the fragmented memories of the past. But Crusoe's creative solipsism proves inadequate by itself for survival. The identities he imposes on the indifferent landscape (troping on snail shells, dyeing baby goats bright red, ambivalently naming the volcanoes after his moods of hope and despair) do not achieve a fertile correspondence. No wonder, after all this hard work, he welcomes the weekend spirit of Friday, who, if he cannot help Crusoe transcend the weary repetition of his life, can at least help him forget it. "Just when I thought I couldn't stand it / another minute longer, Friday came." The human bond formed in the present relieves the sense of life as dull repetition (which his brain breeds). Crusoe makes no attempt to impose a rhetorical value on Friday, to trope on Friday as he did on the other objects of the island. The language is conspicuously simple and direct, free of trope, perhaps expressing an emotion too intense, too deviant, or too private for rhetoric to contain. "Friday was nice, and we were friends." Precisely because this relationship is outside of what language tolerates, "Accounts of that have everything all wrong." Friday also embodies an unrhetorical (unmediated) relationship to the animals which Crusoe appreciates vicariously, in contrast to Crusoe's rhetorical relation (he dyes the baby goat bright red). Friday, then, represents not only human companionship, but the ideal (if not the actuality) of unrhetorical experience, of naturalness. He is the weekend from the rhetorical prison of Crusoe's consciousness. Yet Friday's counter-love is insufficiently other. Though Crusoe's "brain bred islands" he cannot propagate his own kind, even dreams of destroying it. The return to England and the failure of Friday to thrive in that cultural reality (he dies of a European disease) leave Crusoe in a world of empty symbols and paralyzing memories.

Yet this is not the story of a shipwrecked man nostalgic for home, but of someone returned to England, nostalgic for his former island exile, and anxious to set the record straight (which has been distorted as a cultural memory). He complains, as if an actual historical person, of the treatment of his own archetype: "None of the books has ever got it right." He reasserts the uniqueness of his experience: "my poor old island's still / un-rediscovered, un-renamable." The vehicles of cultural memory serve him poorly. In framing her story in the lonely complaints of Crusoe in England, Bishop has not merely reversed convention, making the island the site of noble savagery, the emotional equivalent of childhood wholeness. What Crusoe remembers most about the island is his nostalgia for England. The poem reinforces the inevitability of memory and the elusiveness and unrepresentability of original experience. The apparent opposition between the island and England, between past and present, is undercut ("Now I live here, another island, / that doesn't seem like one, but who decides?"). In both places he experiences a discontinuity between the image and its referent. Baudelaire's sense of objects' "familiar glances" of meaning becomes indifference "or a little malice." Looking at a knife which proved so vital to survival and symbolized his pain ("it reeked of meaning, like a crucifix"), Crusoe complains: "Now it won't look at me at all." The essential parasol constructed on the island by calling up memories of English ones ("remembering the way the ribs should go") fails, once back in England, to signify "parasol" and instead "looks like a plucked and skinny fowl." It seems the real is never known except as it is mediated through nostalgia, yet nostalgia itself deprives one of the real. Problems of representation and problems of memory are thus bound together.

Though tyrannized by internal echoes of the past ("I still can't shake / them from my ears"), Crusoe, back in England, cannot find authentic presence in his island icons. But one reason why they lose their iconic power is precisely the satiation of England against the deprivation of the island. On the island Crusoe was forced to invent culture through apostrophe, to call on rhetoric to fulfill absence and need. Here Crusoe is "surrounded by uninteresting lumber" and bored by "real tea." No Friday ties these objects to human community. The knife, the parasol, the goatskin trousers are symbols of culture in the midst of culture; they have no aura because they fill no absence. The invented objects of the island, though based on memory, had a vital importance for the present, established a thread of life. The museum is the symbol for the past; the objects in it have no present value. Everything is overrepresented in England, a landscape of dead symbols, perhaps a symbol of our contemporary world.

The structure of "Crusoe in England" complicates, by doubling, inverting, disrupting, the chronological relation between a present memory and a past place or event. Yet Bishop does sustain a contrast between the realms the poem juxtaposes; she clearly privileges the first, where iconic memory has value for the present. The passionate center of the poem is the place of need and invention, where Crusoe, dangling above an abyss, finds a home in self-pity. The appeal of an island poverty in which one had to create culture out of memory and ingenuity occurred early to Bishop. Writing in her notebook from Cuttybunk, Maine, in 1934, she remarked:

> On an island you live all the time in this Robinson Crusoe atmosphere; making this do for that, and contriving and inventing . . . A poem should be made about making things in a pinch . . .
>
> The goats are so tame they allow you to hold their pointed chins in the palm of your hand and look into their beautiful yellow eyes . . .
>
> The idea of making things do—of using things in unthought of ways because it's necessity—has a lot more to it. It is an *island* feeling, certainly.[13]

Forty years later, "Crusoe in England" fulfills this promise. It is in many ways more personal than most of Bishop's poetry, a kind of spatial distillation of her many travels—to Key West, Brazil, Haiti, the Galapágos, as well as Cuttybunk. Aruba, particularly, was in the poet's mind.[14] This island is a landscape of memory as well, its fifty-two volcanoes representing the weekly eruptions in a year of Bishop's life, which become icons in memory. Bishop's sense of life as a series of eruptions and survivals, her sense of homelessness, loneliness, longing for children, sexual joy and despair, all find expression in this poem. The distance Bishop retains through her persona and its allusiveness has to do primarily with the wish to set personal feelings and memories in the larger labyrinth of cultural myths. She draws on her wide reading, not only from Defoe but from Melville's "The Encantadas," Darwin's *The Voyage of the Beagle* and his autobiography, Genesis, and Wordsworth. This is a poem less about the poet's ability to transform personal experience to mythic and epic dimension than about the nature of memory as both personal and cultural.

I have explored poems in which Bishop concerned herself with the nature and affects of memory, both as a retentive and a dynamic force. She represents it as a faculty that isolates us from nature's forgetfulness, or liberates us from it. The writer, she early argued in "Dimensions of a Novel," must find a way to represent "experience-time," that human intersection of memory and the continuous present of nature. In "North Haven" (CP, 188–189), one of her last poems, she clearly sets the writer's work beside nature's work, as if to throw off the retentive force of art in favor of its creative force. But memory humanizes the poem, finding its place amid nature's permanence and change, rather than being at odds with it. "North Haven" is one of many poems that attempts to define the place of the artist and his works in terms of a play between memory and flux.

Bishop returned to an island as the locus of memories in "North Haven," a memorial to Robert Lowell. Where Crusoe's southern island is distinctly antipastoral, unwelcoming yet burdened by memory, North Haven appears, at first, as a pastoral escape from history into the presentness of nature. Crusoe speaks from a geographic as well as a temporal distance. In "North Haven" the poet has returned to the island and entertains memory within a context of renewal. But "North Haven," too, is elegiac, its greater optimism founded on a full acknowledgment of temporality. The poem affirms the human capacity to remember, and to change through and with memory. It also makes clear that the act of memorializing experience in art is not a form of mastery over loss.

In 1974 Bishop rented a house in North Haven, an island off the coast of Maine. Her notebooks and comments suggest that the place embodied, for her, a pastoral ideal, where she could be forgetful of personal and public worries. Here she finds the vital, creative necessities of Crusoe's atmosphere in combination with the comfortable solitude of the proto-dream-house. "You can see the water, a great expanse of water and fields from the house. Islands are beautiful." Crusoe certainly didn't think so, but his antipastoral spirit is banished here. Bishop views North Haven as a retreat from the rhetorical redundancy of culture, the kind of thing that left Crusoe so bored at the end of his poem. Having stayed in North Haven while the Nixon impeachment hearings were on television, Bishop admires the island in direct response to her distaste for human history: "Nothing but false rhetoric, bombast, self-righteousness, *repetition*. G. Stein said Americans love repetition. She was right. If this is 'witnessing history'—I'd rather not."[15] Bishop turns away from "history" to the fluent, variable repetitions of nature, which seem free of history, not only political "history" but "personal moods." These two histories, which make up most of Lowell's poetry, are suspended in this apparently timeless world of change without loss or repetition, the two paradoxical burdens of human history: "To have no personal moods at all; to have only the same moods that the weather has here on North Haven Island—that could be the (perfect) temperament, the rest of life? [July 16, 1975.]" And a few days later: "The fir trees between us & the water—that Mrs. Pettit hates so—are the last reality, looking out to the bay—which is quite unreal, vaporous, dream-like—an unknown. Only the fir trees are real—& alive, too—in the strong winds we've been having—moving, rushing, sometimes trying to get away—next to, against the sudden change to an atmospheric, imaginary world—."

This sense of an "imaginary world" free of history was not inconsistent with a meticulous recording of observations. Seeing and dreaming become one; Bishop practices a self-forgetful, perfectly useless concentration: "Well, I have Peterson's bird guide, a book about Pebbles on the Beach, & another Peterson I bought in Camden the night of the 15th—*Guide to Wildflowers*. I want now—now that it's too late—to learn the name of *everything*. [July 1974.]" Bishop goes on for two pages in this journal listing the wildflowers near the house. She fills her notebook with descriptions of North Haven in different times of day and qualities of light, often comparing it to paintings (especially by the Maine painter John Marin.) She seeks to achieve for herself what she imagines painting achieves, a sense of the immediate, continuous present, without the temporal consciousness that excites desire or regret (though her qualifier "now that it's too late" shows how much this will to think in a continuous present is troubled).

But the sense of loss entered into Bishop's imagining of this island even before she conceived of it as the setting for her elegy to Lowell. On Christmas Eve of 1975 she wrote to her doctor, Anny Baumann: "One of the things I didn't get into the villanelle that I feel I've also lost, and that I really regret most of all, is that I don't think I'll be able to go back to that beautiful island in Maine any more—this is too complicated to go into, but it really breaks my heart."[16] "North

Haven" is a poem of return, but it gradually acknowledges the difference between the continuous present of nature and the complex temporality of the human mind, with its sense of loss and will to change. The poet seeks relief from that temporal consciousness by absorbing herself in the simple repetitions of nature. But the poem inevitably returns to, and even values, the human capacity not only to revise, but to memorialize.

Like many pastoral elegies, the poem takes solace in nature's power to renew itself. But there is little hint here that the speaker is mourning. Nature appears oblivious to human loss (in contrast to the nature of "Lycidas," for instance), existing instead as a continuous present in which the poet loses herself in self-forgetful concentration. Gradually, however, the poem introduces other times and other places against which the present takes on definition. "Switching tenses always gives effects of depth, space, foreground, background," Bishop remarked in her interview with Ashley Brown (characteristically tying spatial and temporal categories together).[17] Each stanza of the poem suggests a different temporal attitude. The first designates a present. Marked off from the rest of the poem by italics, this present becomes a timeless visual center to offset the pressure of human memory.

Foreground and distance are marked in this scene before temporal concepts are introduced:

I can make out the rigging of a schooner
a mile off; I can count
the new cones on the spruce.

Having established the horizontal range of distance and nearness, Bishop fills out the vertical poles of sea and sky, mirrored and matched in stillness. She again suspends the human presence, first offering nature's interview with itself. The schooner may suggest human agency, but it is at a distance where it has no emotive power over the scene. The "milky skin" of the bay and the cloud's "carded horse's-tail" (the actual name of a cloud formation) suggest the general animated serenity of the place.

As if growing restless in this peace, Bishop admits her imagination as a faculty projecting change onto what is fixed, rather than, more conventionally, fixing what is mutable. "The islands haven't shifted since last summer, / even if I like to pretend they have." This association of imagination with change becomes crucial at the end of the poem. Here Bishop projects her wishfulness onto the landscape as its own reverie, in which it is lyrically "free within the blue frontiers of bay." But the true priority here is imagination; "nature" is given the circumscribed freedom of art.

This sense of seeing nature as one sees a painting, inferring a dynamic quality within the fixed form, recurs in Bishop's work and notes. In her notebook of 1934 she recorded a dream involving a similar fantasy of flux in still form: "I dreamed last night of paintings that wouldn't stay still—the colors moved inside the frames, the objects moved up closer & then further back, the whole thing changed from portrait to scenery & back again—keeping the same 'lines' all the time."[18] Indeed, in the third stanza nature can "paint the meadows with delight." In this stanza, in which Bishop names the flowers, she narrows the temporal reference and the spatial focus, finding pleasure in a simple act of enumeration. These flowers introduce a very different pace of change from the islands in the bay. Next in this parade toward the human come the birds, who introduce the urge to express. The poem is edging toward memory of the dead friend as the birdsong's "pleading and pleading, brings tears to the eyes." By virtue of personification, the birdsong and the poet's song join together: *repeat, repeat, repeat; revise, revise, revise.* But this is not only a rhetorical joining, Bishop suggests. She displaces the simple dichotomy of nature's presence and the mind's absence and temporal awareness with a fluctuation of shared and distinguishing features.

The main distinction between nature and humanity is personal memory, which occupies the final stanzas of this poem. What the poet remembers most about Lowell is his own remembering. This creates, as in "Crusoe in England," a sense of memory as constant mediating experience. Lowell seemed incapable of simple joys: "('Fun'—it always seemed to leave you at a loss . . .)." The words "leave" and "loss" enter the poem so quietly that their full sadness is felt only as a decay. But whereas the first four stanzas of the poem concerned themselves with return, the last two deal with departure.

Bishop's five-line iambic-pentameter stanzas with third and fifth lines rhymed anticipate the theme of repetition and revision in nature and art. But the final two stanzas, which focus on the dead poet, are much more jagged, full of enjambment, quotation, parenthesis, ellipses, and dashes. Resembling Lowell's style much more than the rest of the poem, they denote a human awareness that cannot match the grace of nature. We "derange" our own work as well as "re-arrange" it; we "learn to kiss" awkwardly. Yet the final stanza regains poise as it returns to a description of nature: "anchored in its rock, / afloat in mystic blue." This image becomes a fixture in the poem, tied to the first image. Lowell is permanently cut loose from this anchor. The ideal of North Haven, and of spatial imagining, is the idea of change within permanence, with an "anchor." But Bishop pulls up this anchor, defining art in terms of the will to change. She ends her poem with the permanence of death, the inability to change ("The words won't change again. Sad friend, you cannot change"), thus refusing the conventional consolations of elegy: the renewal of nature and the permanence of art. Yet the force of resignation may be more appropriate to Lowell than to Bishop. It is her imagination, not that of her "sad friend," which can for a moment "paint the meadows with delight." And while she must, like Lowell, inevitably leave this "haven" of the "north," she can make a memorial to it, and to her friend.

It is chiefly this power of art to memorialize, rather than to master time, that Bishop values. Art can excite memory and thus carry the past as an active force into the present. Because memory is primarily a visual faculty for Bishop, she finds this quality most fully achieved in the visual arts. Her poems that take paintings as their subject help us to understand not only her visual mind, but also her ideas about art's relationship to time.

Art as Commemoration

Although Elizabeth Bishop never analyzed her attraction to the visual arts, she testified to it repeatedly. "I'd like to be a painter most, I think," she remarked to Elizabeth Spires.[1] And she told Ashley Brown, "All my life I've been interested in painting. Some of my relatives painted. As a child I was dragged round the Boston Museum of Fine Arts and Mrs. Gardner's Museum and the Fogg. I'd love to be a painter."[2] She was "very flattered" by Meyer Schapiro's remark that she "writes with a painter's eye" and agreed, in her conversation with Ashley Brown, that she was "more visual than most poets." Bishop's stories and poems are full of allusions to painters—Raphael, Rembrandt, Seurat, Bonnard, de Chirico— which provide a quick glimpse into their visual worlds and a short-hand for attitudes and impressions she otherwise created in words. But it is only in a very approximate way that one can explain how Bishop's love of painting actually influenced her poetic practice. Previous chapters have suggested some of the visual dynamics of her poetry which have analogies in painting.

It is possible to be more precise about Bishop's ideas and attitudes toward the visual arts as she expresses them in poems about particular works. Many of these poems become focused occasions for her reflections on the ontology of works of art and their relationship to time and change. Repeatedly Bishop presents the work as a representation in time, bound to history by its expressive origins, its semiotic nature, and its audience, yet resisting chronology. Often the poems involve questions about the relationship of literary and pictorial values. While Bishop expresses esteem for works of visual art in these poems, she celebrates their power to evoke memory more than their aesthetic mastery. The poet raises the difficult questions of art's ontology within the humblest of contexts. Works minor in scale, achievement, or ambition—a great-uncle's clumsy effort at the sublime in "Large Bad Picture" or his eloquent, miniature sketch of a village in "Poem," an image of a crude tower made of piled-up boxes in "The Monument," a tiny Cornell box containing miscellaneous fragments—draw her attention rather than monumental works. These objects have personal value for the beholder. They are usually tied to the activity of memory, for Bishop the key to art's power to affect us. Yet if art is not a means of transcending the conditions of existence, it is, nevertheless, more than epitaph. The work continues to "live," just as remembering can be a thread of life. By writing about the temporal status of visual art, Bishop joins a long tradition of ekphrastic verse which ascribes to the plastic and graphic media the virtues of permanence, presence, inexhaustible expressiveness, and above all the ability to evoke a moment of life and movement within static forms.

Bishop's special emphasis on the temporal contingencies and semiotic structures that underlie the illusion of art distinguishes her from earlier poets. Her emphasis on the material origins and conditions of the work of art, as well as the historical contingency of artist and viewer, develops a drama within the beholding. Illusion persists, but, like memory, loosed from myths of origin and transcendence into a fractured mirror-world in time. The visual medium activates memory and, by compressing experience, releases it from linear confinement and necessity. It provides a meditative center into which the sense of time can enter and engage still forms without the bitterness of loss. Thus the transcendent unity of the visual space celebrated in the ekphrastic tradition often becomes in her beholding a "compression" of multiple realities. Bishop deidealizes without destroying the mimetic principle of art, disseminating the gaze into a plurality of glances, loosing pictorial from real space without an absolute gap. She converts the ekphrastic opposition between art's eternity and experiential time into a more limited concept of art's commemorative function.

In "Large Bad Picture" (CP, 11–12) Bishop criticizes certain naive aims and readings of representational art, especially its nostalgia and its myths of transcendence. Yet she yields to the mimetic power of the work and ultimately celebrates on her own terms the contemplative and commemorative processes it records. Implicit in her enjoyment of the work is a sympathy with the passions that engendered it. While it fails to meet objective standards of artistic value, the personal value of this painting by a great-uncle remains.

The painting, an early effort by the uncle who went on to create the oil sketch admired in "Poem," is "bad" both in conception and execution. It is a crude imitation of nineteenth-century landscape conventions, its aim of transparency everywhere interrupted by conspicuous schemata: birds "hanging in *n*'s in banks," cliffs "fretted by little arches." The "entrances to caves" suggest diminutive compositional depths to match the cliffs which are hyperbolically "hundreds of feet high" and "masked" by "perfect" waves. The size of the picture is one with its badness, judging from Bishop's general preference for the small and the humble. It presumes a beholder's mastery over the landscape, identifies the beholder with the vast and the sublime, and promises apotheosis. In the large picture Bishop's great-uncle has been caught up in the nostalgic clichés of the sublime. His exotic, remote geography, high receding cliffs, caves, intensely luminous sunset, translucent horizon, and ocean seem a poor imitation of Church, Bierstadt, or Monet (who himself did a sublime Belle Isle series) rather than genuine objects of individual memory.

Bishop hardly dwells on the badness of the picture, however. Her awareness of the picture's conventional nature does not prevent her from ironically participating in its illusionary power.[3] She enters the world of the picture as if it were literally present and creates a narrative about it, expanding beyond visual to auditory sensation.

Though the birds are "hanging in *n*'s," drawn by the most primitive conventions,

> One can hear their crying, crying,
> the only sound there is
> except for occasional sighing
> as a large aquatic animal breathes.

The passage is a parody of Keats's notion that "heard melodies are sweet, but those unheard are sweeter," with a walrus rather than a pastoral piper as the stimulus of imagined sound. No actual observer would hear the animals breathe. The pathos of this crying and sighing reinforces the nostalgic atmosphere of the painting. Bishop mocks the desire for sublimity, describing the ships' spars "like burnt match-sticks" with their putative flames transferred to the eternal "rolling" sunset. Nature sounds a lament rather than an ecstasy, reminding us, perhaps, that the contemplation of eternity is the consolation for death. But Bishop's humor is sympathetic as she portrays the yearning for last (sunsets) and furthest things (the extremities of Belle Isle) against the entrapments of domesticity (this was "before he became a schoolteacher").

The poem's end focuses both the criticism and the sympathy Bishop feels toward this work. The traditionally opposed motives of "commerce" (the public, practical motive of shipping) and "contemplation" (solitary and visionary) merge, each altering the other. Ships, beholder, and artist coincide before the scene. The artist would probably have arrived here by ship, and his original purpose was, as Bishop reveals in an interview with George Starbuck, commercial fishing.[4] The scene itself repeats as narrative the motivation for the painting. The poet admires the work less for its transcendent power than as a link with an ancestor and his gesture of commemoration. "Remembering" is the first word of this poem, and it registers the nostalgic aspect of the painting since what is "remembered" is so stylized and idealized as a vision of eternity. Bishop's poetry develops an alternative to such nostalgia. Yet "remembering" has a positive connotation here as well, not only for the artist but for the viewer who becomes connected to this distant relative through his art. Bishop rehistoricizes "remembering" by framing her description of the painting with details of the artist's life. In other poems Bishop will emphasize this background more fully, locating art's commemorative power within it rather than beyond it.

"The Monument" (CP, 23–25) stresses this value of commemoration over transport. Bishop again explores the paradox between art's crude means and the affective power of its illusions. The poet shapes the opposition as a dialogue, in which one speaker finds only "piled-up boxes," the other "a monument." The defender of the monument gets the final word, finding a role for art which is preservative and commemorative but not nostalgic. Art acts and exists for this speaker within history rather than above or beyond in a space of mastery. The poem also implicitly reflects the relation of words and images, the one interpreting and extending the other. More directly allusive than most of Bishop's poetry, "The Monument" addresses a long tradition of poems about monument making, which includes Coleridge's "Kubla Khan," Shelley's "Ozymandias," Yeats's "Sailing to Byzantium," and Stevens' "Anecdote of the Jar" (itself allusive of Keats's "Ode on a Grecian Urn"). Her version of the monument is particularly suited to a modern age, preserving a place for art after dismantling its idealism.

Bishop's "The Monument" compares most directly to Coleridge's "Kubla Khan," a dream of artistic mastery over nature's laws. Like Khan, Bishop's artist is a prince, a figure of authority, but his decree admits the "conditions of its existence." He is more obscure and less presumptuous than Khan. The poet conjectures that the "artist-prince / might have wanted to build a monument / to mark a tomb or boundary, or make / a melancholy or romantic scene of it . . . ." These are modest purposes: to commemorate, designate, evoke. History has erased his intention. The sea surrounding this monument is not defiantly sunless like Coleridge's, but rather is made of driftwood, already overexposed to the elements.

The monument does not make the past present; it merely stands as a sign of the past. "The bones of the artist-prince may be inside / or far away on even drier soil." Either way Bishop offers no illusions about immortality through art. She does not dictate despair, however, any more than she dictates reliquary worship. "But roughly but adequately it can shelter / what is within (which after all / cannot have been intended to be seen)." The syntactic and descriptive evasion of "what is within" reminds us that this subjective center can only be hypothetical. The recognition of expressive intention within the artifact is essential to its function, however. "Do you see nothing there?" asks Hamlet about the ghost of his father. "Nothing at all, yet all there is I see," replies the Queen. Such is the dialogue of art in this poem. Art exists in a process, to which certain attitudes are preliminary: "Now can you see the monument?" It is the seeing-in or seeing-as which transforms art from mere thing to monument; "what is within" can only be inferred. Perhaps "what is within" is simply the potential to commemorate, which is not really "within" at all. The monument exemplifies the artichoke-like unfolding of the life of a work, its making, its beholding, and its history. The decaying monument simply acknowledges a boundary to human aspiration. Its inscription does not seek to aggrandize as Ozymandias had ("Look on my Works, ye Mighty and despair!"), or to mystify in Keatsian tautology ("Beauty is truth, truth beauty,") but merely to cherish and commemorate:

> The monument's an object, yet those decorations,
> carelessly nailed, looking like nothing at all,
> give it away as having life, and wishing;
> wanting to be a monument, to cherish something.
> The crudest scroll-work says "commemorate".

The dialogue continues by setting the intention of the work against its limitations, both as a work of mimesis and as an object. The monument is no "still unravished bride of quietness"; its representational power has suffered erosion so that its silence is experienced, by the skeptical speaker, as a lack: "'Why does that strange sea make no sound?'" The defender replies:

> —The strong sunlight, the wind from the sea,
> all the conditions of its existence,
> may have flaked off the paint, if ever it was painted,
> and made it homelier than it was.

That decay is not just a matter of physical mutability, but of cultural and perceptual change as well. The image will not answer the question "Where are we?" because it does not recuperate a place. The "view's perspective" cannot become our own. The skeptical speaker is quite legitimately "tired of breathing this eroded air, / this dryness in which the monument is cracking." Art must justify itself against the superior claims of nature. It "holds together better / than sea or cloud or sand could by itself." Art provides order, duration, unity within the flux of nature. But in choosing wood rather than gold as her material, Bishop eschews the idea of mastery or transcendence. She suggests that art not only retains the memory of its natural origins but remains subject to nature.

The monument is a representational object. Bishop describes it at many removes from the original—in a poem about a picture of a wood replica of a landscape with a monument on it. Yet in this layering of representations the dichotomy of art and nature breaks down. The poet's discussion of the image shifts. The monument is exposed to sea and sun, yet that sea and sun are themselves made of driftwood. We can focus this ambiguity (without resolving it) by identifying the source of the poem in a frottage by Max Ernst from his collection *Histoire Naturelle*. Ernst's "False Positions" depicts two long, narrow fretted cylinders, ambiguously juxtaposed on a horizontal, striated base (Figure 1). Fascinated by the form, Bishop made several frottages of her own during her career. Frottage technique involves taking impressions from the grain of wood which seem to suggest other significant shapes, in this case a monument in a seascape. Thus not only the monument but the sea and sky appear to be made of wood, and the second beholder struggles to

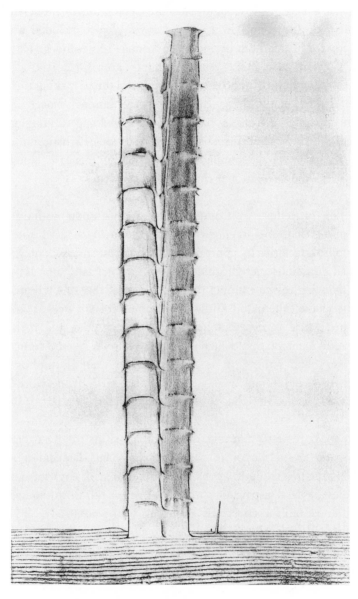

Figure 1 Max Ernst, "False Positions," from *Histoire Naturelle* (Paris: Teufen, 1926). Fogg Art Museum, Harvard University.

see the monument in the impression taken from the grain. (Frottage in a sense becomes the figure for the perception of art itself, its problem of seeing-in.) In *Histoire Naturelle* Ernst included a long apology for his method. In one sense frottage represents an extreme mimesis—art as a literal impression of nature, a sort of fossil, breaking down the distance between sign and thing, making the sign a literal trace of the thing. But the representational aspect of this image separates it from its natural origins, yielding to imaginative invention. As in much surrealist art, the question of artistic authority and originality remains ambiguous, precisely, in this case, along the lines of its representational character. Ernst writes:

> The procedure of frottage, resting thus upon nothing more than the intensification of the irritability of the mind's faculties by appropriate technical means, excluding all conscious mental guidance (of reason, taste, morals), reducing to the extreme the active part of that one whom we have called, up to now, the "author" of the work, this procedure is revealed by the following to be the real equivalent of that which is already known by the term automatic writing. It is as a spectator that the author assists, indifferent or passionate, at the birth of the work and watches the phases of its development.[5]

From an extreme of mimesis, then, frottage shifts to an extreme of expressive art, a mirror of the artist's psyche. The dialogue in Bishop's poem, while it seems to demote art as a copy of nature, also elevates it as a psychic symbol, released both from the natural world and from the conscious intentions of the artist.

As Ernst's title *Histoire Naturelle* also suggests, frottage is deeply involved with questions of the duration of art as opposed to nature. Wood as a medium allows for duration which indexes change (the grain reflecting growth) and is the perfect emblem for dynamic form, "swarming-still." But wood also continues to change even after it is removed from organic life. It has a "life" of decomposition. Bishop contrasts this natural process to aesthetic duration; as art object the monument is seen in a sequence of "now's." "It is the beginning of" something at the end of the poem, even while it is decaying. But in calling on us to "Watch it closely," Bishop also places her monument outside the nostalgia for artistic autonomy. She suggests that the beholder participates in the life of the representational object, even completes it.

The final lines of "The Monument" remove the issues from the observation of a specific work of visual art and offer a more general reflection on the nature and value of art.

> It is the beginning of a painting,
> a piece of sculpture, or poem, or monument,
> and all of wood. Watch it closely.

This gesture of "beginning" at the end of the poem reinforces the antinostalgic view of art that Bishop develops. Art as commemoration has a life in time, a way of growing through its audience.

In "The Monument" Bishop began to explore the relation between historicity and memory, making memory a creative, productive faculty, not merely nostalgic or retrospective. It is not surprising, given this concern, that she translated Octavio Paz's "Objects & Apparitions" (CP, 275–276) and included it in *Geography III*. Paz's poem is a tribute to the art of Joseph Cornell, whose tiny boxes contained miniature fragments of two and three dimensions removed from their contexts and arranged in a surreal space. Bishop was, like Paz, drawn to Cornell's art in later years and made several surreal boxes of her own.[6] Cornell's boxes are marked by a spatial compression and indeterminate reference. Monumentality and symmetry are eschewed for values of compression, understatement, associative freedom. We have already seen that Bishop explores the monumental impulse with a great deal of irony and qualification: the large picture is bad, the "monument" is a crude construction. In *Geography III* Bishop writes about two exquisite and modest miniatures in which the minimal gestures of the artist's hand are inversely proportional to their impact on the beholder. Monuments are made of minutes, without perpetual sunsets; yet they have lasting value.

Paz's poem reads Cornell's boxes as memory chambers. Rather than nostalgically commemorating the past with relics from it, they compress those relics into an infinitely productive shadow world. These are not tombs but "slot machines of visions." We saw that in "Large Bad Picture" and "The Monument" Bishop began, indirectly, to explore the reciprocity between verbal and visual representation. Words introduce narrative extension into images, and images give unity and focus to words. The traditional ekphrastic poem (Keats's "Ode on a Grecian Urn" or Auden's "Musée des Beaux Arts"), which these in many ways exemplify, is hierarchical. It approaches the work of visual art with awe, providing commentary on its enigmas. In Paz's poem the relation between words and images is one of reversal and reciprocity. A translation itself, Bishop's poem highlights the idea of reciprocal translation between the arts as words become visible through descriptive acts and images take on discursive and narrative value. While "Objects & Apparitions" cannot be treated in any direct analysis of Bishop's ideas about the ekphrasis, she does claim it as hers by singling it out, among her many translations, for inclusion in a volume of her work. And it shares many of the features of her own meditations on art: an attention to the humility of the materials that produce a wide imaginative space, a consciousness of the creator, a concern with the activity of memory in relation to representation, and a meditation upon the relation of image to text.

Paz describes Cornell's work not as a copy but as a reversal of nature, which, like all reversals, retains essential elements of its original. Like frottage, Cornell boxes recycle materials to construct an imaginative world. "The reflector of the inner eye / scatters the spectacle." A reversal allows the activity of memory to become productive and indicative rather than belated. Cornell's fragments hurry away from their names just as in metaphor the name hurries away from its denotative meaning and becomes an indeterminate sign. The boxes are not spaces of mastery but of release and freedom. The work then invokes origins, not to recuperate them in illusion's closed mirror, but to pour them into a crucible of meaning and metaphor. Read in conjunction with Bishop's most representational poems, this reversal becomes an implicit feature of representation itself, not merely of the surrealist kind. The power of illusion is not to transport the beholder out of her body, into the unified eternal space of the exact copy. Rather, illusion is a dynamic force, inviting the beholder's associations and memories.

Paz's poem articulates Cornell's reversal of physical laws through a number of tropes of reversal in the writing: syntactic, semantic, figurative. Antitheses of proportion dominate to suggest the relation of constructed to imaginative space: "scarcely bigger than a shoebox," it has room in it "for night and all its lights." Verbal echoes preserve the sense of sameness crucial to opposition: refuse is used, monuments are made of moments. The central chiasmus is, of course, "the opposite of History, creator of ruins, / out of your ruins you have made creations."

The basis for the reversal from ruins to creations is the transition from object to apparition, from thing to eidolon. The loss of material presence becomes a gain of associative potential. The world of necessity and history yields to a more delicate world of illusion, within which a restless motion of metamorphosis—turning, troping, and the weaving and unweaving of memory—replaces the movement of history. The artist is a sleight-of-hand man, putting the laws of identity through hoops. But his space is not comprehensive and consoling. The images are diaphanous, and the beholder has no mastery over them. They weigh "less than light." The poet of particulars becomes the aerial spirit. The "fire buried in the mirror," the "water sleeping in agate" suggest a fugitive energy of life flickering in the still frame of art.

Though specific to the conditions of Cornell's art, this poem incorporates some central themes of Bishop's ekphrastic poetry.

> The apparitions are manifest,
> their bodies weigh less than light,
> lasting as long as this phrase lasts.
>
> Joseph Cornell: inside your boxes
> my words became visible for a moment.

New terms of dependence between images and words inform the end of the poem and challenge ideas of art's mastery. The work of art is not autonomous but contingent upon the beholder's process of unfolding and recreating it. The seeing-in essential to the work of art as object is a dependent quality. Cornell's images depend entirely on the mental space the beholder constructs in response to them. Finding verbal expression for the image gives duration to apparitions ("as long as this phrase lasts"); in turn, the visual fact objectifies the mental space of poetry. This play of silent visibility and articulated invisibility is at work throughout "Objects and Apparitions." Audibility, in echoes, conversations, strummed harp, vocal solos, plays against the muteness of the work of art: the dumb girl, the things running away from their names. Beholding, completed in poetry, becomes the utterance of a silent world.

Bishop's own "Poem" (CP, 176–177) explores, less abstractly, some of the same themes she found in "Objects & Apparitions." The different object of attention naturally produces different concerns, but "Poem" is another meditation on art as a crucible of memories. As her title indicates, the play of words and images is again important as well. "Poem" not only pays tribute to a work of art but, like "Objects & Apparitions," draws out the temporal associations compressed in images. The little sketch is valued not for its autonomy and mastery over time, but for its power to loosen chronology and link us to the past and future.

Bishop's most unqualified delight arises from a minor work by a distant relative. The authority of the painting cannot possibly overwhelm the poet; its value is contingent. Bishop employs a humble rhetoric to match the humility of her subject. But more important, by choosing this low subject to represent the experience of visual art Bishop is able to redefine its impact in pragmatic, relative terms. She celebrates the full charm and evocative power of mimesis as commemoration, without idealizing the space of art as transcendent or recuperative.

"Poem" describes a tiny oil sketch of a Nova Scotia village familiar from childhood. Since a great-uncle (the same responsible for the large bad picture) made the oil sketch, the personal value of the work is primary. "This little painting" is an unqualified pleasure to behold, yet it makes no claims to be a space of aesthetic mastery. The opening of the poem raises questions of value (both commercial and representational) just as "Large Bad Picture" had done at its end. But commerce and contemplation, social and private states, merge here because of a shared reality which the painting evokes. The diminutive size and careless history of the work make clear that this is no immortal monument:

> About the size of an old-style dollar bill,
> American or Canadian,
> mostly the same whites, gray greens, and steel grays
> —this little painting (a sketch for a larger one?)
> has never earned any money in its life.
> Useless and free, it has spent seventy years
> as a minor family relic
> handed along collaterally to owners
> who looked at it sometimes, or didn't bother to.

The subtle economic metaphor introducing the poem works by obvious dissimilarity toward subtle similarity, allowing a value to be ascribed to the work which is entirely free from appropriative instincts. Commerce, as a relation of buying and selling, means more in Bishop's poetry than monetary relations. It includes the impulse to conquest, which taints the large bad picture with its eternal sunset. This picture is neither comprehensive nor consoling, and the response to it is free of the nostalgia so heavy in the earlier work. Not only the diminutive size but the status of the work as a sketch reduces the magisterial claims of art. It offers no recuperation of lost worlds, no glimpse of eternity. The world it depicts was "yet-to-be-dismantled" and has long since been dismantled when Bishop remembers it through the painting. But she sees the transience of the scene as part of its beauty. Not worth the dollar it resembles, the painting is "Useless and free." Again Bishop emphasizes the value of freedom over that of mastery and textual captivity. It is free in requiring no purchase, something "that we get for free," as the poem later tells us. The life of the work, which the poem sketches at the outset, is not bound, like our own lives, to obligation and demand, or to necessity. It allows us to dwell in a free aesthetic space of imaginative extension, but not of mastery.

Yet the painting's likeness to the dollar bill is not merely a matter of color and size. Both are representational (though in different senses), standing for a substantial presence which is never actually cashed in. And both move "collaterally." The word choice serves Bishop in two ways. In a monetary context, it means "of or relating to or being an obligation or security to another to secure its performance." If the painting is "free" this definition should not apply. Yet all representational art is collateral for life, or the memory of it, as money is for gold. Bishop brings forward a second definition, however: "belonging to the same ancestral stock but not in direct line of ascent." This definition suggests that the "commerce" of the sketch has a positive connotation: it permits a connection with family and with a fellow artist-beholder who is also a relative. Further, the term "collateral" points to the alinear, though not atemporal, quality of art's dissemination.

The first stanza of the poem thus establishes the status of the painting as a physical object or commodity—"useless and free" yet historically contingent. But these same qualities will become part of the work's value, part of its ability to extend our own lives. The next stanza explores the work as mimetic object, hovering on the threshold between painterly surface and illusion and exploring the work's semiotic activity. Though charged with recognition, the poem does not become absorbed in the world of illusion. Schemata are not transparent but rather everywhere divert attention from illusion back into surface. This very awareness of the composition, while it interrupts the perfect unity of the illusionary space, extends the life of the artist in a beholder's consciousness. What might have seemed a liability becomes an asset:

It must be Nova Scotia; only there
does one see gabled wooden houses
painted that awful shade of brown.

The other houses, the bits that show, are white.
Elm trees, low hills, a thin church steeple
—that gray-blue wisp—or is it? In the foreground
a water meadow with some tiny cows,
two brushstrokes each, but confidently cows;
two minuscule white geese in the blue water,
back-to-back, feeding, and a slanting stick.
Up closer, a wild iris, white and yellow,
fresh-squiggled from the tube.
The air is fresh and cold; cold early spring
clear as gray glass; a half inch of blue sky
below the steel-gray storm clouds.
(They were the artist's specialty.)
A specklike bird is flying to the left.
Or is it a flyspeck looking like a bird?

The stanza moves from background, the continuous present of
Nova Scotia and its dull brown houses, to detailed foreground (the
cows, the iris). This prepares us for the personal recognition of the
next stanza, where Bishop introduces various dimensions of time.
The record of this beholding clearly contradicts Gombrich's claim
that surface and illusion are mutually exclusive in the eye of the
beholder. Awareness of schemata does not block illusion. The enjoyment of the beholder is precisely in the play between depth and
surface; the poet relishes the activity of seeing in the bristol board
and the marks of paint an absent landscape; brushstrokes become
cows almost at once. Bishop forgets neither the scale of the picture
nor its surface marking as she recalls the landscape in memory. An
element of uncertainty remains to mark the difference between
picture and lost world. Similarly, she breaks the autonomy of the
illusionary world by marking the traces of artistic activity, which
place the image in history. Someone squiggled the iris from the tube;
the steel-gray storm clouds were someone's specialty, though this
"artist-prince" is "far away."

The play of tenses provides an important index to the temporal
awareness of "Poem." Past and future pressure the present tense of

the painting's scene. The genre of landscape enhances this sense of continuity. Indeed, landscape has been the emblem of continuity in English literature. But Bishop emphasizes the ephemeral objects over enduring geological forms: flowers, mortal geese and cows, the "yet-to-be-dismantled elms." She admires the power of the sketch to catch them in their passing. The composition emphasizes the horizontal, whereas the uncle's large bad picture was all verticals. Landscape presents an unusual subject for ekphrastic poetry since landscape traditionally represented duration in nature rather than the "still moment." Even Auden's "Musée des Beaux Arts," which includes a great deal of landscape description, centers around a moment of human action. In Bishop's poem there are no eventful moments—no pursuing lovers, no funeral procession, no human figures at all. But she apprehends the landscape sketch as if it were a still moment. The iris, the cows, the elms become the transient events the picture preserves, their mutability the only implied action. The moment of artistic creation is another "still moment," caught in the squiggled paint and brushhairs. The unitary visual space of the picture, then, does not recuperate a single past but evokes a diversity of moments for the beholder.

The third stanza connects pictorial to real space through a process of recognition, but reasserts their difference by separating the time of painting, the time of beholding, and the times of the various objects. All "coincide" in the painting, but do not resolve into a unity. The fourth stanza returns to the work as created and historical object, now linking this aspect of its identity to its illusion. In the process Bishop reintroduces the narrative association that began the poem, adding dialogue to this hybrid of visual and verbal values:

A sketch done in an hour, "in one breath,"
once taken from a trunk and handed over.
Would you like this? I'll probably never
have room to hang these things again.
Your Uncle George, no, mine, my Uncle George,
he'd be your great-uncle, left them all with Mother

when he went back to England.
You know, he was quite famous, an R. A. . . .

The *plein air* spontaneity of the work seems crucial to Bishop's appreciation of it. What pleasure does the spontaneous, quick sketch offer over the highly contrived, premeditated, and labored painting? Certainly not the pleasure of realism. The schemata are just as artificial and just as primitive in this picture as in the large one. But the sketch is made in closer proximity to the perception. Done "in one breath," the picture matches the fugitive nature it records. But the breath of composition is only one measure of art; it lives beyond its origin and enters an imaginative space which telescopes time ("Your Uncle George, no, mine"). Bishop presents a pluralistic, time-critical, reciprocal notion of representation. The work of art establishes a repository for memories. In it one finds the place depicted, the painting's own making and history, and even the particular history that brought it serendipitously to this threshold of contemplation. The separation of the real, compositional, and imaginative space allows for creative new connections, and the linear sense of time yields to coincidence. The final stanza of the poem describes this process:

I never knew him. We both knew this place,
apparently, this literal small backwater,
looked at it long enough to memorize it,
our years apart. How strange. And it's still loved,
or its memory is (it must have changed a lot).
Our visions coincided—"visions" is
too serious a word—our looks, two looks:
art "copying from life" and life itself,
life and the memory of it so compressed
they've turned into each other. Which is which?
Life and the memory of it cramped,
dim, on a piece of Bristol board,
dim, but how live, how touching in detail

—the little that we get for free,
the little of our earthly trust. Not much.
About the size of our abidance
along with theirs: the munching cows,
the iris, crisp and shivering, the water
still standing from spring freshets,
the yet-to-be-dismantled elms, the geese.

Emotionally the passage pursues the simple rhythms of loss and gain, reduction and expansion. But it exemplifies the compression it describes, containing in twenty lines the rudiments of a complex theory of art's ontology.

"Coincide" is a carefully chosen word in this poem, for it centers the play between spatial and temporal concepts. Two things or events can coincide spatially or temporally. Bishop does not superimpose these, but allows spatial coincidence to have meaning as a connecting force through time. The figure for this connectedness is family relation, the work of art as a family relic. The poet of "Over 2,000 Illustrations and a Complete Concordance" was closed out experientially from the timeless, autonomous scene of nativity, from the "family with pets." But the poet of "Poem," no longer nostalgic for origins, is brought into the scene by family connection and, conversely, feels her family connection through the work of art.

Syntactically, the things that coincide here are not just two looks, but art "copying from life" and "life itself." They coincide in the mental space established by memory and representation. The dichotomy takes a further turn as "Life and the memory of it" become coincidental; all temporal priority is erased in spatial convergence. When life and the memory of it turn into each other, we are freed momentarily from the feeling of belatedness and loss. The bristol board, the space of art, is not transcendent or unitary. The final images of the poem clarify this special antinostalgic view. Bishop uses abundant participial adjectives to characterize the sustained action of the pictorial world. To behold is to unpack the temporality inherent in spatial images, though that temporality is not linear or one-directional. The dynamic space evoked in the beholding of a frozen image includes past, present, and future as a multiplicity of durations. "The munching cows, / the iris, crisp and shivering, the water / still standing from spring freshets, / the yet-to-be-dismantled elms, the geese" suggest many moments beyond the pictorial frame. The dynamic space of art, with the temporality which beholding brings to it, becomes one with a wider consciousness of life. If Bishop gives up the ideal unity celebrated in ekphrastic poetry, she broadens considerably the range of consciousness which a work of art "compresses."

The final stanza has returned to the question of value introduced at the beginning of the poem and continues the economic metaphor in the image of earthly trust. The value of art is commensurate with its size here, but size is measured not in terms of commodity value but of commemorative value. As such, spatial and temporal concepts again converge; our earthly trust is "About the size of our abidance / along with theirs." Bishop resists the nostalgic impulse within illusion for mastery over time, but engages memory as a source of creative vitality and a supplement to the limits of existence.

Epilogue:
Maps and Mirrors

Among the many images of representation in Bishop's writing, two predominate: maps and mirrors. The map, Bishop tells us in her epigraph to *Geography III,* provides "A picture of the whole, or a part, of the / Earth's surface." It orders the observable world into an intelligible visual scheme that reflects a political structure as well as a geological one. The mirror's appeal is its power of exact replication and its suggestion of a shadow world. As a vehicle of self-reflection, it frames and objectifies identity. While Bishop's poems delight in the process of mapping and mirroring the world, they question the promise of visual mastery by reminding us of the historical dimension in which maps and mirrors exist. Her treatment of these images serves as an index to her views on the pleasures and limits of all representation.

By placing "The Map" (CP, 3) at the beginning of *North & South* and subsequently of the *Complete Poems,* Bishop tempts readers to approach it cartographically, as a diagram for reading her work. But in responding to this analogy we must recall the sense of change and process that pervades Bishop's poems and pressures even her early work. A careful reading of "The Map" reveals how fluent, uncertain, and even historical the map, and the poem, can be. If Bishop finds herself more allied with the mapmaker than the historian, she also makes clear how much these means of beholding overlap within the changing, unschematic surface of the earth to which the map ambiguously refers. Her map is not a vehicle of mastery but one of imaginative engagement, a way of seeing in and through time.

If we are to consider the ways in which a poem might be like a map, we must first acknowledge that Bishop treats this map almost as though it were a poem. It possesses illusionistic as well as diagrammatic properties. She approaches the map as a reader of signs but also as a beholder of a picture. She finds not the determinate shapes of a diagram, free of perspective, but the indeterminate signs of a fiction, made out of desire and subject to the play of a beholder's interpretive glance. The map's orders do not exclude the process which is the usual domain of the historian.

> Land lies in water; it is shadowed green.
> Shadows, or are they shallows, at its edges
> showing the line of long sea-weeded ledges
> where weeds hang to the simple blue from green.
> Or does the land lean down to lift the sea from under,
> drawing it unperturbed around itself?
> Along the fine tan sandy shelf
> is the land tugging at the sea from under?

The map raises issues of control, first in terms of the relations within the map, later in terms of the beholder's and creator's relation to the earth's surface which the map depicts. To see a map as a poem is to loosen relations of dominance, to allow a flow of direction and interpretation and to reject the imperial stance. It also loosens the relation of sign to referent, resulting in a freedom from fixed realities, along with an anxiety about exceeding them. What the map does not offer is a directive. With the open, meditative syntax and the redundant rhymes, this map is not a transparent diagram but, like a picture or poem, bears an uncertain relation to the real.

The middle stanza of "The Map," in a simple language of cause and effect, at first idealizes the imaginative stance of the map, suggesting the object's stability and the beholder's control:

> The shadow of Newfoundland lies flat and still.
> Labrador's yellow, where the moony Eskimo
> has oiled it. We can stroke these lovely bays,
> under a glass as if they were expected to blossom,
> or as if to provide a clean cage for invisible fish.

These are shadows, not shallows, the beholder decides, and the signs are established by their direct connection to the inhabitants of the place they represent. But this whim exposes the will of the beholder. And the "as if" in the lovely vision of blossoms and the "invisible fish" returns us to the arbitrariness of the map and the movement of life under the frame.

After this point, the poem explicitly separates places from their "names" as linguistic and cartographic mastery become excesses detached from object or cause:

> The names of seashore towns run out to sea,
> the names of cities cross the neighboring mountains
> —the printer here experiencing the same excitement
> as when emotion too far exceeds its cause.

Again, Bishop presents feeling exceeding the boundaries of form. Grasp is restored in the image that follows: "These peninsulas take the water between thumb and finger / like women feeling for the smoothness of yard-goods." But this female image of sensuous and intuitive judgment contrasts with the map's traditionally rational and imperial posture. These yard-goods can be formed to almost any contour. And these relations occurring between portions of the map are even more indeterminate than those which can occur between mapmaker and world or beholder and map.

In the final stanza of "The Map" Bishop emphasizes the internal, fictional relations of the map and their difference from factual relations of the world. But while fictional relations allowed the beholder to experience tranquillity and control in the middle stanza, the shift from sea to land in the final stanza introduces a new anxiety. The speaker returns, after an open, unrhymed middle stanza, to the redundant rhymes of the first stanza.

> Mapped waters are more quiet than the land is,
> lending the land their waves' own conformation:
> and Norway's hare runs south in agitation,
> profiles investigate the sea, where land is.

The "conformation" reverses rather than confirms. Instead of a perspectiveless diagram, Bishop imagines a space agitated by many perspectives. Here, too, the beholder has entirely removed interpretation from denotation, reading the map as if it were an illustration. This has been an impulse throughout, to read the map illusionistically (as a mirror) rather than as an aggregate of knowledge, and to separate that illusion from its referent. The poem continually questions a sign's relation to its object. "Are they assigned, or can the countries pick their colors?" What connection does the imagination have to reality? How contiguous are its figures? This is also a question of control, political and creative. "Topography displays no favorites" suggests the judiciousness of a control which holds to no single perspective. But North has certainly been featured if not favored in this poem, and if it is "as near as West" it is also as far, since the map's images connect nothing tangible. "More delicate than the historians' are the map-makers' colors" because more subtle and more fragile. The historian's contours are those of necessity and contingency, of the determinate, temporal world. The mapmaker's outline does not supersede or master the historian's realm of time. The map may represent an ideal of perspectiveless, unchanging totality, but as an object of contemplation and expression it is always drawn back by its beholder into history, time, the many active displacements of perspective. Thus Bishop, as mapmaker, is always also historian.

If there is a visual analogue to Bishop's "The Map," it should be Vermeer's *The Art of Painting* (Figure 2), which is similarly con-

Figure 2 Jan Vermeer, *The Art of Painting*. Kunsthistorisches Museum, Vienna.

cerned with the relations between history, topography, and representation. But the aesthetic and thematic similarities between the two works serve to highlight their fundamental difference in attitudes toward mastery. Vermeer's painting absorbs a complex world into a form of spatial knowledge.[1] Bishop's "The Map," and her poetry generally, continually intercept that knowledge with the sense of unmasterable flux and plurality.

Vermeer's smooth surfaces, his precision and restraint, are easy to associate with Bishop's descriptive art. But Vermeer's allegorical canvas is a kind of paradigm of his intentions. It portrays a painter whose back is to us so that we cannot determine the focus of his gaze. Is it toward the map which covers much of the wall (and is marked with Vermeer's own name and the word "descriptio"), or toward the woman dressed as Clio, goddess of history, who is posing for the portrait? The composition absorbs both images, geography and history, into the spatial mastery of the painting. Vermeer makes an analogy between the map and his own activity by marking the map with his name. Is painting diagrammatic, like a map? But the other objects in the room are representational in different ways. On the canvas represented in the painting, the painter has begun an emblematic portrait of Clio. Other objects in the room are neither iconic nor diagrammatic but simply contextual. In Vermeer's painting these different forms of representation do not confuse the beholder or compete for dominance but resolve themselves within the artist's vision. Representing himself within the scene, Vermeer is at once observer, interpreter, and maker of this scene, participating in its contingent, experiential reality but also moving out from it into various forms of contemplation. In their way of juxtaposing forms of representations—emblematic, narrative, descriptive—Vermeer and Bishop suggest that art is both map and view, that these flow together. But in Bishop this produces a "dazzling dialectic" rather than a stable form of knowledge. The two artists share a preference for description over narration, for spatial over sequential ways of absorbing the breadth and complexity of the world, of bringing the distant near. But Bishop resists claiming visual mastery. She is far less confident about the power of art to transcend the limits of the human gaze or to represent historical reality as visual knowledge. Bishop does not import the historical world into the immediate scene with a map, but introduces the awareness of life's flux and stress into the visual diagram. If the map is pictorial in Bishop (as it is in Vermeer), it is not in order to bring knowledge into visual immediacy but to subject knowledge to human contingency.

Description is, for both Bishop and Vermeer, a primary way of understanding the world, one that is capable of accommodating its historical nature. The general devaluing of description in our time and the priority of mental over sensuous awareness have led critics to defend Bishop by ignoring or dismissing her descriptive qualities as a mask for emblematic or discursive ones. Bishop's poems are certainly a record of consciousness shaping a visual experience, but they are also an evocation of something seen.

Reflective surfaces served, in Dutch painting, to celebrate description as a form of objective knowledge. A placid pond or lake could bring heaven and earth together in an ideal continuity that seemed free of artistic intervention. A judiciously placed mirror could reveal objects and situations outside a subjective gaze. Bishop's poems, too, are full of mirrors, but they tend to evoke mystical and psychological themes alien to Dutch objectivity. The reality that Bishop's mirrors reflect is too fluctuating and elusive to be mastered in description. The aspiring priest of nature in "The Riverman" (CP, 105–109) longs for a "virgin mirror" which can reflect the river's spirit and thus give him knowledge of it. But all his mirrors are fogged, his magic blocked by cliché, narcissism, and debased ideas of beauty in the culture around him.

> I need a virgin mirror
> no one's ever looked at,
> that's never looked back at anyone,
> to flash up the spirit's eyes
> and help me recognize them.
> The storekeeper offered me
> a box of little mirrors,
> but each time I picked one up
> a neighbor looked over my shoulder
> and then that one was spoiled—
> spoiled, that is, for anything
> but the girls to look at their mouths in,
> to examine their teeth and smiles.

"The Map" and "The Riverman" explore different urges for mastery: in the first, to diagram reality; in the second, to reflect it exactly. A great deal of Bishop's poetry is taken up with questioning one or the other impulse, sometimes both. Bishop's "Sonnet" (CP, 192) however, published in the last year of her life, explores an opposite urge, for freedom, which pulses through her poems but is seldom their focus.

> Caught—the bubble
> in the spirit-level,
> a creature divided;
> and the compass needle
> wobbling and wavering,
> undecided.
> Freed—the broken
> thermometer's mercury
> running away;
> and the rainbow-bird
> from the narrow bevel
> of the empty mirror,
> flying wherever
> it feels like, gay!

Like many formal poets, Bishop uses poetic constraints antithetically, to allow for more energy in release. Here the sonnet is reduced to a dimeter line to draw the boundary between form and formlessness. The dimeter rhythm also highlights the poet's ambivalence and the dazzling dialectic between form and freedom. The bubble and the compass represent troubled states which arise often in Bishop's poetry: within structures of measurement and direction the spirit feels divided and undecided. The mercury and the rainbow-bird suggest solutions: break the bindings, release life into its naturally amorphous state. But the poem reminds us that this release of energy and movement can only be appreciated through constraining form, through organized images and sounds. The tension between "caught" and "freed" energies marks the pleasure of poetry.

The images in "Sonnet" are particularized so as to keep the reader's attention on the dynamics of "caught" and "freed" rather than on a spiritual metaphor. Yet they are all instruments of measurement in some way. Omitting an object to be captured or freed in measurement, Bishop suggests that measurement itself, at least for the poet, is an ambivalent impulse. Within the urge to measure and master lies the paradoxical urge to release.

The last image of "Sonnet" is different from the others in that it deals with reflection rather than measurement. The "empty mirror" shines up the opposite of what the Riverman sought—not a presence but a void. At the extreme of freedom lies emptiness, which can be a joy to contemplate. But the "rainbow-bird" has no existence independent of the mirror. It is an effect of light breaking against the bevel, the corner that marks the frame. If there is a sexual meaning to "gay" at the end of the poem, Bishop does not embrace it as her identity. It arises when the mirror is empty, rhymes with "away," and marks the freedom from a label.

"The Map" and "Sonnet" mark the poles of Bishop's career and the extremes in her questions of mastery, the world "caught" under glass, the spirit "freed" from measurement and representation. I have argued that each of these extremes is highly qualified—the map as diagram is uncertain and limited; the sense of freedom depends on the prior constraint of form. The wish to master reality—in art, thought, or life—is not forsworn, but questioned and curtailed.

We might do better, in seeking a paradigm for Bishop's poetry, to consider Jerónimo's house, that makeshift, temporary dwelling, a "gray wasps' nest / of chewed-up paper / glued with spit" suspended around "writing-paper / lines of light" (CP, 34). Jerónimo is master of his poemlike house, but not of the hurricane that drives him from it. The poet rediscovers this "wasps' nest" in Santarém and at the end of her career claims it as a souvenir of her journey.

Notes

Index

Notes

Introduction

1. An earlier version insisted on the more sentimental "azure eyes" as the focus of lost love.

2. Randall Jarrell, "The Poet and His Public" (1946), reprinted in *Poetry and the Age* (New York: Farrar, Straus and Giroux, 1972), p. 235.

3. John Hollander, "Elizabeth Bishop's Mappings of Life" (1977), reprinted in *Elizabeth Bishop and Her Art,* ed. Lloyd Schwartz and Sybil P. Estess (Ann Arbor: The University of Michigan Press, 1983), p. 247.

4. Ibid.

5. Vassar Rare Books and Manuscripts, Recorded Observations, 1934–1937.

6. Ibid.

7. Elizabeth Bishop to Marianne Moore, 1938. Rosenbach Museum and Library, Philadelphia.

8. Elizabeth Bishop, "The Country Mouse," in *Elizabeth Bishop: The Collected Prose* (New York: Farrar, Straus and Giroux, 1984), p. 13. Subsequent references will be made within the text, abbreviated CPR.

9. Vassar Rare Books and Manuscripts.

10. Denis Donoghue, *Connoisseurs of Chaos: Ideas of Order in Modern American Poetry* (New York: Columbia University Press, 1984), p. 269.

11. *Vassar Journal of Undergraduate Studies* (May 1933), pp. 102–120. Reprinted in Schwartz and Estess, eds., *Elizabeth Bishop and Her Art,* pp. 271–272.

12. *Vassar Review* (February 1934), pp. 5–7. Reprinted in Schwartz and Estess, eds., *Elizabeth Bishop and Her Art*, pp. 273–275.

13. Elizabeth Bishop to Robert Lowell, July 11, 1951. Houghton Library, Harvard University.

14. Elizabeth Bishop to Anne Stevenson, March 20, 1963. Washington University Special Collections.

15. May 20, 1955. Houghton Library.

16. Randall Jarrell early emphasized Bishop's visual qualities, especially her power of conveying things seen, and many have taken up his line of thought. Anne Stevenson followed his lead in her groundbreaking book, *Elizabeth Bishop* (New York: Twayne, 1966). Nancy McNally ("Elizabeth Bishop: The Discipline of Description," *Twentieth Century Literature,* 11 [Jan. 1966], 189–201) considers Bishop an impersonal but highly perceptive observer. Jan B. Gordon ("Days and Distances: The Cartographic Imagination of Elizabeth Bishop," *Salmagundi,* 22–23 [Spring/Summer 1973], 294–305) complains that Bishop reduces life to mere objective observation. Jerome Mazzaro continues the debate ("Elizabeth Bishop and the Poetics of Impediment," *Salmagundi,* 27 [Summer/Fall 1974], 118–144), arguing that her descriptive method is an acknowledgment of relativity. Sybil Estess tries to strike a balance by describing the interplay of reality and imagination ("Elizabeth Bishop: The Delicate Art of Map Making," *Southern Review,* 13 [October 1977], 705–727). Marjorie Perloff places Bishop among those modern poets who at their best treat the particular as numinous rather than representational ("Elizabeth Bishop: The Course of a Particular," *Modern Poetry Studies,* 8 [Winter 1977], 177–192). Thomas Travisano's recent book, *Elizabeth Bishop: Her Artistic Development* (Charlottesville: University Press of Virginia, 1988), published after the manuscript for this book was complete, discusses Bishop's development from an abstract symbolist isolation to a descriptive orientation toward history and geography. Robert Dale Parker in *The Unbeliever: The Poetry of Elizabeth Bishop* (Urbana and Chicago: University of Illinois Press, 1988) defines the changes in Bishop's style more thematically, as a movement from "wish" to "where." My argument differs from his in exploring the perceptual and epistemological implications of certain themes and in arguing that Bishop's vision is open, fluent, and ambivalent rather than either charming or bleak. My book is distinct from all previous studies in its emphasis on the drama of meaning of the beholder in Bishop's poetry, which underlies her visual technique.

17. I first argued this point in a lecture presented at the Bunting Institute, "Lost in Correspondences: Memory and Representation in Elizabeth Bishop," April 17, 1984. These ideas were corroborated and placed in a feminist/deconstructionist context by Lee Edelman in "The Geography of

Gender: Elizabeth Bishop's 'In the Waiting Room,'" *Contemporary Litera-ture*, 26, no. 2 (Summer 1985), 179–196.

18. For a discussion of change as a theme and practice in Bishop's art, see Barbara Page, "Shifting Islands: Elizabeth Bishop's Manuscripts," *Shenandoah*, 33, no. 1 (1981–82), 51–62, and Jane Shore, "Elizabeth Bishop: The Art of Changing Your Mind," *Ploughshares*, 5, no. 1 (1979), 178–191.

19. Many critics have noted Bishop's play with perspective, but few have dealt adequately with the intentions behind style. Some discussion of this question occurs in David Bromwich, "Elizabeth Bishop's Dream-Houses," *Raritan*, 4, no. 1 (Summer 1984), 77–94. My ideas about the grotesque style and meaning in Bishop's poetry were inspired by Helen Vendler's now famous essay "Domestication, Domesticity, and the Oth-erworldly," *World Literature Today*, 1 (Winter 1977), 23–28. After com-pleting this book I read Helen McNeil, "Elizabeth Bishop," in *Voices and Visions* (New York: Random House, 1987), pp. 395–425. McNeil makes use, as I do, of Freud's concept of the "uncanny" in describing the structure and impact of Bishop's poems. Joanne Feit Diehl discusses Bishop's attitude toward the sublime in a feminist context in "At Home with Loss: Elizabeth Bishop and the American Sublime," in *Coming to Light: American Women Poets in the Twentieth Century*, ed. Dianne Middlebrook and Marilyn Yolom (Ann Arbor: University of Michigan Press, 1985), pp. 123–127).

20. See especially David Kalstone, *Five Temperaments: Elizabeth Bishop, Robert Lowell, James Merrill, Adrienne Rich, John Ashbery* (New York: Oxford University Press, 1977), pp. 12–40.

21. The most truly biographical work thus far, however, has come from David Kalstone, *Becoming a Poet: Elizabeth Bishop with Marianne Moore and Robert Lowell* (New York: Farrar, Straus and Giroux, 1989). The book frames and comments upon the long correspondence Bishop had with these two writers.

1. *"Active Displacements in Perspective"*

1. David Hockney, quoted in Lawrence Wechsler, "About Time, About Space, About David Hockney," *California* (October 1981), p. 105.

2. Bishop made several sketches and water-colors of window views as well as writing poems from this perspective. Traditional Renaissance perspective is itself based on a window technique, in which a glass placed before a subject becomes the surface on which the ordering of the subject takes place, while its transparency gives the illusion that the actual order and unity of nature have been perceived. The angled windows (as opposed to central perspective) of which Bishop was fond drew attention to the isometric design of space.

3. Lorrie Goldensohn has discussed this technique of miniaturization in her thoughtful article "Elizabeth Bishop's Originality," *American Poetry Review,* 7, no. 2 (March/April 1978), 18–22. But Goldensohn sees this as a means of control; the poem does not allow the sense of control much space, however.

4. Bishop's notebooks suggest her simple visual enjoyment of this image, independent of its function in the poem. "These hot mornings the street sprinkler goes around about 9:30. The water dries off very rapidly, but very beautifully, in *watermelon* pattern—only wet-black on grey, instead of darker green on brighter green" (Vassar Rare Books and Manuscripts).

5. Elizabeth Bishop to Anne Stevenson, January 8, 1964. Washington University Library.

6. T. S. Eliot, *The Complete Poems and Plays: 1909–1950* (New York: Harcourt, Brace, 1971), pp.12–13.

7. William Carlos Williams, *The Collected Earlier Poems* (New York: New Directions, 1966), p. 353.

8. Ashley Brown, "An Interview with Elizabeth Bishop" (1966), reprinted in *Elizabeth Bishop and Her Art,* ed. Lloyd Schwartz and Sybil Estess (Ann Arbor: University of Michigan Press, 1983), p. 297.

9. John Ashbery, "The Complete Poems" (1969), reprinted in *Elizabeth Bishop and Her Art,* p. 201.

10. Elizabeth Bishop to Anne Stevenson, March 20, 1963. Washington University Library.

11. Whenever self-reflection is at issue (and especially when it is so literal as it is here), contemporary critics are inclined to invoke Jacques Lacan. His theory of "the mirror stage" would seem to provide an explanation or analogue for this poem, anticipating the themes of "In the Waiting Room." In Lacan's theory the mirror is the threshold of perception and self-consciousness, of the imaginary and the symbolic, the place where the child recognizes herself as an other. Mature subjectivity requires a further stage (which Lacan calls the symbolic) in which "the subject integrates into the symbolic system and asserts itself there, through the exercise of a true word" (Jacques Lacan, "Le Seminaire I" [1953], quoted in Umberto Eco, *Semiotics and the Philosophy of Language* [Bloomington: Indiana University Press, 1984], p. 203). Bishop's poetry emphasizes the instability of this "mature" stage. Perhaps because mirrors are a part of adult life as well as the life of children, that threshold experience of the self remains active. Indeed, the words here are not the mastering "I am an Elizabeth" (which prove so unstable in "In the Waiting Room") but "I am not that staring man." The speaker refuses to accept the image before him as his image. The linguistic "I" resists the specular "I," the I as bodily,

social being. The verbal whitewash blocks out or (in Derridean style) puts under erasure the external image as a way of disowning it. It declares its immateriality ("What do I do? / —Collect no interest") and the limited freedom and agency this implies ("otherwise what I can"). This second person can never express herself directly, for she exists "between your eyes and you" at the threshold between inner and outer worlds (not, clearly, in some securely interior first-person space).

12. Bishop's poetry is certainly influenced by Wordsworth's *Preface to Lyrical Ballads,* which she studied and took notes from during her college years. (See College Notebooks, Vassar Rare Books and Manuscripts.) Wordsworth argued his purpose: "to choose incidents and situations from common life . . . and, at the same time to throw over them a certain colouring of the imagination, whereby ordinary things should be presented to the mind in an unusual aspect; and, further, . . . to make these incidents and situations interesting by tracing in them, truly though not ostentatiously, the primary laws of our nature." William Wordsworth, "Preface to Lyrical Ballads (1850)," in *Poetical Works,* ed. Thomas Hutchinson, revised by Ernest de Selincourt (London: Oxford University Press, 1936), p. 734. But Bishop's approach allows her to find rather than create this interest.

13. Elizabeth Bishop to Anne Stevenson, January 8, 1964. Washington University Library.

14. Bishop's letters to friends indicate how habitually she imagined looking at things from odd points of view. In a letter to Robert Lowell (November 18, 1947), she describes the swimming pool of the Hemingway House in Key West at night: "The swimming pool is wonderful—it is very large and the water, from away under the reef, is fairly salt. Also it lights up at night—I find that each underwater bulb is five times the voltage of the *one* bulb in the light house across the street, so the pool must be visible to Mars—it is wonderful to swim around in a sort of green fire; one's friends look like luminous frogs" (Houghton Library). While she focuses on the swimming pool, Bishop draws attention to the reef, the lighthouse across the street, even to Mars.

15. Travel Notes, Vassar Rare Books and Manuscripts.

16. With this theme in mind, "Song" may be read as a rewriting of "Pleasure Seas."

2. Attractive Mortality

1. Elizabeth Bishop to Robert Lowell, September 8, 1948; Houghton Library. "Sometimes I wish we could have a more sensible conversation

about this suffering business, anyway. I imagine we actually agree fairly well—it is just that I guess I think it is so inevitable & unavoidable there's no use talking about it, & that in itself it has no value, anyway."

2. January 8, 1964; Washington University Library.

3. I differ particularly with Robert Dale Parker, who, in response to early emphasis on the pastoral pleasures of Bishop's work, reads her as a poet of terrors. See Robert Dale Parker, *The Unbeliever: The Poetry of Elizabeth Bishop* (Urbana and Chicago: University of Illinois Press, 1988). Bishop's work insists on an emotional and conceptual openness to the contradictions in life. She is not her unbeliever who, with his eyes closed, projects a malevolent will upon the sea. She is the clear-eyed poet who sees a rusted capstan as a blood-stained crucifix, but also sees the hirsute begonia brightening the black translucency, the luminous rocks in their bezels of sand despite bleak March winds. Bishop's poetry is not merely gay in the presence of barbarities, of course. The humor is often black. But her imagination resists tonal as well as conceptual stasis; it acknowledges a perpetually dividing heart.

4. In contrasting an ideal, autonomous, timeless, and totalizing mode of thought to a temporal, mortal, pluralistic existence, Bishop often implicitly draws upon gender distinctions. Her "fleshed, fair, erected indivisible" "imaginary icebergs" and "stiff and idle" "final thoughts" are clearly phallic, and in many poems plurality, metamorphosis, decenteredness are associated with female experience. One can argue that Bishop's grotesques, open to change and contradiction, resisting dualities of mind and body, self and world, reflect a female consciousness. Bishop does not idealize, abhor, or attempt to master the body, as the male-dominated culture sometimes does. Instead, she confronts the challenge our corporeal, historical being makes to all fixed and totalizing forms, all illusions of immortality. But while the poet seems sometimes to invoke gender distinctions, she is by no means consistent in her use of them. Women as well as men in her poems express the fear of life, the longing for cultural mastery or aesthetic and conceptual transcendence. Male as well as female beholders confront an elusive, contradictory, mutable, and recalcitrant reality. Bishop's misfits are of both sexes. While I consider psychosexual aspects of Bishop's vision where they seem most prominent, I do not make this issue the center of my argument because Bishop herself avoided any static alignment of consciousness and gender. The will to autonomy, to transcendence, is , for her, as universal as mortality. It includes but is not explained by gender.

5. March 20, 1963; Washington University Library.

6. As a young poet Bishop took up almost obsessively the metaphysical conceit of the eyes as expressions of the heart and windows of the soul.

The fascinating though awkwardly baroque "Three Sonnets for the Eyes" (CP, 223–224) is representative of her early insular treatment of the eyes as the center of an inwardly defined, timeless identity. As Bishop left behind her metaphysical style and took up a symbolist rhetoric, the eyes increasingly became symbols of problematic or elusive identity. She abandons the conceit altogether after *North & South,* except when Crusoe encounters the inexpressive, horizontal eyes of the billy-goat, which refuse altogether to fit the idea of a transcendent or profound (vertical) identity. What Bishop continues and develops, to displace the essentialist conceit of the eyes gazing inward or heavenward, is a narrative of looking, staring, glimpsing.

7. Marianne Moore praised Bishop for the phrase in a letter: "'battered moonlight' is not hackneyed!" Vassar Rare Books and Manuscripts.

8. Vassar Rare Books and Manuscripts.

9. Notebook, Vassar Rare Books and Manuscripts.

10. Just as "The Weed" reimagined Herbert's suffering heart, "The Fish" reimagines Melville's struggle with nature. He is more like Moby Dick than Bishop's minimal, mock-heroic rhetoric would suggest. Melville anticipates Bishop's deep regard both for the homeless skeptic yearning for meaning and the naked reality which eludes it, a restless, endless flow which may conceal nothing behind it. Bishop conspicuously avoids the sublime massiveness, the august rhetoric, the encyclopedic quality of Melville, preferring a plain, anecdotal style with the humble figurativeness of the simile. Her trimeter line, punctuated with an occasional dimeter, suggests the voice of a storyteller more than an orator, like Melville only in her love of detail and fisherman's practicalities.

11. Vassar Rare Books and Manuscripts.

12. Bishop told Marianne Moore that she was inspired by Picasso's *Guernica.*

13. October 17, 1938; Vassar Rare Books and Manuscripts.

14. Vassar Rare Books and Manuscripts.

15. Ibid.

16. Parker, *The Unbeliever,* pp. 98–99.

17. Vassar Rare Books and Manuscripts.

18. Ibid.

19. Ibid.

20. Many of Bishop's poems include confrontations between landlord and servant classes ("Faustina, or Rock Roses," "Twelfth Morning; or What You Will,") or between dominant and subjected cultures ("Arrival at Santos," "Brazil, January 1, 1502") in which the observer is affronted by the discovery of an alternative culture or will where she had assumed a primitive blank slate on which to impose her own will or imagination.

3. Imaginary Heights, Invisible Depths

1. Vassar Rare Books and Manuscripts.

2. Another prototype may be from Bronte's *Jane Eyre* (1847; New York: New American Library, 1960), p. 129. Jane shows Mr. Rochester a painting of an iceberg "piercing a polar winter sky" with "a colossal head, inclined towards the iceberg, and resting against it," anticipating Bishop's analogy with the iceberg and the soul. Indeed, Jane decorates the head with a white flame crown "gemmed with sparkles," suggesting Bishop's "jewelry from a grave." Jane describes the act of painting the picture as "one of the keenest pleasures I have ever known." The pleasure is presumably one of freedom from human contingency, emotional volatility, and other forms of bondage.

3. Harold Bloom, Foreward, in *Elizabeth Bishop and Her Art,* ed. Lloyd Schwartz and Sybil Estess (Ann Arbor: University of Michigan Press, 1983), p. x.

4. Denis Donoghue, *Connoisseurs of Chaos: Ideas of Order in Modern American Poetry* (New York: Columbia University Press, 1984), pp. 259–260.

5. Joseph Summers, *"George Herbert: His Religion and Art:* Its Making and Early Reception," *George Herbert Journal,* 5, no. 1–2 (Fall 1981/Spring 1982), pp. 17–18.

6. Vassar Rare Books and Manuscripts.

7. Elizabeth Bishop to Anne Stevenson, January 8, 1964. Washington University Library.

8. Vassar Rare Books and Manuscripts.

9. Ibid.

10. Steven Knapp, *Personification and the Sublime: Milton to Coleridge* (Cambridge, Mass.: Harvard University Press, 1985), pp. 106–110.

11. Washington University Library.

12. Vassar Rare Books and Manuscripts.

13. Ibid.

14. Ibid.

15. Houghton Library.

4. Excursive Sight

1. January 8, 1964. Washington University Library.

2. Elizabeth Spires, "The Art of Poetry XXVII: Elizabeth Bishop," reprinted in *Paris Review,* 23, no. 80 (Summer 1981), 75.

3. Vassar Rare Books and Manuscripts.

4. Ibid.

5. Elizabeth Bishop to Marianne Moore, May 14, 1942. Vassar Rare Books and Manuscripts.

6. January 8, 1964; Washington University Library.

7. Henry James, *The Art of Travel*, ed. Morton Dauwen Zabel (Garden City, N.Y.: Doubleday, 1958), p. 18.

8. Vassar Rare Books and Manuscripts.

9. Ibid.

10. Ibid.

11. Henry David Thoreau, "Walking" (1862), in *The Portable Thoreau*, ed. Carl Bode (New York: Viking, 1947), p. 593.

12. Quoted in Thoreau, *Walden*, in *The Portable Thoreau*, p. 336.

13. Ralph Waldo Emerson, *Selected Writings*, ed. Brooks Atkinson (New York: Modern Library, 1940, 1950), p. 906.

14. Lawrence Buell, *Literary Transcendentalism: Style and Vision in American Renaissance* (Ithaca, N.Y.: Cornell University Press, 1973), p. 187.

15. Emerson, *Selected Writings*, p. 906.

16. Thoreau, *A Week on the Concord and Merrimack Rivers* (1849), in *The Portable Thoreau*, p. 226.

17. Blaise Pascal, *Pensées*, no. 139, (New York: Dutton, 1958), p. 39.

18. Lee Edelman ("The Geography of Gender: Elizabeth Bishop's 'In the Waiting Room,'"*Contemporary Literature*, 26, no. 2 [Summer 1985], 179–96) and others have challenged Bishop's repeated claim to literal truth, seeing that claim as a way of distracting us from her rhetorical purposes or pretending that language can be transparent. In fact, the argument goes, the poems are self-conscious constructs that testify to the abyss of language. But we can respect Bishop's insistence on the factual basis of these poems without becoming naive literalists. The details of her poems are "true" as absorbed and transformed by the beholder's mind and again by memory and poetic invention.

19. Spires, "The Art of Poetry XXVII: Elizabeth Bishop," p. 62.

20. Rosenbach Museum and Library, Philadelphia.

21. Washington University Library.

22. Bishop remarked about the indrawn "yes" of Nova Scotian dialect in a letter to James Merrill. Vassar Rare Books and Manuscripts.

23. Helen Vendler, "The Domestication, Domesticity, and the Otherworldly," *World Literature Today*, 1 (Winter 1977), 23–28.

24. Vassar Rare Books and Manuscripts.

25. Joanne Diehl reads the poem darkly, finding in the sun a cruel force that toys with nature and humanity. Joanne Diehl, "At Home with Loss: Elizabeth Bishop and the American Sublime," in *Coming into the Light: American Women Poets in the Twentieth Century*, ed. Dianne Middlebrook and Marilyn Yalom (Ann Arbor: University of Michigan Press, 1985), pp. 123–

137. Certainly the coyness of the big paws and teasing manner frame a fearful symmetry. The sublimity of the sun absorbs all the feeling from earlier images of exposure and threat in the poem. But the poem is equinoctial as well as the sun; it turns from this austere sublimity to a renewed, affirmative power of imagination and engagement with fate rather than mere surrender (as in "giving up the ghost") of imagination to fate.

26. In fact the images for this poem may have come out of Kings as much as Genesis. Attached to Bishop's drafts for the poem are excerpts from Kings describing the consumption of the polis by fire. Vassar Rare Books and Manuscripts.

5. Memory's Eye

1. Charles Baudelaire, "The Painter of Modern Life," in *Strangeness and Beauty: An Anthology of Aesthetic Criticism, 1840–1910*, vol. 1, ed. Eric Warner and Graham Hough (Cambridge: Cambridge University Press, 1983), p. 213.

2. Vassar Rare Books and Manuscripts.

3. Ibid.

4. "Dimensions of the Novel," Vassar Rare Books and Manuscripts.

5. This poem, and others by Bishop, complicate Emerson's simple formula: "the eye is the first circle; the horizon which it forms is the second; and throughout nature this primary figure is repeated without end." Ralph Waldo Emerson, "Circles" (1841), in *Selected Essays*, ed. Larzer Ziff (New York: Penguin, 1982), p. 225. Emerson's concentric circles have no trace of temporality, but Bishop's intersecting circles exhibit retention and repetition rather than expansion. Emerson bypasses memory altogether. "In stripping time of its illusion, in seeking out what is the heart of the day, we come to the quality of the moment and stop duration altogether." "Paris, 7 A.M." does not locate a moment at all, immanent or transcendent, but loses it to the redundancy of time.

Bishop's poem also bears comparison with Baudelaire's "Paysage," in which the poet looks out from a high window at a wintry urban scene. But unlike Bishop, he achieves an aesthetic transformation of the scene and with the visionary power of the child makes the world over in his imagination. Baudeliare's clock towers spar with the sky. Yet even Baudelaire's idealism is haunted by its opposite. The proximate poem in *Les Fleurs du Mal* is "L'Horloge," which warns: *"Souviens-toi que le Temps est un joueur avide / Qui gagne sans tricher, à tout coup! c'est la loi."* ("Remember. Time the gamester (it's the law) / Wins always, without cheating."

6. "Quai d'Orléans" is dedicated to Margaret Miller, a fellow student at Vassar who lived with Bishop in Paris for a time. Miller was injured in an automobile accident, for which the poet may have felt responsible. It is likely that the weight of memory in the poem is due to this or another incident between Bishop and Miller, though the occasion of memory's impact is entirely suppressed in the poem.

7. Houghton Library, Harvard University.

8. Vassar Rare Books and Manuscripts.

9. January 8, 1964; Washington University Library.

10. Elizabeth Spires, "The Art of Poetry XXVII: Elizabeth Bishop," reprinted in *Paris Review*, 23, no. 80 (Summer 1981).

11. "Dimensions of a Novel," Vassar Rare Books and Manuscripts.

12. George Starbuck, "'The Work!': A Conversation with Elizabeth Bishop," in *Elizabeth Bishop and Her Art*, ed. Lloyd Schwartz and Sybil Estess (Ann Arbor: University of Michigan Press, 1983), p. 319.

13. Vassar Rare Books and Manuscripts.

14. In a letter to Robert Lowell on December 14, 1957, Bishop wrote of a trip: "Aruba is a little hell-like island, very strange. It rarely if ever rains there and there's nothing but cactus hedges and prickly trees and goats and one broken-off miniature dead volcano." Houghton Library.

15. These and the following excerpts are from Vassar Rare Books and Manuscripts.

16. Vassar Rare Books and Manuscripts.

17. Ashley Brown, "An Interview with Elizabeth Bishop," reprinted in *Elizabeth Bishop and Her Art*, ed. Schwartz and Estess, p. 298.

18. Vassar Rare Books and Manuscripts.

6. Art as Commemoration

1. Elizabeth Spires, "An Afternoon with Elizabeth Bishop," reprinted as "The Art of Poetry XXVII: Elizabeth Bishop," *Paris Review*, 23, no. 80 (Summer 1981), 79.

2. Ashley Brown, "An Interview with Elizabeth Bishop," in *Elizabeth Bishop and Her Art*, ed. Lloyd Schwartz and Sybil Estess (Ann Arbor: University of Michigan Press, 1983), p. 296.

3. Bishop's interest in the illusionary and narrative elements of painting is revealed in her comment to Robert Lowell (September 8, 1948; Houghton Library) about Auden's "Musée des Beaux Arts": "What I really object to in Auden's 'Musée des Beaux Arts' isn't the attitude about suffering—you're probably right about that—it's that I think its just plain inaccurate in the last part—the ploughman & the people on the boat will rest to see the falling boy any minute, they always do, though maybe not

to help. But then he's describing a painting so I guess it's alright to use it that way."

4. *Elizabeth Bishop and Her Art*, p. 314.

5. *Histoire Naturelle* (Paris: Editions Jeanne Bucher, 1926): Portfolio of 34 collotype plates after pencil frottages of 1925 by Max Ernst; VIII, les fausses positions. (see Figure 1.)

6. In an interview Bishop responded to Elizabeth Spires's question about "a shadow-box hanging in the hall. Is it by Joseph Cornell?" Bishop responded: "No, I did that one . . . Cornell is superb. I first saw the 'Medici Slot Machine' when I was in college. Oh, I loved it . . . When I looked at his show in New York two years ago I nearly fainted because one of my favorite books is a book he liked and used. It's a little book by an English scientist who wrote for children about soap bubbles." Elizabeth Spires, "The Art of Poetry XXVII: Elizabeth Bishop," p. 79.

Epilogue

1. My discussion of this work and of Dutch art generally depends upon the revisionary interpretation of Svetlana Alpers in *The Art of Describing: Dutch Art in the Seventeenth Century* (Chicago: University of Chicago Press, 1983), pp. 119–163.

Credits

is reprinted by permission of New Directions. The publisher generously allowed me to print all of "The Attic Which Is Desire" without a fee.

The Art of Painting by Jan Vermeer is reproduced with permission from the Kunsthistorisches Museum, Vienna. "False Positions" by Max Ernst is reproduced with permission from the library of the Fogg Art Museum, Harvard University.

Index of Poems

General Index

Bishop, Elizabeth (*continued*)
on sexuality, 57, 64–65, 72, 74, 83–85, 87, 122, 145, 148, 250n4; natural imagery, 57–64, 67–69, 80, 100, 106, 144, 165, 171; interest in optics, 63; on love, 65–66, 73–75; homoeroticism of, 72–73; on pain and suffering, 75, 77, 79–80, 249n1; as lesbian, 84; and the infinite, 90–126; on the sublime, 91–92, 94, 103, 105–107, 119, 125; role of the imagination, 92–93, 98, 101, 119, 132, 136, 139, 150, 156, 168–169, 171, 212; use of personification, 101; foreground and background in landscape, 103, 106, 109, 211; landscape smells, 110; on God, 115; figurative geography of, 116–119, 234; on maps, 116–117, 190, 234–237, 239, 242; travels, 127–130, 208; on home and homesickness, 128, 132, 136, 152, 154, 156–157, 159, 165, 167, 208; on cognition, 129–130, 150; use of archetypes, 132, 134–135; use of history, 134, 148, 150–152, 157, 209–210, 234–235, 239; on sin, 145–147; determinism of, 158–160; childhood, 175, 187–200; use of icons, 191–200, 207–208; on painting, 212, 214–218, 226–231, 255n3; on monuments, 218–220, 222–225; interest in frottage, 220; sketches and watercolors by, 247n2; openness to contradictions in life, 250n3; metaphysical style, 250n6; factual basis of her poems, 253n18

INTERVIEWS: with Ashley Brown, 26, 211, 214; with Elizabeth Spires, 128, 161, 187, 214, 256n6; with George Starbuck, 201, 217

JOURNALS AND NOTEBOOKS: 3–4, 34, 60–61, 71, 90–91, 97–98, 100, 103, 114–115, 124, 129–132, 136, 151, 176, 187, 207–210, 212, 248n4, 249n12

LETTERS: to Anny Baumann, 63, 76, 210; to Robert Lowell, 8, 46, 124, 186, 249n14, 255n14, 255n3;

to James Merrill, 253n22; to Marianne Moore, 5, 130, 161; to Anne Stevenson, 8, 20, 27, 46, 50, 112, 127, 130, 161–162, 187

POEMS: *See* Index of Poems

POETRY COLLECTIONS: *A Cold Spring*, 75, 92, 97, 102–103; *Complete Poems*, 234; *Geography III*, 32, 92, 116–118, 139, 159–160, 173, 183, 200–201, 223, 234; *North & South*, 48, 67, 92, 94, 97, 184, 234, 251n6; *Questions of Travel*, 75, 116, 138–139, 187, 193, 200

POETRY READING NOTES: 37

POSTCARDS: 151

PROSE: "After Bonnard," 72–73; college essays, 176–177; "The Country Mouse," 6; "Dimensions of a Novel," 187–188, 208, 254n4; "Gerard Manley Hopkins: Notes on Timing in his Poetry," 7; "In the Village," 188–190; "Memories of Uncle Neddy," 47, 85; "Primer Class," 190–192; "The Sea & Its Shore," 186–187, 200; "Time's Andromedas," 7

TRANSLATIONS: "Objects & Apparitions" (by Octavio Paz), 223–226

Blake, William, 41, 96
WORKS: *Songs of Innocence*, 188
Bloom, Harold, 96
Bonnard, Pierre, 73, 214
Boston, Mass., 117, 127–128, 160, 214
Brazil, 48, 75, 80–83, 85, 117, 128–129, 138–149, 152–153, 173–174, 208, 242
Bromwich, David, 247n19
Brontë, Charlotte
WORKS: *Jane Eyre*, 252n2
Brown, Ashley, 26, 211, 214
Buell, Lawrence, 151
Bunyan, John
WORKS: *The Pilgrim's Progress*, 97
Burke, Edmund, 110

Cabo Frio, 41
Cain, 82
Cape Breton, 103–109
Carnival, 75–78, 80, 83–86

derived from, 5–6, 8; and melodrama, 53; and Bishop's vertical iconography, 91; visionary awareness in, 103; elegiac meditation in, 105, 109; and solipsism, 200–201; nature as secular paradise, 203. *See also* Transcendentalism
Ruskin, John, 8

Santarém, 129, 173–174, 242
Santos, 129, 138–142, 152–153, 173–174, 251n20
Schapiro, Meyer, 214
Seattle, Wash., 128
Selkirk, Alexander, 149
Seurat, Georges, 34, 214
Shakespeare, William, 39
    WORKS: *Hamlet*, 219
Shelley, Mary, 47
Shelley, Percy Bysshe, 53, 96
    WORKS: "Mont Blanc," 94; "Ozymandias," 218–219
Shore, Jane, 247n18
Sidney, Philip
    WORKS: *Astrophel and Stella*, 32
Spenser, Edmund, 145
Spires, Elizabeth, 128, 161, 187, 214, 256n6
Starbuck, George, 201, 217
Stein, Gertrude, 209
Stevens, Wallace, 8–9, 37, 44, 96
    WORKS: "Anecdote of the Jar," 218; "Poetry Is a Destructive Force," 172; "Sea Surface Full of Clouds," 34; "Sunday Morning," 106, 108; "The Sun This March," 172
Stevenson, Anne, 8, 11–12, 20, 27, 46, 50, 112, 127, 130, 161–162, 187, 246n16
Summers, Joseph, 97
Surrealism, 9, 15; Bishop's interest in, 26–28; and frottage, 220, 222; in Cornell's boxes, 223, 225
Symbolism, 10, 21, 29; Bishop's early use of, 5, 9, 15; Bishop's skepticism of, 8; in "The Weed," 59; in "The Bight," 184–185

Tennyson, Alfred, 28
Thomas, Dylan, 124
Thoreau, Henry David, 90, 151
    WORKS: *Walden*, 149; "Walking," 142–143, 148, 158; *A Week on the Concord and Merrimack Rivers*, 158
Transcendentalism, 2, 116, 150; Bishop's romantic vision related to, 5–6, 8, 10; and facts, 149; and organic form, 151. *See also* Romanticism
Travisano, Thomas, 246n16

Vassar College, 13, 127, 176, 255n6
Vassar Journal of Undergraduate Studies, 7
Vendler, Helen, 166, 247n19
Vermeer, Jan
    WORKS: "The Art of Painting," 237–240

Whitman, Walt, 102
    WORKS: "As I Ebb'd with the Ocean of Life," 169
Williams, William Carlos, 9, 20
    WORKS: "The Attic Which Is Desire," 22–24; "The Rose," 73
Wollheim, Richard, 193
Woolf, Virginia
    WORKS: *The Waves*, 177
Worcester, Mass., 123, 127
Wordsworth, William, 6, 8, 26, 96, 106, 114, 154, 175, 179, 203, 208
    WORKS: "I wandered lonely as a cloud," 204–205; "Lines Composed a Few Miles above Tintern Abbey," 111; *Lyrical Ballads*, 188; "Ode: Intimations of Immortality," 123–125, 167; Preface to *Lyrical Ballads*, 249n12; "Resolution and Independence," 111–112; "The Ruined Cottage," 105; "The Thorn," 105
World War II, 59, 64–65

Yeats, William Butler, 82, 175
    WORKS: "The Circus Animals' Desertion," 90–91; "Sailing to Byzantium," 93, 218

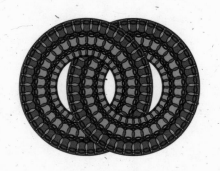

Miss August

miss august

nin andrews

CavanKerry ◈ Press LTD.

CavanKerry Press Ltd.
Fort Lee, New Jersey
www.cavankerrypress.org

Publisher's Cataloging-in-Publication
(Provided by Quality Books, Inc.)

Andrews, Nin, author.
Miss August / Nin Andrews. — First edition.
pages cm — (Notable voices series)
ISBN 978-1-933880-62-4

1. Coming of age—Southern States—History—20th century—Poetry.
2. Transgender people—Southern States—History—20th century—Poetry.
3. Racism—Southern States—History—20th century—Poetry.
4. Race relations—History—20th century—Poetry.
5. Upper-class families—Southern States—History—20th century—Poetry.
6. Southern States—Race relations—History—20th century—Poetry.
7. Narrative poetry.
8. Novellas. I. Title. II. Series: Notable voices.

PS3551.N444M57 2017   811'.54
QBI17-900017

Cover illustration by Laura Powers
Cover and interior text design by Ryan Scheife, Mayfly Design
First Edition 2017, Printed in the United States of America

NOTABLE VOICES
CavanKerry ❦ Press

CavanKerry Press is proud to publish the works of
established poets of merit and distinction.

CavanKerry Press is grateful for the support it receives
from the New Jersey State Council on the Arts.

Also by Nin Andrews

This book is dedicated to my beloved Jim
and to the memory of Mary Walker and Diane Frank.

Contents

Four

Red Buckle Shoes

———————

THE WAR

Gil

When I was a boy back in the 50s and early 60s, my folks talked about THE WAR all the time. They weren't talking about Vietnam, even though our neighbors, the Burtons, who lived one farm over had three sons who were drafted, and all three came back home in body bags. They weren't talking about the Cold War, even though we lived through the Bay of Pigs and the Cuban Missile Crisis. I remember hiding under my desk during duck-and-cover drills, expecting the Russians to bomb my school, Robert E. Lee Elementary, any minute then. They weren't talking about the Korean War, even though my daddy said that Mr. Maupin (we said it, *Moppin*), lost his arm over in Korea. Mr. Maupin liked showing off his prosthesis, which was the coolest thing. It had little knife and fork attachments, so he never needed silverware. They weren't talking about World War II, even though my daddy had worked in the military supply department and was stationed in San Francisco. He never left the country once, but the way he told it, you'd have thought he was on the front lines at D Day. And they weren't talking about World War I, but my daddy's father, my granddaddy, Mr. Leonard P. Simmons, was wounded in action and earned himself a Purple Heart, which he wore til the day he died, even if it was, according to my mother, a tiny foot-wound and self-inflicted.

No, when my folks said THE WAR, they meant the Civil War.

In my early years I thought THE WAR happened yesterday. Or maybe the day before. I knew it was a while ago. But I didn't think it happened in the 1800s. My father said a war inside a country never ends, unlike a war against, say, England or Germany or the Japs or Vietnam. That's why it was THE WAR. Always in caps.

But it was Mama who explained that THE WAR never ended because the South never buried all its dead. Mama was superstitious like that, and sometimes at night after she had an extra whiskey or two or three—she said it was rude to count, but I always did count. Sometimes, after her third drink, she'd look out the living room window, swaying a little, one hand on her hip, the other holding a cocktail glass with a few melted ice cubes in it, and say something like:

Look out yonder, Gil. You see that man? She'd point out past the alfalfa field, past the black walnut trees draped with vines and say she was sure she'd seen a gray man out there. Don't you see him? she'd ask. No ma'am, I said. But her gray man was out there, sure as the grass is green. And he was dressed in a Confederate uniform because that's what all ghosts wore in Lessington, Virginia. My daddy would tell Mama there wasn't a thing to see but dusk coming down to meet the earth.

Mama got mad then, the red flaming up like someone struck a match in her cheeks. I did, too, see a gray man, she said. I saw him clear as day. Sometimes she'd rush out the front door and wander down the dirt road. Later, when she came back inside, I'd ask, Did you find your ghost, Mama? She'd answer, I most certainly did. She'd tell me how that ghost was out there, searching for somebody he loved: a wife, a lover, a son. Somebody long dead. No doubt about it. Then she'd ask, Isn't it the saddest thing? To be lost in time like that? Stuck in a war long past? I'd nod, Yes, ma'am. It sure is sad.

One

Chinquapin Hill Farm

The Day You Was Born

May Dee

Lawd it was dark the night you was born, Gil Simmons. Sure enough it
was. Dark as the devil hisself. Not a star shining. Not a cricket or a tree
frog singing. Not a hound dog moaning. Your pa was out of town. And
it was hot. Lawd it was hot. I was so scared the doctor wasn't coming. I
couldn't take a breath without feeling it catch like a fishbone in my throat.
Your mama, swollen big as a prize sow, was laying up in the bed, hollering,
The baby's coming May Dee! It's coming fast. Yes you was, too. Coming
feet first. I seen your heel slip out. *Lawd have mercy,* I prays. I didn't know
whether to reach in and pull you by the ankles or wait. Then the doctor
knocks. *Praise be to God.* But when he brings you into the world, you all
blue. I thinks to myself, *That baby done changed his mind.* He gone on back
to God. Just like them other babies done. Then you let out such a howl.
Loud enough to wake the dead. And the coonhound started wailing, and
the rooster started crowing, even if it was the middle of the night. You
kep' on howling, too. Like you was never gonna stop. And I knew. You was
sorry you'd come. I felt how you was. I didn't blame you none. Lawd no.
But I loved you. I loved you like you was my own.

My Story

Gil

I was a born nobody—my days so dull, I lay in my bed and watched dust rise. I listened to insect songs. And kept things to myself. I remember two silver dollars in my bedside table. A snow globe I wanted to climb inside. My pony, Annabel, that I didn't ride. And more whippings than I can count. After a while I didn't feel a sting. I learned there is a reason to lie. Not to ask. Not to tell. Not to flinch. Anybody asked, I said, *Nothing happened.* And nothing did. My friend, Sarah Jane Lee, she disagrees. She says I suffered. She says she did, too. And I thought she was the happy one. *Nuh-uh,* she shakes her head. She blames the South for everything wrong in our lives; everything bad, everything rotten or bitter as turnip greens. *Come on up to New York,* I say. *Leave that place.*

Nah, she says. *I can't live any place else.* She gets a way-off look in her eyes. *Besides,* she says, *folks up North don't talk right.*

Dream

Sarah Jane

One night I dreamt you was stepping out of the crick where we caught crayfish as kids, your hair wet, slicked back, and you was grinning wide. I was so happy to see you. Together we lay on the flat stone by the pawpaw tree, the two of us, pale ghosts beneath a full moon. I had so many questions to ask, Gil Simmons, but you said *hush.* I reached out to touch your face, and when I woke, I felt the past on my skin like hot breath.

The Story of Gil Simmons

Sarah Jane

People still talk about Gil Simmons. They say, *That boy was one strange bird*. They say, *He wasn't right in the head*. They say, *His daddy ought to have taught him a thing or two*. These are Lessington, Virginia folks, mind you. When I was a girl, they shot deer frozen in their headlights and stray dogs that howled at the moon. They flew Confederate flags in their front yards. They spoke to God and ghosts and called black folks niggers. And they closed the public schools. *Don't let the coloreds in our classrooms*, they said. *Restrooms either*. But Gil, they thought, was the strange one. *Stranger than a faggot*, they said. Still do. I smile, light up a cigarette, and say, *Define normal, if you will.*

Chinquapin Hill Farm

Gil

I still dream I'm a boy looking out of my window or wandering the farm where I grew up. In the distance, I see horses swishing their tails and grazing in white-fenced fields. I see Mr. Maupin and Otis, the farmhands, leading a pregnant mare to the barn. Caleb, the gardener, is waving birds away from the cherry trees while Fran, the laundress, hangs a load of sheets on the clothesline. Thelma, the cook, arrives in a Yellow Cab. Wearing a white uniform and a cap, Thelma bows her head and walks to the front door with quick, mincing steps. She always looks scared. My daddy insists she wear that cap because, as he puts it, *I don't want any wiry hairs in my food.*

How'd you get so black? I asked Thelma once, back before I knew better than to ask questions like that. Thelma was as black as a moonless night. Daddy said even coloreds don't want to share their classrooms or restrooms with negroes as dark as Thelma. *But Thelma,* he said, *is one nice old negress. And she sure can cook.* Mr. Maupin agreed. *I reckon she's the nicest darkie I ever knowed,* he said with a grin.

Summertime I slept with the windows open and woke to Thelma's sing-song voice, *Morning, Mrs. Simmons. Mornin' Otis. Morning Mr. Maupin. Mornin' Caleb.* They never answered her. Caleb would be telling Mama, *Them birds is going to strip your cherry trees clean, Mrs. Simmons. You best buy me a net to cover them up.* Mama, dressed in jodhpurs, a riding hat and jacket, just nodded. But she wasn't listening. She never did listen to the help. Later, she would blame Caleb for our bare cherry trees. So would May Dee, my black nanny, who bossed all the other servants. And my folks, too. When she wasn't bossing, May Dee sang hymns like Mahalia Jackson. She paused only to swear and cuss out Thelma who, she told Mama once, dried the silverware on her sleeve.

Your Mama's Friend

Sarah Jane

The first time I visited Chinquapin Hill Farm was a week after Mama and me moved from Oiselle Isle (we called it Why Sell) in South Carolina—off the coast near Charleston. Mr. Simmons gave me a lift to the farm. I sat in the back seat of his Buick, my window rolled down, wind flapping my bangs, while I stared at the back of his head—his pink neck so fat, it overflowed his collar like crust over a pie tin. And I wondered why he was what Grandpa'd called *your mama's friend.*

Mr. Simmons talked the whole time, his voice a fly buzz in my brain. *Those are our alfalfa fields,* he said, when we got close to the house. *Alfalfa makes a fine hay for the thoroughbreds.* He pointed at the horses, grazing in the pastures—brown horses, spotted horses, and a white mare—they was the prettiest things I ever laid eyes on. *And over yonder, you see those little gray houses, Sarah Jane?* Mr. Simmons asked. *They used to be slave homes. After that, there were sharecroppers living in them.* I looked at the row of shacks with paint peeling. One had a door swinging loose on its hinges. It looked like a mouth letting out a dark scream.

Meeting Sarah Jane

Gil

It was a June morning, already hot as a skillet, and I was still in my PJs when my daddy drove up, opened the back door of his Buick Roadmaster, and a girl with yellow hair and red tennis shoes climbed out of the back seat and squinted up at the house. (My father always made children and colored folks sit in the back seat.) *Gil*, he called out. *Come on down here and meet our new friend, Sarah Jane Lee*, as if it was nothing unusual, him bringing me a girl to play with and calling her *our* friend. Especially when he was always trying to make me play with boys and calling me a sissy. But the day he took Sarah Jane Lee's pink hand in his and led her into the dining room, and May Dee served us sweet tea and a slice of jelly roll with powdered sugar on top, he smiled down at me like a benevolent god. I thought maybe there was a god hearing my prayers after all—I'd always wanted a girl to play with. Sarah Jane ate without a word, holding her fork like a pitchfork and shoveling jelly roll into her mouth so fast, it was gone before I could blink. *You like another slice, sweet pea?* May Dee asked her. *Yes'm*, Sarah Jane said, her eyes fixed on the cake. *Ain't she just as cute as a minute?* May Dee smiled, her hands on her hips as she watched Sarah Jane down her third slice of jelly roll. Then she drank three cups of sweet tea and burped out loud. Didn't even say excuse me.

Ya'll always have a maid to serve you sweet tea and cake? she asked later.

No, I said. But I lied.

Déjà Vu

Sarah Jane

In my mind I see Gil Simmons the same as I seen him that first day. Seeing him was like looking into a mirror. Like the feeling of running a comb through your hair after a storm, and nothing snags.

That Sarah Jane

May Dee

It was a fine day when she done showed. Came when the magnolias was in bloom. She was a happy tune, that girl was. Running loose all day long, helping Otis with the cows, going barefoot in the horse barns. The pig sty, too, til I tells her *put some shoes on*. The girl talk so fast, words come out her mouth, faster than spray from a shook Co-Cola bottle. I can't catch a word. Gil, he just watch, sitting quiet-like on the porch them first days. Then he ask her to come in the house and play awhile. Sometimes she do.

Nine Bathrooms

Sarah Jane

When Mama and me moved from Oiselle Isle to Lessington, one of the first things we learned is how many folks was still fighting the Civil War. Especially the Simmonses. They blamed the North for all their problems including taxes, old age, and the rising murder rate. Even the tomato wilt and the raspberry blight got blamed on General Sherman and the burning of the South. Mr. Simmons liked to brag that his great-granddaddy was a general, wounded in the Battle of Cedar Run. He said the world woulda been *a whole helluvalot better off* if the South had won that war.

Mr. Simmons said his home at Chinquapin Hill Farm was the oldest plantation in the South. (He was a liar, too. I learned that quick. Or, as Gil put it, *he was prone to exaggeration.*) But the house was big—it was the biggest house I ever been inside, with white pillars, lace curtains, nine bathrooms, and twelve black servants—only we called black folks *colored* back then. When I first visited, Gil took me on a tour, and I counted bathrooms. *Ya'll sure don't have to hold it none*, I said, and we laughed and laughed. Then I asked what all them servants did when he was at school. Gil paused. Then he grinned real wide, *They clean the bathrooms, Sarah Jane. Duh-twang.*

The Servants

Gil

My friend, Sarah Jane kept asking how many servants we hired at Chinquapin Hill Farm, and I said twelve. But the number changed with the seasons,
and I never was sure how many to count. I just knew that if anything had to
be done, the servants did it, quietly and without asking. The cooking, the
cleaning, the shopping, the mowing, the farming, the gardening, and the
serving. There was so much serving back then. You name it, they served it:
tea, coffee, ice cream, cookies, cakes.

If I was sick, May Dee came to my bedside every hour with a Coca Cola
(Co-Cola, she called it—*You wanna a nice cold Co-Cola now, Gilly boy?* she'd
ask) and gave me saltines and a baby aspirin and took a rag soaked with
witch hazel to rub my back. *You be fine real soon*, she said. Anything I needed, May Dee took care of. But my parents ignored me and the goings-on
of May Dee and the servants, unless something wasn't done right, or was
missing or broken. Then they blamed the servants—usually the newer
servants who were not members of the main staff—and fired a few, who
were quickly replaced. Servants were like disposable tableware. As my
daddy put it, there were always more where they came from.

Horse Dreams

Sarah Jane

It was early morning after a hard rain, and everything was green and shiny, like the whole world had a fresh polish on it, that first time I seen Mrs. Simmons riding her white horse, Leda. The two of them looked like they was one soul, flying over the fields. Seeing her on that horse was seeing my dream. It was like *I* was riding, and the wind and sunshine was on my face, the saddle between my legs. When Leda jumped a fence, I rose up on my toes and felt myself lift clear out of my skin. *Let me ride one day,* I prayed then. *Let me ride like Mrs. Simmons.* When Mrs. Simmons came back in the house, I asked her straight out, *Can you teach me to ride?* She didn't answer me.

I told Mama on the way home that I wanted a horse real bad. She patted my head. *When I was your age,* she said, *I wanted a pony, too,* her voice, a sad music. Like she was telling me my dreams was nothin I'd ever own.

Luncheons

Gil

Mama wore riding clothes year round, her blond hair tucked up in a net beneath a helmet, her jacket buttoned below her bosoms, jodhpurs flaring above her knee-high boots. When she wasn't in town or asleep, she was at the barn. Thelma served her luncheons in the tack room, and when he was home, my daddy and I ate at the long mahogany dining room table. We barely spoke. When my father did talk, he started with, *Son?* as if it were a question. But when he was away on business trips, I ate in the tack room with Mama, sitting on a bench beneath racks of saddles, smelling of saddle soap and horse sweat, watching her stab peas or slices of roast beef before she placed her china plate on the floor for Sissy (short for Sisyphus), her Bluetick Coonhound to lick clean. Once in a while, I asked her a thing or two. Sometimes she'd answer. Usually she just stared past me, out past the mud creek that looked like a dirty orange string, past the fields where Leda grazed, and the grasshoppers sang and stripped clean the alfalfa leaves.

Confederate Gil

Sarah Jane

Don't listen to what others say, Mama said. *Judge for yourself what's right or not.* Because back then, people gossiped. It's a fact. They gossiped all day long. Everyone in Lessington had a tale to tell that might have been true. And might not have, too. Like the one Mama's beautician, Louanna Shiflett, told about Gil's mama. She said Mrs. Simmons planned to have an ample family, but all she got was a graveyard of preemies and Gil.

And that ugly little Gil, she said, *never looked like he was fully here. He was so pale and thin, he was almost see-through. The town doctor, Dr. Repolt, says Gil Simmons was bit by a black widow when he was a bitty thing, and the boy barely survived. He was so white, the doctor said he looked like he'd been dipped in Clorox.* Rumor had it that Mr. Simmons wasn't really his daddy. Instead, folks around town said Gil was the son of a Confederate soldier. So he was part-ghost. Everyone laughed at that. On Halloween Gil's mama dressed him in a gray flannel sheet. *Ghosts aren't gray,* I said. *Yes, they are, too,* Gil answered me back. *In the South, they are. Casper is a Yankee ghost.*

My Father's Research

Gil

My father took long business trips back then. If he wasn't meeting with one of his political groups like The Defenders of State Sovereignty and Individual Liberties, he was retracing the path of the War so he could write a book one day. When Sarah Jane asked what he did, and why he was away so often, I said he was a historian. History, I explained, is something you have to search for. And you have to search, not once but many times. That's what the word, research, means: searching over and over again. But my father hadn't found what he was looking for yet. He said he would be famous when he did. And everyone would agree at last that the South should have won the War. And the North was to blame.

I imagined my father coming home with a Confederate soldier in hand who could tell us things we didn't already know. Mama always said there were loads of Confederate ghosts around, still fighting the War, or wandering the countryside, looking for their loved ones. She could hear them at night. And their ghost dogs, too. Howling for everything they lost, she said. And everything we want back again.

Only Gil

Sarah Jane

In those days life didn't happen unless I told Gil so. I talked to him all day long, and after I went home, I talked to him in my head or on the telephone. No matter what I said, Gil didn't laugh or make fun. He never said, *You're crazy, Sarah Jane.* Not when I hung upside down from a tree limb like a possum or when I grabbed ahold of the electric fence, saying, *I don't feel nothin. You try it.* And he didn't. He didn't say nothin when I played horses all day long, galloping in circles, eating oats from Leda's bucket and licking the saltlicks in the pasture. I told Gil I wanted to be a horse when I grew up. I wished it every time I wished. I even dreamt I was a pony, running through tall grass, sucking water from the crick. I rolled in the dust. I bucked riders off my back.

Who do you want to buck off? Gil asked.

Everyone, I said. He nodded and listened so close, I could hear him listening. I still can.

Cocktail Parties

Gil

All the fancy folks in Lessington came to our cocktail parties at Chinquapin Hill Farm back then. It took a whole week to get the house ready. Servants vacuumed, waxed, and polished until the floors shone, and not a speck of dust rose in the air. Before the guests arrived, May Dee dressed me in a navy suit with a red bow tie and said, *Stand up straight, Gilly boy, like the young man you is.* And Mama made me practice shaking hands. *Don't be limp-wristed like a lady,* she said. I squeezed her moist, lotioned hands. All night I watched the guests and tried to stand like the men. And laugh and walk and cross my legs just like them.

Usually there were the same guests—including Mr. Boone Williams, the president of The Lessington Bank and Trust—my father was a trustee at the bank. Mr. Billy Ray Harding, the Lessington mayor. And Mr. Austin Byrd, a distant cousin to Senator Harry Byrd and my father's Charleston College friend. My father was a good Southern Democrat, involved in local politics, and always bragging about the time he met Governor J. Lindsay Almond. He said it made him proud to shake the governor's hand. All our party guests were supporters of the Bryd Organization, which I thought had something to do with real birds like the Audubon Society. My father was on a lot of boards, too, which meant everyone kept saying, *Your daddy is a real fine gentleman,* while he stood by and grinned. They all wanted something from him. Everyone knew he had Mama's money to give. And he was generous with his friends.

Them Parties

May Dee

Them parties was a big mess a' trouble. Miz Simmons hadda hire extra help to clean and serve. She put me in charge, saying the whole place had to be spotless. *Make sure y'all is all dressed in white*, she said. *Everything's got to be just right.* It was, too. So shiny clean you could eat straight off the floor. One time Gil drop his toast butter-side down before the party begin, and I says to him, *Go on and eat it.* And he do.

After the party's done, it take us half a night to clean up. When I finally puts my feet up and leans back with a cup a' coffee, Mr. Simmons be coming down the steps and ask me to fix him a nightcap. That's when I says to him, *Get your own damn drink, Mr. Simmons. I'm dog-tired.*

The Southern Bell

Sarah Jane

The first night I ate supper at the Simmonses', opera was playing on the turntable. *Sounds like a lady being strangled*, I said. Nobody smiled. There was roast beef on a silver platter and crystal glasses of sweet tea and a vase of zinnias in the middle of the table. A lime-green caterpillar was eating them flower petals, one by one. Mr. Simmons kept talking and talking like he did. Gil didn't say nothin. Mrs. Simmons never ate a bite. She sipped wine and stared out the window. When the meal was over, she rang the southern bell, a copper bell shaped like a lady in a large skirt with one leg for her dinger. Thelma, dressed in a white cap and apron, came running to the door. *May I help you, Miz Simmons? Ya'll care for dessert now? Coffee? Custard? A nice slice of pecan pie?*

Yes'm. I said. *I care for it.* Mrs. Simmons glared at me. But I wanted everything Thelma said.

That Little Southern Gal

Gil

Even now if I talk to Sarah Jane on the phone, my partner says, *I know who you're talking with. It's that little Southern gal.* And I think how Sarah Jane and I used to answer for each other, and fool folks. That's how alike we sounded when we wanted to. We finished each other's sentences and read each other's minds, which was easy to do with Sarah Jane—she only liked two things in life, food and horses. She ate like a half-starved hound. Sometimes, when no one was looking, she licked her plate. But she never gained a pound. May Dee used to say, *I worry about that girl—she musta got worms in her.* May Dee made her swallow dropperfuls of wormwood oil, followed by warm milk. The taste, Sarah Jane said, pinching her nose, was like a bad odor all up inside your head and clear down to your toes.

Bacon Grease

Sarah Jane

I was hungry all the time back then. So whenever I visited the Simmonses, I snuck into the kitchen, hoping the servants wouldn't be down there. Thelma caught me every time. *What you doing, Miss Sarah Jane?* she asked me. *Nothin,* I lied. When I thought her back was turned, I dipped my finger in the tin of bacon grease Thelma kept on the stove, stuck it in my mouth, and sucked. *You say grace before you eat that?* Thelma asked. *Yes'm,* I lied. *I said it to myself. Lord make me thankful for the bacon grease.*

Wishes

Sarah Jane

At the end of the day at Chinquapin Hill Farm, I sat outside as the sun slid behind the oak trees. The hills turned from blue to black while I waited for Mr. Simmons to give me a lift home. *You think I slipped his mind?* I asked May Dee.

There's no telling with that man's mind, May Dee said. Sometimes I stayed past dark, the backs of my legs, cold on the stone steps. Gil sat beside me, picking scabs off his knees and singing, *Oh, I wish I was in the land of cotton . . .* Or, *Jimmy crack corn and I don't care, My master's gone away . . .* them folk songs we learned at school. Sometimes we chased milkweed seeds that blew around the yard. Every seed caught in the air, Gil said was worth one wish. We'd run around catching all them wishes. *What're you wishing for?* Gil asked me whenever I caught one. But he already knew. When he closed his fist around a silky seed, he'd never tell his wish. *I can't,* he said. *I just can't, Sarah Jane,* his paper-white skin, pink as a rose.

Sarah Jane's Swim Suit

May Dee

The time I catch my Gilly boy in Sarah Jane's swimsuit, that little flowered suit with ruffles like a tutu, I prays, *Lawd, don't let Mr. Simmons see this.* There be so much going wrong at Chinquapin Hill Farm. I tell you the truth. And there I seen Gil twirling like a ballerina, right when I comes in to tuck him in. Wearing her pink flip-flops, too. I don't say nothin. I just stands in the doorway. When he seen me seeing him, he stop hisself real quick. I says, *Get on in the bed now and switch off the light.* That day, he and Sarah Jane been swimming in the mud pond after school—that brown, nasty water full of frogs and leaches and snapping turtles. Water moccasins, too. Lawsy be, you never catch me down there. Dead or alive. Gil neither, if it hadn't been for Miss Sarah Jane. *You ain't a scaredy cat, is you?* she tease him. *Nu-uh*, Gil say. He be doing whatever Sarah Jane doing back then. Trying his best to be her friend.

Two

May Dee

Lost Things

Gil

Mama had a knack for wandering around the house, taking off her things wherever she went, dropping her pocketbook in the vestibule, her boots on the patio, her diamond rings by the kitchen sink. She left her clothes in a heap in her bathroom, earrings on top of the phone book, wine glass by my bed. But she was always sure the servants were stealing. *You know how light-fingered they are*, she'd sniff. Or, *I've just been robbed blind.* Mornings, as soon as she woke, I'd hear her calling out, *Where's my purse? Where's my engagement ring? Where's my brand new brooch? I left it right here last night!* Servants would rush upstairs like a wave rising from below. *Yes'm?* they asked. *May I help you, Miz Simmons?* their faces scared, looking like God was throwing His dice again, and luck would never be theirs. Only when the missing items were located, and May Dee stood over Mama, asking, *This what you looking for, Miz Simmons?* did the servants recede, back into hallways, shadows, and basement rooms.

The Secretary

Sarah Jane

Mr. Simmons collected spooky things. He had a ceiling-high cabinet in the living room called the secretary where war relics and ghosts was kept. There was a mud dauber nest in the top corner and a smell like moldy bread rising and metal boxes of musket balls, belt buckles, gold buttons, and pieces of uniforms, some gray and some blue. One time Gil picked out a three-ring bullet, lodged in a piece of wood with a stain on it. *That stain right there is Confederate blood*, he said. *The bullet went clear through a man's heart.*

How do you know? I asked, but he didn't answer—just kept on talking. *The man's name was Solomon James Halstead,* he said. *Mama knows him. That's one of the ghosts she sees wandering out in the cornfield. He's been out there since the War of Northern Aggression.*

What war are you talking about, Gil? I asked.

That's just another word for the Civil War, Sarah Jane, he said, staring at me like I didn't know nothin. Just then his daddy walked in, looking mad, and making little ticky noises with his tongue, like a rattlesnake was stuck up in his head. *As long as I live, Gilbert Rhett Simmons,* he said, *nobody calls it the Civil War in this house.* He grabbed ahold of Gil so tight, he left black-and-blue fingerprints on his white-white arms.

Southern Culture

Gil

Sarah Jane used to tell me things about slavery that I didn't learn from school or my folks. She talked in a whisper even when the door was closed. She said her neighbor, Miss Alice, told her that if a slave tried to run away, he could be beaten or even lynched. She said Miss Alice once saw buzzards circling before she saw a colored man, hanging from a tree limb, left there for the birds to eat. When I asked my daddy if that was so, he asked, *Who have you been talking to?* Then he paused and added, *There have always been bad folks, Gil. But the South is a refined culture where people take care of each other, no matter who they are and how they fit into society. Coloreds included.*

Colored or Black

Sarah Jane

The day I called May Dee *black* was after my babysitter, Miss Alice, said she was a black woman, not a colored lady. May Dee corrected me right quick. *I ain't black, Sarah Jane,* she said. *I'm a colored lady. I'm a negro lady. But I ain't no black lady. Now you take Thelma,* she said. *That woman is black. Pitch black.*

Caleb Johnson's Grandfather

Gil

It was one of my father's favorite stories: the tale of Caleb Johnson's grandfather. Caleb's grandfather, my father said, was proof that the Southern man is better than the Yankee, but I never did hear Caleb tell the story.

My father insisted that Caleb would be happy to tell anyone who asked him how his grandfather was the son of a sharecropper before he went up North after the War to find a new life. He left the South with a whole herd of other negroes who were looking for Eden. *But them Yankees*, Caleb Johnson said (or at least my father said he said), *didn't talk to the colored man on the street, much less look him in the eye.* Caleb's grandfather traveled from city to city, trying to find work. He lived in New York, Boston, Syracuse. No one would give him a decent job. *Jews, dagos, chinks, spics*, my father said, *they were all hired before the colored man.* Mr. Johnson traveled from city to city before he settled in Chicago where he worked at a meat-packing factory until he had an accident—cut three fingers off his right hand. That's when he took the first train home. *Yep, he still called Virginia his home after all those years. He came on back here to Chinquapin Hill Farm, and asked for a job. Now, how's a man going to work on a farm with one hand?* my father asked. But Mr. Johnson stayed on the farm til he passed, living down in one of the sharecropper huts. *Because that's how we treat folks in the South*, my father bragged. *And his grandson, Caleb, he's been working here since he was a boy. He and his daddy both will tell you Virginia is home. They know it's the Southern man they can trust.*

How White Trash Talks

Gil

Mama never paid much attention to Sarah Jane and me, but she did comment that Sarah Jane talked like a farmhand. She worried that the two of us were beginning to sound the same. *She talks like white trash, the poor thing*, Mama said. *That girl needs to learn proper English.*

She needs to talk proper, I agreed. Mama glared at me.

Properly, she corrected me. But I loved how Sarah Jane talked. I mimicked her every time we played. I loved her, *ain't* and *cain't* and *ya'll*. Her double negatives—how when she didn't like ketchup, she announced, *I never cared for no ketchup on my dawgs. I don't like no tater salad neither.*

I don't take no ketchup on my dawgs neither, I said, even though I loved ketchup, even if ketchup was the only reason I ever ate a hotdog.

When a Man Turns Bad

May Dee

I get to wondering how a man turns bad. Like apple cider going hard, then to vinegar. Happen to all the men I known. You take Mr. Simmons. Now that man never been no saint. But in them early days, when I first come to Chinquapin, he had his dreams. Like men do. He say he gonna to be a famous writer. He gonna to write the real story of what happened in the War. Set the record straight. He typing on that Smith Corona in his den day in and day out, the typewriter so loud it coulda woke the dead, dinging the way it did. I don't know how a one of us slept.

When Mr. Simmons wasn't in his study, he was outside with Mr. Maupin cutting trees. The man love his chainsaw. Love it til the day he cutting a limb off an old oak tree—he clumb up in it, and his arm gave way. That chainsaw cut into his leg. Buzzed down to the bone. Mr. Maupin and Otis carried him up to the house, blood soaking his pants, Mr. Simmons moaning like a bitty child. Before the doctor come, he downed most of a fifth a' whiskey. He never did stop drinking since that day. He taking pain pills, too. He goes from one doctor to the next—musta seen every doctor in town. Every one of 'em gives him a prescription. He got a whole medicine cabinet full of them little brown bottles with white caps. Demerols the ones he likes. Popping 'em like candy and chasing 'em down with a swig of whiskey. He give up his typing. After the accident, he just sit around. Acting nasty. I asks him whatever happened to that book you been writing, and he say he working on it longhand. But his hands is short and stubby like they always was.

Which is nicer to the colored man, the South or the North?

Gil

my father asked May Dee every now and again, an ugly gleam in his eyes. May Dee never answered him. But one day she shook her head. *Mr. Simmons*, she said, *I seen a child's boot down at the river just the other day. A yellow boot. Stuck on a log jam. Looked like a child mighta drowned in there. And I get to thinking. My cousin's boy, Bobby Hearn, he gone missing. Been two weeks now. Nobody seen hide nor hair of that boy. You know how it is when a colored boy don't come home like he sposed to? You have to ask yourself. Is the sheriff knocking on doors, asking who seen that child last? I don't think so, Mr. Simmons. I don't think so.*

Mr. Simmons

Sarah Jane

Gil's father was as mean as a stepped-on snake, especially when he been drinking. *Don't mind Mr. Simmons, Sarah Jane,* May Dee used to say. *He's just talk.* But I did mind him. How he leaned up against the doorjamb in the room where Gil and me was playing cards and watched us like a hunter in a stand. He said things like *Gil, are you running your mouth again, Boy? You know what I'd like to do one day? Cut that tongue clear out of your head. Make you quiet as sleep.* Then he laughed, shook his head and said, *I'm just joshing, Sarah Jane. Don't look at me like that.* I looked at Gil instead, his skin blue-tinged like something living underwater. I never knew how he got any air in them days.

Nabs

Gil

Sarah Jane knew things. And knew not to ask. Playing nurse, she checked my bruised arms and back, and one time, a shiner so bad, my eye was swollen tight. *That was a mean lickin' you done had,* she said. Or, *Nah, that's nothin, Gil.* Or she just shook her head and asked, *You want to share my nabs?* And pulled a packet of nabs from her trouser pocket, the cracker crumbs spilling out of the plastic. *I love my nabs,* she said, licking the salt from her hands. I loved her nabs, too. But I loved her anger more—there in her quivering lip and her hot, quick breaths.

Stories

Gil

Alone in my bedroom I made up stories about running away from Chin-quapin Hill Farm. In one I stole Mama's MasterCard and moved into a Howard Johnson's where I spent my days sampling ice cream and laying by the pool. In another story I convinced May Dee to steal me away in a Yellow Cab. She always did say, *White folks don't know how to raise their own children.* Maybe one day she'd save me, I thought. And we'd run away together, move to Richmond or New York City. But in most of my stories I left on a spaceship with Sarah Jane and May Dee on board. Sometimes we landed on a planet where space folks traded clothes and faces and bodies. Everyone on the planet was destined to be an angel, but in the meantime we could be whoever we wanted. I turned into Sarah Jane Lee, and she was a palomino pony, galloping across the alien landscape. May Dee was a bird that sang hymns all day long. At night we slept on our bellies so our wings could grow.

Twin Souls

Gil

Sometimes Sarah Jane couldn't come over to visit, and I missed her because I didn't have other friends. And besides, we were what May Dee called twin souls. Which meant we both liked crustless grilled cheese sandwiches cut in triangles, (squares never did taste right), and our favorite other things were angels, horses, the numbers 2 and 9, and snow. But we argued about the color of 9, which I said was blue, but she was sure it was white. How could 9 be white? I'd still like to know. But Sarah Jane said it was simple as a fact, just like pink is a 2. I had to take her word for it. She was the only one who knew the color of numbers and music. How it was scary to feel too good or taste something real sweet like ice cream, which is why I said I never ate ice cream or egg custard pie or caramels. I said, *I don't care for them, thank you very much.* So did Sarah Jane. Back then we even shared lies. But the best part was when she stayed overnight when her mama was out of town. I couldn't sleep. Neither could she. We snuck into the kitchen and ate bowl after bowl of vanilla ice cream. The taste, so cold, so pale, so light.

Hide and Seek

Sarah Jane

Gil's favorite game back then was hide and seek. We played it for hours in his huge house that stunk like Johnson's floor wax and Old English furniture polish. His house was so big, I never could find him. I was easily distracted by the china bowl of chocolates in the front hall that were for guests only (I didn't count as a guest no more). *Give me a hint*, I'd say, my mouth full of bonbons. Gil would promise to hide in a bathroom the next time. But there was too many bathrooms. Every one of them with a vanity, a peach-colored marble top, and a cabinet full of monogrammed towels. But this one day I slipped into the servants' bathroom that was down in the basement, covered myself in towels, curled up and took a nap. It was May Dee who found me. She opened the door and stared at me like she was seeing a cockroach. Then she gave me a talking-to. *Girl,* she said, *didn't your mama teach you nothin? This room is for coloreds. Don't let me find you hiding in my nice clean towels again. You hear me?*

The Death of Charlie Dee

Gil

May Dee wasn't like the other colored folks in Lessington, Virginia. She liked to associate with white people, and I mean, only white people. And she liked to talk about her dead husband, Charlie Dee, who she said almost was white, *God rest his soul*. She talked about Charlie Dee so often, I can still hear her voice in my head. *Gilly boy,* she said, *do you know my Charlie Dee coulda been your uncle? No one woulda knowed no better. That's how white he was.*

That's how come Charlie Dee got hisself hired as head cook over at the Lessington Country Club where everyone but the waiters got to be white, or pass, one or the other. If they'da found out he was a colored man, they'da fired him quick as they could spit, but he cooks so fine, nobody asked no questions. Like why his hair was nappy. Nappy like mine, May Dee said, rubbing her head. She never did use relaxers in her hair like the other colored ladies did.

Charlie Dee made the best spare ribs in town. And butter biscuits and pecan pies. That man could cook. Mmmmhmmm. He making good money too. There's bad money out there. Bad money walking the streets. Charlie Dee never touched no bad money. Not in them early days. But after a while he doing so fine, he start loaning money out when folks asks—colored folks always be needing a little cash. I says to him, Charlie Dee, don't be doing that. I don't want no trouble now. But they pays that money back. Charlie Dee, he make sure of that. They pays him back and pays him back. And they kep' on paying him back, too.

Pretty soon Charlie and me is living so fine, he bought hisself a baby blue DeSoto sedan, and drives all over town. He riding over to the houses of folks who owe him more than they can pay him back—no accounts, he calls them—and Charlie Dee be waiting in the dark. After a while, neighbors get to talking. They don't nod or say hello no more. Some spit when they pass our home. They toss lit cigarettes on our leaves in fall. I be scared halfway to death, but not Charlie Dee. He don't fear a thing. Not til he took sick one night, and his heart started racing, his face flushed red, and his soul flew out of his mouth like a sparrow chased by a tomcat.

Suddenly I had no one but the ceiling to talk to. Folks don't feel sorry for me. Not one iota. They don't bake me no pies or bring me no fried chicken or chitlins or black-eyed peas with bacon or potato pork casseroles like I loves. Pastor Elmer Rose don't even pay me a visit. Shoot, the man refuse to hold a funeral for Charlie Dee. And the mortician, Sammy T. Bells, he won't lay Charlie Dee to rest in the colored cemetery. He say a man act white on earth, he gonna be black as coal in hell, sure as the sun rise in the east. Mmmhhhmm. And you know white funeral homes don't bury no colored man in Lessington, Virginia, even if his corpse is as white as Charlie Dee's. As white as your daddy and your mama and your friend, Sarah Jane Lee. Even if he did work at the Lessington Country Club. I had to drive Charlie Dee's dead body, smelling ripe as an old melon on a hot day in July of 1953, all the way to Leesburg where his brother works for a funeral parlor that buries folks like him, no questions asked.

May Elsa Dee

Gil

Her full name was May Elsa Dee, and Mama said she arrived at Chinquapin Hill Farm like a Mary Poppins—that is, if Mary Poppins had been a black lady. She said May Dee came in a Yellow Cab one hot summer night when Mama was seven months pregnant and sitting out on the patio, watching the bats swoop over the yard. It was in the year of the drought, and that time of day when no-see-ums rise up and feast on your bare skin. May Dee eased out of the cab and stood in the tall grass, balancing her weight, first on one leg, then the other. *She looked perfectly regal,* Mama said, *like she already owned the place.* May Dee turned, picked up a small red suitcase, a straw purse, and a Sunday hat, and ambled slowly up the path to where Mama was sitting. *My name is May Elsa Dee,* she said, *and I understand that you folks is looking for someone to care for your child.* Mama said she hadn't advertised for help. But May Dee said that when a white lady is having babies like popcorn, word gets out. And she sure would like *a nice cold Co-Cola, and room near the baby's, thank you very much.* The truth is my mother had been having miscarriages, not babies. (May Dee knew that. In a town like Lessington, everyone knew everyone's business. And they especially knew it if it was a secret.) But May Dee told Mama she knew how to make a baby stay inside til its time comes. After May Dee moved in, Mama stayed in the bed, day and night, doing just what May Dee said. If it hadn't been for May Dee, Mama said, I would never have been born.

Taradiddles

Gil

What taradiddles she tells, my father said whenever he heard May Dee talking about Charlie Dee. *Don't ever believe what colored people say.* He didn't believe May Dee was ever married to Charlie Dee, even if she did take his last name. Because Charlie Dee, he said, had all kinds of women, riding around town in his Chrysler DeSoto, living on his loan collections and leftover cooking from the Lessington Country Club. *But he did look white,* my father said. *Even if everyone knew he was colored except for Charlie Dee himself. May Dee was right about one thing. The folks over at the Lessington Country Club loved his cooking.*

Some liked his liquor, too—a sweet corn whiskey he sold on the sly, but he drank most of it himself. When he was good and drunk, he beat May Dee. Neighbors said you could hear them screaming and carrying on on those summer nights when the windows were open. That's why some folks think May Dee might have killed Charlie Dee. Killed him when he was drunk or out cold. Of course everyone—at least everyone in the colored neighborhood—was relieved to find out Charlie Dee was gone. Better dead than alive, they agreed. Who was going to question that?

But after Charlie Dee was gone, so was his money. Neighbors began to question why May Dee left town, and with his body, too. May Dee said she was just taking him back where he came from, back to his folks in Leesburg. But she knew there was talk. May Dee is one smart colored woman. When she came back to Lessington, she sold Charlie Dee's blue DeSoto and got a cab to bring her over to Chinquapin Hill Farm. When she arrived, she was carrying a red suitcase and several black bags. Your mother never mentions those bags. I guarantee it wasn't clothes she brought with her. Your mama wasn't one to ask questions. She invited May Dee in like she was a long lost friend. When I asked her about it, she said, You know what the scripture says about taking in angels. *Like she thought May Dee was sent by God.*

One day, not long after you were born, Sheriff Dicky drove up to the farm, asking if he could speak with May Dee and search the premises. Whatever for? *your mama asked. And when he said he suspected May Dee of taking things that didn't belong to her, your mama said,* That's stuff and nonsense. Unless you have a warrant, you best be running along. *And he did run along, but he came back a few days later, warrant in hand. He never found a daggone thing. Not a red suitcase, not a black bag, not even a Sunday hat. No, when May Dee knew Sheriff Dicky was coming, she covered her tracks. If there's one thing a colored woman knows,* my father said, *it's how to hide whatever she's done when the law comes a-knocking.*

Three

The Sound of a Soul

Miss Alice

Sarah Jane

When Mama and me first moved to town, I stayed over at Miss Alice's when Mama was working. Miss Alice was related to my grandpa's fishing friend, Mr. Abe. She lived just over the railroad tracks behind our home on a street of tiny gray shacks where every house looked the same. Pretty soon everyone in the neighborhood knew my name—I was the only white girl running down that street. Miss Alice was a retired school teacher with a white cat named Puff and no accent. She told me the first day we met that she was black, not colored. But she didn't sound Southern or black. She sounded whiter than my own mama and me. Folks around town called her an Oreo, meaning she was black on the outside and white inside. Miss Alice taught school in Philadelphia before she moved to Lessington to take care of her aging father. She stayed on to teach history in the public schools and *to help young black children imagine a better life*, as she put it.

It was Miss Alice who taught me how to speak *correctly*, even if I only spoke that way when I was in her home. Every day when I visited Miss Alice, she gave me what she called *grammar and elocution lessons*. She didn't allow me to say words like *ya'll* or *reckon* or *crick*. She was always correcting my accent, too. *I don't want to be falling asleep and waking up in the middle of the same sentence while you drawl on, Sarah Jane,* she told me. A Southern accent, she said, makes a person sound dumb. *And you don't want to sound stupid now, do you?* The truth is, I liked drawling. I liked saying things just the way I do. But I listened to Miss Alice because I wasn't allowed to play with Puff or have chocolate chip cookies and milk until she said so. Not until I spoke *properly* for at least fifteen minutes. Sometimes fifteen minutes lasted a whole afternoon because I couldn't say my words like she wanted me to, clipping the beginnings and ends like the ears and tail of a fighting dog.

Grandpa's Funeral

Sarah Jane

Gil asked why me and Mama left Oiselle Isle, South Carolina. I didn't want to talk about it. I didn't want to tell him how we lived with my grandpa two blocks from the sea in a rusty, old doublewide that leaked and smelled like low tide. How Grandpa and his colored pal, Mr. Abe, was fishermen—up at dawn and out on the boat every day of the week before Grandpa took sick with the cancer. Mama quit her job at the Piggly Wiggly and stayed home, watching over him. I watched him, too. Watched his eyes sink into his head, his nut-brown skin fade to the color of a chicken skin before you toss it on a skillet. He got a odor to him like old broth and rotten eggs stirred together. Mama said that's the smell of death hovering close. The night he passed, Mama cried so hard, we had to wring the tears out of her sheets in the morning.

The cancer sucked the life out of Grandpa and all the money out of our bank account. If Mr. Simmons hadn't come down for one of his visits like he did, Mama wouldn't have been able to afford a funeral. We'd have thrown Grandpa into the sea and let the fish eat him. That's what Mama said. But Mr. Simmons took my grandpa's corpse to the finest funeral parlor on Oiselle Isle. Before they buried him, Grandpa looked so nice, laid out in his casket and wearing a brand new suit, I thought they put the wrong fella in there. At the cemetery, when they lowered the casket into the dirt, Mama would have dove in after it if Mr. Simmons hadn't grabbed her by the wrist. She turned to him then, sobbing and moaning, and wrapped herself around him like a morning glory around a fence post, not caring when the wind blew away her black velvet hat.

Mr. Abe

Sarah Jane

Grandpa said God never did him no favors. If it hadn't been for Mr. Abe, he'd have been done for long ago. Mr. Abe, he said, had special powers— he could feel a good fishing day like it was some kind of weather. And he always knew where the fish was swimming. Grandpa said Mr. Abe could see them fish flickering beneath the waves. What Grandpa didn't say was the sun had burnt holes in his own eyes so he was half-blind. I'd watch him at the end of the day, fingering coins, counting his change.

But Grandpa was right when he said Mr. Abe could see things. He saw Grandpa was sick long before we knew. *Take him to a doctor, Miz Lee,* he told Mama. But Grandpa wouldn't go. It was Mr. Abe's wife, Jewel, who cared for us in the end, bringing by shrimp casseroles, sweet potato pies, and prayers. So many prayers. Before he died, she and the entire congregation at the Assembly of God Church was praying for our souls. That's why Mama said I should never say a bad word about *them folks.* They was there when we was down and out, she said. And so was Mr. Simmons.

Ugly Daddy

Gil

It was your daddy who found Mama a job over at the John Deere dealership, Sarah Jane told me once.

Doing what? I asked.

Sitting behind the service counter. Answering the phone and looking pretty is all. That's how come we moved from Oiselle Isle. Mama was out of work. She said she couldn't find a job to save her hide. Said your daddy walked right in and saved us. He promised if she moved to Lessington, he would take care of her and me both. Find her a home and work, too. Now he walks into our house any time of day or night. Like he owns the place. Don't even knock. 'Walk right in, sit right down,' *Mama sings,* 'baby let your hair hang down.' *Only your daddy don't have no hair.*

Naw, I said. *He's as bald as a newborn. And a whole lot uglier.*

We broke down laughing at how ugly my daddy was.

Crazy Mama

Gil

When I was a boy, I had two mamas. Regular Mama and Crazy Mama. Regular Mama was my mother until 1960, the year Father Pitt, a retired priest from Chicago, drove into town in a two-tone Chrysler Town & Country station wagon, full of marble statues of angels, Virgin Marys, and three baby Jesuses. Father Pitt moved into a brick house on Water Street across from Christ Episcopal Church, set his statuary out in the front yard and introduced it to passersby. Everyone talked about Father Pitt because he was the first Catholic to make his home in town. My daddy didn't care for him. He said we didn't need Catholics moving down south. And besides, there was bird shit all over his statues, and he figured that was some kind of commentary from above. But Mama disagreed. She said that seeing those Jesuses and saints and angels out there in the sun and the rain, and yes, even with bird shit decorating them, made her feel like it was Christmas all year long. It made her think about the Lord and his minions. She took up driving us into town and talking with Father Pitt every chance she had. She must have told him about all the babies she lost and how much she wanted another child because Father Pitt told her miracles happen to those who believe. He asked, *Do you have faith enough to move the mountains, Mrs. Simmons?* Mama looked out at the Blue Ridge and blinked.

One night the Virgin Mary came to Mama in a dream and promised if she turned Catholic, she could have all the babies she wanted. In her dream, my mother said, babies grew like apples on trees. That's why she converted. And why she made an appointment with Dr. Repolt who prescribed her some new, special pills. The next thing we knew, Mama *was* pregnant. And with four babies. She was so happy, she told everyone in town that she wasn't having a baby, she was having a litter. God was making up for lost time. But when she was a few months along, those babies fell out of her like peas from a split pod. Her hair started falling out. Daddy said her mind left with her hair and those babies. And Regular Mama left too.

Playing Saints

Sarah Jane

One day Mrs. Simmons said if Gil and me acted real nice, we could turn into saints, complete with halos and the stigmata. She said it like she knew. Like she wasn't just fooling with us. Gil said she was right—it sure could happen, and he knew exactly how. First, he said we'd feel our foreheads get hot and glowy, and people would shade their eyes just to glimpse us. Next our hands and wrists and feet would sting before the skin broke open in small wounds. Then we'd start blessing people. They'd kneel before us and say *Amen*. But first we had to wear the right clothes. The statues of saints in his mama's church wore long stone gowns. So we snuck into his mama's room when she was out riding and dressed up in her nightgowns. I remember Gil in his mama's white nightie, waving his arms, shouting, *Let your light so shine before men, Sarah Jane!* It was a hot day, and his cheeks were bright red. He looked as pretty as a bride. I told him so, and his face shined.

Summer Nights

Sarah Jane

Summer nights Mama and Mr. Simmons sat out on our back porch, smoking and drinking cocktails after Mr. Simmons brought me home. Mama made me sit with them for a spell. Mr. Simmons spent the whole time trying *to educate me*, as he put it, bragging about his family bloodline that traced back to the Order of the First Families of Virginia. He talked about the different battles in The War like the Battle of Fredericksburg and Chancellorsville when Robert E. Lee outfoxed the North. He said there were Confederate colored soldiers, too. All the while he'd be touching Mama, one hand on her knee. Once, when he whispered something in her ear, making her giggle, I couldn't take it no more. I asked real loud, *What about the slaves that got whipped? What about the lynchings?*

Mr. Simmons stopped smiling and Mama gave me a warning look. *The War wasn't about slavery, Sarah Jane*, Mr. Simmons said, his face turning watermelon-red. *It was about tariffs. It was about the Southern man's right to self-rule. We Southerners don't like the federal government interfering with our ways. Do we, Sue-Anne?* he asked Mama. Then he added with a grin, *You know they only lynched criminals, Sarah Jane. Some white folks were lynched, too. The way I see it: lynching is a whole lot cheaper than the electric chair. And quicker too.* When he said that, he gave me a wink.

I couldn't look at him no more. But whatever Mr. Simmons said, my mama just nodded, her eyes soft and dumb, like the light had gone out in her head.

Tadpoles

Sarah Jane

The day Gil and me caught a bucket of tadpoles down at the crick below the cow pasture, Mr. Simmons bet us five dollars we couldn't grow a single one into a frog. I took two tadpoles home in a Mason jar that day and carried them over to Miss Alice's. *Don't be filling that jar with faucet water, Sarah Jane*, Miz Alice said. *Put them in a glass bowl and bring new water from the creek every few days.* For two months Miss Alice and me and Puff, her white cat, spent our afternoons watching them tadpoles. One afternoon they had little arms and was clinging on to a stick Miss Alice brought in from the yard. Another day their tails was gone. They looked up at us with bumpy eyes. Then a week later, two tiny green frogs hopped out, right at the same time. Puff pounced, quick as a heartbeat, and ate them up without hardly a crunch. *That's nature*, Miss Alice laughed, slapping her leg. But I wanted Puff to give me back my frogs.

Mr. Simmons didn't believe a word of it when I said my pollywogs was frogs before the cat ate them up. He said I had to prove it if I wanted my five bucks. I had to show *evidence*. Now how was I going to do that? I asked. I wanted to tell him right then and there how sometimes there ain't no proof of what's been. Maybe that's why the past gets made up again and again.

A Melon Seed

Gil

Now isn't it strange, Mama asked once, *that a pretty lady like Miz Lee never married in the first place?* That's when I realized Sarah Jane didn't have a daddy, which is one reason the parents at Foxfield Academy didn't allow their children to play with her. That, and she lived on the wrong side of town, only one street over from the colored neighborhood.

But the day Mama said Miz Lee was pretty was the first time I ever looked at her and decided she *was* pretty, even if she was old. She must have been thirty-five at least. But her hair was silky smooth and blond and not all done-up like most ladies back then, and her face didn't have any wrinkles or brown spots. And her waist and ankles were so thin, she would have looked girlish if she didn't have a bottom the size of two sugar melons side by side.

Once, when I asked Sarah Jane what happened to her daddy, or why her mama didn't have a husband, Miz Lee answered for her. *Sarah Jane*, she said, *came from a melon seed. A man didn't have nothing to do with it*. And she said that was the way she liked it. I believed her. I wanted to anyways. I thought Sarah Jane must be the luckiest girl alive, not to have a daddy like I did.

My Mama's Hair

Gil

Mama was always saying, *The world is just so unfair.* Especially on the mornings when she looked in the mirror and tried to figure out what in God's world she was going to do with her hair. No matter how much she curled and permed and sprayed it in place, her hair hung limp as Johnson grass that's been bit by a new frost, and there was no bringing it back to life. But there was this one day when Mama went to a new salon, Cathy's Cut and Curl. When she came home her hair was poodled up so tight, it looked like May Dee's. That day May Dee couldn't help herself. She said it out loud: *Lawdy be, Mrs. Simmons. Looks like you and me is related after all.*

Mama looked startled at first, like she was going to cry. Then all at once she and May Dee broke out laughing. It was the only time I ever saw Mama laugh like that. She and May Dee got to laughing so hard, they were sobbing, their laughter and sobs rising in waves. Bigger and bigger waves, until they couldn't stay standing up, and they collapsed onto the linoleum—May Dee in her uniform and nurse's shoes, and Mama in her town clothes—her pink pencil skirt and matching purse, the two of them holding their stomachs, kicking their lady-legs, gasping and giggling and gagging on that wet, hot Virginia air.

Beauty Parlor Day

Sarah Jane

Most days Gil said his mama never looked in the mirror. If she did, she just sighed, *So help me God.*

Is this a beauty parlor day? Gil would ask her, hoping she'd say yes. He and me loved going to the Downtown Beauty Shop on Fisher Street. Mrs. Simmons would give us two quarters, and we'd slip over to the Ben Johnson's Five and Ten and buy sacks of penny candy and Juicy Fruit gum, then eat and chew it all up while Miss Bettie Jo Morris, the beautician, gave Mrs. Simmons a tight set. Once, when the beauty shop was empty, Miss Morris gave me a set, too. Turned my hair into an upside-down tulip. She showed me how to wrap my hair in pink rollers, pin it up tight, and spray it with Aqua Net. I practiced on Gil's bangs, curling them up nice. I made him look pretty as me that day before every curl on our heads blew out on the long ride home.

Spitting Image

Sarah Jane

One morning when I was visiting Gil, I overheard his mama in the vestibule. *Is Sarah Jane that academic research you've been doing?* she asked. *Why the girl is a spitting image of your sister, Evelyn.* Mr. Simmons didn't answer. He told Mrs. Simmons I was welcome at Chinquapin Hill Farm whenever my mama needed a sitter, and he didn't want to hear another word about it. I was happy he said that because I loved the farm. There was so much happening at Chinquapin, and there was oodles of folks and horses and barn cats and a coon dog named Sissy and Thelma's cooking. On Saturdays Thelma made gingerbread with white sauce, sweet enough to make my eyes burn. She let me taste the sauce, hot off the stove. Mr. Simmons liked her sauce, too. He stuck his big hairy hand in the bowl, licked his finger, and stuck it back in again. Didn't even use a spoon. After I seen that, I didn't want no more. But Mrs. Simmons never ate sweets. Sometimes she peeked in on Gil and me. If I looked up, I seen a sadness inside her like a genie, all curled up in the bottle she was stuck inside.

Hair Spray and God's Minions

Gil

Your mama was a pretty thing, back before she married your pa and spent all them years trying to have babies. That's what May Dee said. *She even won a beauty contest when she just a girl of sixteen or seventeen.* May Dee said she was a dogwood or cherry or some other kind of blossom queen. I wanted to know what kind of blossom she was, but if I asked, Mama would just say she was God's blossom. I didn't want to hear her talk about God because once Mama started her God-talking, she never stopped. She talked on and on about God's miracles and virgin saints who levitated and the holy men who got the stigmata, bleeding out of their palms and ankles just like Jesus did—those were her favorites. She said their blood smelled like roses and attracted bees in the summertime. When they died, their corpse didn't even rot. Sometimes she thought she was getting the stigmata herself. I had to admit she did smell like roses. That might have been her floral-scented soap. And the bees did like her. They circled her head like a buzzing halo, but I think it was her Revlon hairspray that drew them. They hovered around her, and she let them buzz and buzz. Sometimes one of her bees flew around me. *Don't you swish my bees away now*, she said. *The bees are God's little minions.* Then she'd glare at me as if to ask, who was I to say otherwise?

The Sound of a Soul

Gil

My daddy hated religious zealots. He particularly disliked it when Mama was praying for our souls. *Let the Lord take care of that, why don't you?* she asked him whenever he was in a pickle. He just said *hmph,* and walked away.

Mama, he said, was filling my head with notions, and he was worried I'd grow up afraid of sixes, spilled salt, birds flying into the house, and God only knows what all else because there wasn't a superstition she didn't know and spout off. Mama was like a Methodist, a Christian Scientist, and a Catholic, all mixed up into one, which was even worse than being a Baptist, according to my daddy. He especially didn't care for her stories. He didn't believe she had a poodle once that could count. (She insisted she'd say *three*, and the dog would *yap, yap, yap.*) And she owned an owl that was an angel in a cage. (*Yes, it is an angel*, she said, even after it took sick, lost all its feathers, and rolled over onto its back, talons to the sky.)

And he didn't believe her father was run over by a car either. According to Mama, one day a car ran over her daddy, severed his head from his body, but he survived. Why? Because she prayed. *Yep, that's right*, she said. And her father's head snapped back onto his neck.

It made a little noise when it reattached, a noise she will never forget, like the air between his head and his neck was escaping fast with this *whoosh* followed by a sticky slap of skin. *Once you hear a sound like that*, Mama said, *you never forget it. That's the sound of a soul going back inside where it belongs. At least for a little while.*

Life after Death

Sarah Jane

It was Mrs. Simmons who said she had proof there is life after death. It was a few months before she went into the asylum when she told me and Gil how her daddy died and came back to life. *He came on back with news from the other side*, she said. Gil's father told her not to tell Gil and me that story. He said Gil had enough nightmares as it was. And he said that he, for one, didn't believe a word of it. But Gil and me made her tell that story again and again when Gil's daddy wasn't home. She told us how her own father was run over by a car, and his head was severed clear off his body. But a miracle happened, and the head reattached. I asked her if there was tire tracks on her daddy's neck, and she said she was mighty glad I asked her because as a matter of fact there was. Them tracks never went away. God left tracks just to show folks how close death is, how it's breathing down our necks every minute we're alive. *Or it's driving over our necks*, I said, and she said, *Yep. That's a fact.* She said her daddy never did seem himself after the accident. *A man who sees God*, Mrs. Simmons said, *is never the same man.* She said it was as if his head was still in heaven, so he could see the other world. He taught her to see it, too. *It's right here each time you blink,* she said, *and then it fades into the air. Seeing it is a spirit-art. That's how you see ghosts. And angels. And how you learn death isn't half-bad. You don't need to be afraid of taking your last breath. Because that's when life really begins.*

Mama's Superstitions

Gil

Mama practiced every superstition known to man, and made up a few, too. I never knew which she believed in, and which she said just for fun, or to make my daddy mad. Years later, I can still recite them one by one. Here are just a few of them:

If you spill salt, toss it right hand over left shoulder, or bad luck will happen to you or someone you love.

If you eat a piece of pie, save the point for last, and wish on it. Your wish will come true, but only if you don't eat another bite before dinner time. (*In other words, don't be eating my bonbons, Gil.*)

If you wake before 7 a.m. on the first day of the month, say *bunny bunny* before saying another word. If you don't, you won't escape the bad luck that is already blowing your way. (Not unless you walk backwards down the front stairs seven times, saying the Lord's Prayer with every step.)

If you're in a car, and a train passes overhead, duck or an accident will happen, and all the passengers will die. You will read their names in the newspaper. You will dream or see their faces in your window for seven weeks.

If a bird flies into your house, death will follow soon. Or worse, you will want it to. Nothing can be done once death enters the premises.

If you see a ghost walking down a beach, leave immediately or you will be washed out to sea. Or your house will. And all of your relatives.

If you wake on the wrong side of the bed or feel a crick in your neck when you first open your eyes, remember your dreams. Otherwise a ghost will borrow them for a few days or weeks. He will not want to give them back. When he does, they will feel drab like an old towel, sucked clean of softness and life.

The Dead Colt

Sarah Jane

Seemed like everything at Chinquapin Hill Farm went sour the week Mrs. Simmons' mare, Leda, was due to foal. Mrs. Simmons moved into the barn to keep watch and never did go back to the house. Not after Leda gave birth to a dead colt and hemorrhaged internally, the blood running out of her onto the sawdust floor of her stall. By the time the vet came, it was too late. Leda had to be put down. Mrs. Simmons was holding her head when Leda collapsed on the ground. I stood by and watched when Mr. Maupin and Otis tied the dead horses' legs with baling twine and loaded them onto the flatbed of the truck. The next day we all drove out past the cornfield to where Mr. Simmons had had a pit dug, and we buried them horses. I remember Mrs. Simmons staring past us, glassy-eyed. She didn't speak for weeks afterwards. Whenever folks asked her a question, she inhaled quick and straightened up, like she was sucking all the words back inside where she kept them safe beneath her folded arms.

Talking to Jesus

Gil

How's your mama? Sarah Jane asked whenever she came for visits in the weeks after Leda died. I didn't want to tell her that Mama was gone. That Mama had stopped eating and wouldn't sleep in the house. May Dee fussed over her all the time, offering her saltine crackers and spoonfuls of chicken soup and *a nice cold ginge-ale*. All Mama drank was wine. She said that the Lord made her water into wine, so all she needed was *the Lord's drink*. Then one afternoon Daddy and Mr. Maupin carried her to the car, and my father drove her off to the mental hospital. Before she left, she was sitting out on a folding chair in front of the barn, rocking and muttering to herself. *Who you talking to, Mama?* I asked. *I'm talking to God,* she said, *but He won't listen to me anymore. And besides, He's not very nice.*

The Nut House

May Dee

Mr. Simmons drove poor ol' Miz Simmons over to the nut house one day. But he the one they should have locked up. Thrown the key away, too. First time she went in, I says to myself, why Miz Simmons be better off in a hospital. Maybe they feed her something, put some meat back on her bones. And stop them voices she got in her head. She got all kinda folk talking in there. Jesus and the devil, too, I reckon. But when she come back home, musta been two months she gone—she thin as a scarecrow. Lawd what a sight. Her mind, too, empty as a dried-out gourd. She still know me, but she don't know Caleb or Mr. Maupin or Otis or Sarah Jane. Act like she never seen a one of them. But she remembers Mr. Simmons. Like she scared of him now. She says to me, *May Dee, I can't be living here like I used to. I'm not home in my own home,* her eyes wild, the whites showing. But she did stay on. A lady like Miz Simmons don't have no place else to go.

Four

Red Buckle Shoes

A Time like This

Gil

I never imagined this time would come, folks were always saying back in those years. They swore they'd never allow colored children in the same classroom as their sons and daughters. Or in the same swimming pools either. I remember my father's friend, Mrs. Richardson, saying in her thick British accent, *I will nevah, nevah allow my daughtah to swim in the same watah as a niggah.* She sent her daughter, Beverly, to a prep school outside of DC. Private schools sprouted like mushrooms all over the South. By the time integration was enforced in our county, my father and his country club cronies had started Foxfield Academy, a small brick building at the edge of a cornfield. Robert E. Lee, the public school, was closed as part of the Massive Resistance. The academy filled up so fast, they had to give entrance exams. Only the rich and well-connected got in. And Sarah Jane Lee. She had a special voucher. My daddy made sure of that.

Color

Gil

On Sarah Jane's first week at Foxfield Academy, Mary Teeters, one of the popular girls in our class, told everyone that her daddy saw Miz Lee coming out of The Good As New, Lessington's used clothing shop. She said only negroes shop at The Good As New. That's how she knew Sarah Jane was wearing a colored girl's hand-me-downs. Mary Teeters father owned Teeters Department Store, downtown on Main Street. Mr. Teeters gave Mary's friends discounts. Some days Mary Teeters and her girlfriends came to school wearing matching dresses and red buckle shoes with frilly white bobby socks. I'd catch Sarah Jane eyeing them. She said she'd didn't mind *one whit* what Mary Teeters said or what she and those mean girls wore. *And besides that*, she said, *Mama says color don't matter—not the color of your dress or the color of your skin.* When Sarah Jane said that, she tossed her blond pigtails defiantly and glared at me with her blue, blue eyes—eyes as blue as a July sky. I nodded, *yep.* Like I agreed. But I knew, and she knew. Her mama wasn't right.

Envy

Sarah Jane

At Foxfield Academy I wanted things I never knew I wanted. I wanted those fancy rich mamas in their nylons and high heels to see me and wish their own daughters was as pretty as me. They was always bringing in cupcakes and cookies and giving us rides on field trips to places like Monticello or Manassas where the guide talked about Thomas Jefferson and the Battles of Bull Run. And I wanted all those freckled blond boys in their white collared shirts and tan trousers to give me a St. Christopher medal because that's what boys gave you when they asked you to be their girl. By the time I left Foxfield Academy, I had a whole drawer of St. Christophers—I never gave back a single one. And I wanted the girls to envy me, and I thought they would, if only I could wear pastel-colored blouses and poodle skirts and red buckle shoes like they did. I wanted them to envy me so bad, I'd feel them burn.

History Class

Gil

In fifth grade, we studied the Civil War. My daddy came to school to lecture us, only he made sure we called it the War of Northern Aggression. Waving his hands in the air, he told how my grandfather was a general, wounded at the Battle of Cedar Run. He said General Sheridan and his Yankee troops swept through Virginia, burning homes and barns and killing livestock, turning all the old folks and women and children out of their homes, into the cold, just like they were Indians. Just like they didn't fear the same Lord as the Union soldiers. He said that if we went on down to the river behind the schoolyard, we'd find relics. That's how close the War came to where we stand today.

That afternoon my daddy stayed on to talk to the history teacher, making sure she knew what he called *the right facts about the War*. At recess Sarah Jane and I found a piece of an old rotten shoe, bullet casings, and a tin pot by the creek below the playground. My father nodded approvingly. *Now this is definitely a piece of a shoe from the 1800s*, he said, patting Sarah Jane on her blond head. *You children are touching history now.*

The Price of Red Buckle Shoes

Sarah Jane

When I was a girl, Mama said, *Sarah Jane, you get what you pay for in life. If something looks too good to be true, or if it don't smell right, it's wrong.* But I wanted things real bad. I specially wanted a pair of red buckle shoes from Teeters Department Store. At Teeters the shoe salesman x-rayed your feet with a fluoroscope so he could find you a perfect fit. Gil said you could look through a porthole and see the bones in your feet move when you wiggled your toes. That way you knew if you had growing room. Some days Mr. Teeters himself would help out in the shoe department. Rumor was that Mr. Teeters had a thing for pretty girls. If you let him kneel down in front of you while he slid your shoes on and off and stared up your skirt, he'd give you shoes for free. Sometimes he snuck his hand up there for a touch. It was true. I never told a soul about it. Years later, I think of red buckle shoes every time a man reaches for my crotch.

Lipstick

Gil

Sometimes I'd sneak into Mama's dressing room and take out her lipsticks, open the tubes one by one, and read the names: *Victory Red, Whisper Pink, Pouty Peach*. Victory Red was the color of Mama's lips the night she dressed in black velvet for a Christmas party and flew into such a rage, her words went as red as her mouth. Whisper Pink was the morning after when everything was quiet again. I could hear May Dee humming her first hymns of the day. But Pouty Peach was the one Sarah Jane and I liked best. Sarah Jane put it on one afternoon before she sang in the Christmas musical. The color matched her barrettes and popbead necklace. But when the performance began, the lipstick was gone. Sarah Jane had an orange smear on the sleeve of her white blouse. I thought how May Dee always said, *Pretty things, Gilbo. They don't never last.*

My Father

Sarah Jane

In fifth grade our class took a field trip to Washington, DC, and I got sick on the bus ride and threw up all over Joey Preston who was sitting by me, holding my hand. He'd just asked me to be his girl, but he didn't like me after I puked on his new plaid pants. That was fine by me. I had to take a ride home early with Mrs. Wynette, one of the class chaperones. She covered the car seat with plastic before giving me a ride back. I remember fishing the house key from under the doormat, letting myself in our front door. Mama was still at work, but I lied to Mrs. Wynette, said Mama was just upstairs taking her nap. Alone, I felt sicker than I already was. The house was all tore up. There was dirty dishes in the sink, and the radio was left on with Elvis singing, *It's now or never, come hold me tight, Kiss me my darling, be mine tonight.* A man's coat hung on the banister. Upstairs, Mama's bed was unmade, her red dress slung over the rocker, gold buttons scattered across the floor. A pair of men's black socks lay on the night stand. When Mama came home that night, I made her say what I always knew but didn't want to. *Yes, Sarah Jane,* she said. *Gil Simmons is your half-brother.* I couldn't look at Mama then. I hated her real bad. I hated Gil, too. I hated Mr. Simmons worst of all.

The Power of Mean

Sarah Jane

I remember the day after I found out about Mama and Mr. Simmons. I stayed in my room, watching yellow jackets bump across the ceiling. *You ever going to get out of bed?* Mama asked. I didn't answer.

I remember thinking, *I don't care what you say, Mama. I don't have to listen to you no more.*

I remember thinking, *I want to get out of this town. Go back to Oiselle Isle where I belong.*

I remember thinking, *I am so ashamed of you, Mama.* And, *Why do you keep on with that man?*

I remember thinking, *Can't you tell Mr. Simmons just to leave us alone?*

I remember thinking I'd tell him myself, *We don't need your help no more. We do just fine by ourselves.*

I remember thinking, *I will never call that man my daddy.*

I remember Mama knocking and knocking, saying she was bringing me a supper tray. *I ain't hungry, Mama,* I lied.

I remember saying, *I ain't hungry* for a whole week.

I remember thinking, *I'm so hungry I could bite a person in two.* I felt mean, too.

I remember thinking, *I like being hungry and mean.*

I remember being in school and saying to Mary Teeters, *You think you're so special. Well I got news for you.*

I remember saying to Delia Parks, *Your mouth is as big as a barn door. And your rear end is, too.*

I remember telling Gil Simmons, *Find someone else to sit by, why don't you? I'm done with you.*

I remember telling Tucker Johnson, *You got a nose so big, you could snort peanuts.*

I remember telling Thomas Bodette, *You're so ugly, I bet your mama mated with a rhino.*

I remember thinking, *I'm popular now. Everyone, even the teachers is nice-ing up to me.*

I remember thinking, *So that's what being mean does for you. If you're almost thirteen. And right cute, too.*

Riding with Mr. Simmons

Sarah Jane

When Mrs. Simmons was away at the mental hospital, Mr. Simmons hung around the horse barn, shooting the breeze with Otis and Mr. Maupin. He knew I didn't care for him, and he also knew how bad I wanted to ride. Some days he'd saddle up Gil's pony, Annabel, and let me ride around and around the ring, giving me pointers on how to hold the reins, develop a good seat, and post. And what to do if the pony tried to buck or run loose. One day he saddled up Juno, the bay mare he bought for Mrs. Simmons after Leda died, and we went on a trail ride over the fields and into the woods. On the way back, he took off at a canter across the cow pasture. I raced after him, squeezing Annabel tight and giving her a good kick. She broke into a gallop, her neck long, her little pony-legs stretching out in big strides. I held on to her mane and laughed out loud. *This*, I thought, *is flying*. At the end of the ride, Mr. Simmons lifted me out of the saddle, his gold tooth glinting in the sun, his blue eyes soft and glowy. That day I seen the man my mama loved.

Lucky Sarah Jane

Gil

I knew it was only a matter of time before Sarah Jane Lee became one of the popular girls. Because Sarah Jane fit into life like blue in the sky. Like water in a glass. Like her cowgirl legs in the tiny breeches she wore. It was no wonder she always took first prize. She beat me at Go Fish and checkers and Crazy Eights. And sang the solo in the Christmas concert. *She's just lucky is all,* May Dee said. *Why can't I be lucky?* I asked. I watched Sarah Jane close, and I tried to do what she did. And like what she liked: purple and snow and grilled cheese and Piglet and horses. Horses liked her back. They snorted and hung their heads out of their stalls when she came close. They took grass and sugar from her bare hands, nibbling carefully with their big yellow teeth. And when she talked to them, saying, *You pretty thang,* she claimed she could hear them answer. I believed her, seeing how they pricked their ears forward whenever she spoke. Even Annabel, my mean pony, let her ride her bareback. When I tried, Annabel bucked me off, and I landed on my backside. *Some of us just got all the charm,* Sarah Jane laughed. *And some of us don't got none.*

Mean

Gil

One day in sixth-grade lunch period, Sarah Jane said to me, *You cain't sit with me no more, Gil.* I didn't ask why not. I picked up my tray with a bowl of tomato soup and three packets of saltines, like I always ate, and was just walking away when Joey Preston elbowed me. Red soup splashed on my white school shirt and dripped down my pants. Everyone laughed until Miss Tabb, the teacher sitting at the head of the lunch table called out, *All y'all hush up now. There's nothing funny about spilled soup.* She dabbed my shirt with a paper napkin and sent me to the nurse's office where I searched through the box of old clothes smelling of pee and dirty socks. I finally found a grass-stained shirt and a pair of clean trousers, three sizes too big. When I went back to the cafeteria, Mary Sue Coles dared Joey Preston to yank my pants down, and he did. Everyone started cheering and pointing. I was so embarrassed, even my legs blushed. I remember searching out Sarah Jane with my eyes, thinking only she could help me out now. But she wouldn't even look at me. I knew why. I needed her too much.

Not One Lick

Gil

One day I told May Dee that Sarah Jane was the girl I loved. The next day Sarah Jane let Joey Preston kiss her on the lips at recess. I couldn't love her after that. I told May Dee, *I don't care one lick if I ever lay eyes on Sarah Jane Lee again.*

Not one lick, May Dee nodded. *Not one lick.* When she said it, it was true.

Dream

Gil

One night I dreamt I snuck inside Sarah Jane's house. I stole the Mason jar full of coins off her kitchen counter. She sat there on the Naugahyde couch watching me, eating a pickled egg. *I didn't do it*, I said, *I didn't steal a penny*, even though the jar was still in my hand.

What's wrong with you, Gil Simmons? she asked. *Why can't you be like everyone else?* I woke in a sweat, wondering, *How could I ever explain?* I felt all wrong—like a fish trying to fly. Like a rabbit trying to run with the wolves. Like a frog trying to sing with the whippoorwills.

Five

God's Mistake

The Sad Time

May Dee

What was I like back then? Gil asks me on the telephone sometimes. And I says to him, there was good times. And there was sad times.

Sometimes I wanted to shake you. I wanted to shake that little Sarah Jane, too. She walking around with her little pink nose in the air. Like she too good for us. Not even stopping in to say hello before she head on down to the barn and ask Mr. Simmons or Otis if she can ride that little pony you owned. *Oh please*, she ask, sweet as can be. *May I ride Annabel today?* Not a man living ever say no to that girl. She got them all wrapped around her little finger. You especially. If you wasn't staring after her, you was hiding in your bedroom. Sometimes I heard you crying. It was enough to break my heart—you all shut up inside, like you was living in a tomb. Sadness like a tide rising up in you. And in me, too.

Practicing Snow

Gil

The year everything went wrong in my life was the year Mama taught me what she called *the art of prayer*. She said prayer could make everything better. All you had to do was sit for a spell, close your eyes, and bring one wish into focus. She said everything else in your mind had to leave. And she meant everything. *It's best to start simple,* she explained. *Start with something like the weather. Like a day of sunshine. Or rain.*

I started with snow. Even if we did live in Virginia, and it was Indian summer the day I began.

I practiced snow at breakfast and lunch and in the school cafeteria when I sat by myself, eating my bologna sandwich and Wise Owl potato chips. I practiced snow after school when Sarah Jane couldn't come to Chinquapin. Sometimes I'd touch that snow and taste it. I'd roll imaginary snowballs and build imaginary snowmen. If I did it right, I could feel my toes turn blue, a chill traveling up my arms and legs. Nights I pretended I was sleeping in snowbanks. I kept the windows open, even when the rain blew in, even when the curtains looked like ghosts in the wind. I dreamt of walking in deep snow, the whole sky filled with snowflakes, falling on my face and on my bare arms and legs. Then one night in November it did snow. Fat, wet flakes blanketed the town.

When I told Mama I made it snow, she smiled. *Of course you did. But don't tell a soul. Okay, Gil?*

Snow

Sarah Jane

One day Gil Simmons bet me a dollar we'd get a foot of snow. He said he could see the snow falling before it fell. I said, *Naw, you cain't see nothing, Gil. It ain't gonna snow*. But he said, *Yes, it is, too, Sarah Jane,* and he bet me another dollar we wouldn't have school the next day.

That night it did snow, and by morning there was so much snow, the neighbor's chicken coop caved in. Two trees toppled over on the power line. I didn't get out of bed because we didn't have no heat or electricity, and the house was an ice cube. Mama lit the wood stove and made coffee, and she said Mrs. Wimberly, the old lady who lived down the street, died in a car wreck. Her tan station wagon slid over to the other side of the road, right into oncoming traffic. Two teenagers was in intensive care over at the Mary Washington Hospital. Mama said Mrs. Wimberly was old and British, and she always did drive on the wrong side of the road, but I blamed Gil. *Gil made it snow,* I told Mama. And when he phoned me and said, *I told you so,* and wanted me to pay up, I couldn't believe it. Neither could Mama. She said she didn't want me paying a dime to Gil Simmons. I said, *I won't Mama. Gil Simmons ain't my friend no more.* And he wasn't. Not for two whole weeks.

The Year Prayer Wasn't Enough

Gil

Whatever you want, Gil, you just pray for it, Mama said. But by the year I was twelve, I knew. Prayer wasn't enough. That was the year everyone in school turned mean, and Mama developed a conscience, as she put it, which meant she was always out. If she wasn't at a meeting for the citizens of Bartow County or delivering cans of Dinty Moore Stew to the local soup kitchen, she was checking on old Mrs. Holloway, the widow the next farm over who had a habit of getting lost in her own home. *Your mama,* my daddy said one night as he poured himself a whiskey, *has developed a penchant for trying to save lost souls.*

Does she save any? I asked. *Nope,* he said as he rattled the ice in his cocktail glass before adding, *She tried to save me once. And you can take a looky here and see how that worked out.*

God's Mistake

Gil

God makes mistakes. Even as a boy, I knew. I hated how everyone says God is perfect and great and all that kind of stuff. I wanted to say to them, Look around, why don't you? Look at all the folks who aren't who they say they are. Not a bit like it. All the sick folks, all the ugly folks, all the mean folks, all the folks who look half-baked. All the folks who think if they can just get a new hairdo, a new car, a new dishwasher, they'll be just fine, thank you very much. I feel sorry for them. I really do.

Sometimes I wonder if anyone feels okay in their own skin. Nobody wants to admit they're all wrong. So they make up stories. Or pray. Or lie. Or they drink cocktails at five o'clock. Like my daddy did. Whiskey on the rocks. Lots of whiskey. Not many rocks. It doesn't make a man into somebody else. Just makes him mean.

Me? I don't pretend. I blame God. I say, *God, you made one big old mistake when you made Gil Simmons.* But he won't answer me. You know how God is.

Fishing

Gil

Of course my daddy knew something was wrong with me, even if he didn't say it out loud. I could hear it in his voice when he said my name. I could feel it like a hay rash all over my skin when he looked my way. I could taste it like an old penny on my tongue when he asked, *What you been doing, Son,* and I said, *Nothing,* like he knew I would. I knew there was some answer he wished I had.

May Dee made him stop beating me in the house. But he kept on when we were outside. Like those days he took me fishing in the Appomattox River. I hated fishing. I hated everything about it: the long walk through the swamp grass and cattails, tall as my ball cap, the ticks and chiggers crawling up my legs, the deer flies burrowing in my hair, the cold river water and slimy rocks, and the sun beating on the top of my head, hot as the flat of an iron. And I hated catching fish most of all. I would never slip the bloody hook out of a fish's mouth. My father tried to make me, slapping me hard, his face turning dark red like the Virginia clay. *You going to live your life in a pair of white gloves, Gilbo?* he asked me. I didn't answer. But I thought to myself, *Yes Sir, I sure am.*

Slut

Sarah Jane

My pretty little slut, Mr. Simmons called Mama one night when she answered the door, wearing nothin but a pink slip. He kissed her on the neck and started sucking on her like a vampire, his hands cupping her ass. He didn't see me in the rocker by the wood stove. He kept kissing and calling her names like *hussy* and *little cunt,* saying them words soft and sweet like other folks say *darling* or *sweetheart.* Mama didn't say nothin to make him stop. She never put up a fuss. But when Mr. Simmons caught sight of me, he began to blush. I gave him my best stink eye. Mama turned and said, *It's past your bedtime, Sarah Jane. Get on upstairs now.* When I was going up the steps, I heard Mr. Simmons laugh and say real quiet, *You raising her up right?* And she answered, *I do my best.* I wanted to shout, *You sure don't. Not with that man in the house.*

A Pillar of Society

Gil

Sometimes after my father hit me, I cried until he sent me away to think about what I'd done. If we were fishing, he made me sit up on the bank next to the pawpaw trees on the sunlit rocks where copperheads sunbathed while he kept casting his line. Back then I wished that time didn't move as slow as a river snail oozing over the rocks. That the sun didn't burn me pink as Hawaiian Punch. I wished I was allowed to talk to my daddy—or even hum. My father said, *If you start your yacking, Gil, the fish will hear you, and they won't bite.*

You ever stick your head underwater and see what you hear? I asked, opening and closing my mouth like a trout.

Don't you give me any lip, Son, he said.

He wanted me to be as quiet as he was. To grow up and be a man with nothing between my ears but the sound of the river and a mosquito buzz or a crow cawing in the pines. He wanted me to become what he called *a regular pillar of society.* That's the term he used for men he admired. I pictured them, my daddy's men, as statues in the park, silent and lonesome. I pictured myself as a yappy little poodle dog, peeing all over their cold, stone feet.

Baptism

Sarah Jane

One day when I'd been sassing her, Mama said she'd had *enough*. I wasn't her nice little girl no more. And what I needed was to know the Lord. I answered her back that God sure didn't help Mrs. Simmons none, and she said, *Now aren't you getting too big for your britches, Sarah Jane?* She drove me over to the Park Street Baptist Church to have me Christianized. I had to take lessons twice a week. I remember there was a smell of wet tennis shoes in the church basement and a red-haired preacher with a greedy shine to his eyes. Looked like he wanted to eat me. On the day of my baptism, he held my butt and dipped me back in the water. I came up sneezing. *That's the devil leaving you,* he said. *Now you is God's little gal.* Does God have little gals? I wanted to ask. But I knew he wished I was his instead. Just like I knew being pretty was all I had. Not Jesus. Not God. My mama taught me that.

Riding Lessons

Gil

Sarah Jane, Sarah Jane, I still sing her name in my mind like it's music. She's a habit I never outgrew. I used to worry she would leave one day and never be back. But even when she was mean at school, she kept coming over to Chinquapin because my father and Mr. Maupin let her ride Annabel. My father gave her lessons some days. I watched from my bedroom window—Sarah Jane in a tiny pink T-shirt and jeans, riding around and around our ring while my daddy called out, *Press your heels down, Sarah Jane. Grab ahold of the reins, not the mane.* She rode in tennis shoes even though Mama said she shouldn't be riding without boots and a riding hat. But Sarah Jane liked the wind in her hair, and she didn't care for boots. *Will you teach me how to jump?* she asked. *Can I show Annabel at the state fair?* My father smiled and patted her head. Whatever she asked for, she got.

After her riding lesson, Sarah Jane came up to the house and waited for a ride home. I waited with her like old times. We listened to The Beatles, Peter, Paul and Mary and The Chiffons on the radio, singing along with "He's So Fine," and "Love Me Do" while we played gin rummy. *Are we friends?* I asked one day. *Will you come over on my thirteenth birthday?*

Okay, she shrugged.

My birthday was in August. No one from school would know.

Miss August

Gil

My thirteenth birthday was during a heat wave on a day so sweltering, Otis put ice cubes in the chicken water to keep the hens laying. Mama took a long cold bath but complained she was sweating before she even toweled off. I sat in front of the box fan, a wet rag on my forehead, waiting for Sarah Jane. *What if she forgot?* I worried. That morning my parents had to go to town to do some kind of *important business*, as they called it. I watched them climb into the back of a black Lincoln Continental, and Ellis, the new chauffeur, dressed in a navy-blue uniform, drove them slowly away, down the newly-paved road. The fact that they had to go together meant they were in worse moods than usual. I was glad when they were gone, glad they didn't remember my birthday, and glad, too, that Sarah Jane was coming over, and we would eat Thelma's lemon cake, even if I didn't have a thing else planned.

But when Sarah Jane knocked on the door and stood out on the front porch, her blue dress blowing against her legs in a gust of hot wind, a half-smirk on her lips, I thought for the first time maybe my father was right. *Someday you are going to outgrow playing with Sarah Jane Lee,* he said, adding, *Boys and girls don't stay just friends.* I didn't know what to do with her, not after I opened the box she brought me with a baseball glove inside, even though we both knew I didn't play ball. She said her mama picked it out and looked away, embarrassed. We wandered aimlessly around the house, opening closets and drawers, searching for something, like maybe a game of Life or Clue. Whenever Sarah Jane saw a servant she didn't know, she said, *Oh, look, a new one! You got so many new folks helping ya'll out. Do they know it's your birthday?* I looked out the window while Sarah Jane asked every new servant his or her name and acted like they were

[97]

her new best friends. I thought of how May Dee always said *Miss Sarah Jane, she got to learn to mind her own cotton pickin' business one day.*

After a while, we wandered into my daddy's den, the only room I wasn't allowed inside, with wood paneling, a portrait of General Simmons in a Confederate uniform, and my father's stale scent of whiskey, talcum powder, and B.O. *We can't go in there*, I said, but Sarah Jane stuck her tongue out at me and walked on in. *This room is cool!* she announced and flopped down on the brown shag carpet—that shag must have been six inches tall at least. She waved her bare feet in the air and started singing, *Happy birthday to Gil!* That's when May Dee walked in, carrying a pitcher of iced tea with four inches of sugar on the bottom. She stirred the tea with a silver spoon, making little clinky noises, and poured two glasses before asking, *What ya'll doing in your pa's room, Gil? You know you ain't s'posed to be in here.*

It's my fault. Sarah Jane giggled. *Gil told me we wasn't allowed, but I love this room. Don't you, May Dee? It's the only cool place in the house.* May Dee shook her head and gave me a look that said, *You're going to be in a whole heap of trouble, Gilbo.*

As soon as May Dee left, Sarah Jane picked a *Playboy* magazine from inside my father's desk—like she already knew it was there—opened the magazine and started flipping pages, stopping to stare at the slick, naked ladies. I sat down beside her. *Lemme see,* I said. She snatched the magazine away and started teasing, *You can't look! You can't look!* Then she opened it up and placed the *Playboy* in front of me. And we both looked. And looked. And looked.

We stopped at the centerfold of Miss August, the two of us staring at her together, holding our breath. Miss August lay naked on a beach with nothing but the ocean behind her, sand granules sticking to her oiled buttocks and thighs, her back slightly arched, the bright, day all over her bare skin. And I mean...all...over. And I knew suddenly. I could never...ever...see enough...of Miss August.

After a while, Sarah Jane stood up. *I gotta go,* she said. *I don't want to see no more nudey ladies.* But I didn't move. I couldn't. I felt as if I was under a spell, a spell of Miss August, a spell of recognition. It was as if—how can I say it? I could feel Miss August unfolding inside me, and it was me who was lying on my back on a beach far away with the sun on my sandy skin, my soft hips, my plump breasts.

Yes, I thought. *Yes!* It felt so true, so right. I knew then. Or maybe some-one inside me knew...who I really was. And what I wanted to be when I grew up.

Gil in a Dress

Sarah Jane

Mr. Simmons came home one night and found Gil wearing his mama's red cocktail dress. Or he found Gil in his mama's flowered bra and pantyhose. Or he found him wearing her black high heels and not a stitch else. Everyone in Lessington tells this story, and everyone tells the story different. They keep on telling it, even if it happened decades ago. May Dee, too. *I heard the hollering,* she says. *And I rushes upstairs, and there I seen it. Gil in his mama's pink dressing gown, cowering like a whipped puppy dog. If I hadn't been there, the man mighta kilt that boy.*

It was true. Gil was so beat up, he couldn't go to school the next day. Mr. Simmons had taken a belt to him—his back and legs was red-striped. A week later, Gil was shipped off to a boarding school in North Carolina—some prep school run by Mrs. Simmons' brother. Gil never did come back to Foxfield Academy. I missed him all the time. We all did. Even Mr. Simmons was sorry he was gone. The man needed someone to beat on. But May Dee was saddest of all. She stopped her singing and started fussing over every room in the house, top to bottom. It was so quiet when I visited Chinquapin Hill Farm to ride Annabel. Like all the rooms was hollowed out. Wiped clean of dust and song. Nobody and nothing was living there no more. Mrs. Simmons moved back into the horse barn. Slept on a cot in the hayloft like she did during foaling times. Mr. Simmons left on one of his long trips. Even May Dee got a place in town. My mama pulled me out of Foxfield Academy and put me in public school where I belonged. The public school had just opened up again. I made new friends, friends who talk like I do. Some was colored girls. And some wore used clothes from The Good As New. But no one was a friend like Gil Simmons was.

What Did I Know?

May Dee

Did you know about Gil? Sarah Jane asking me years later. *Did you 'spect something wrong?*

Course I did. I known before I known. I seen it. I didn't want to, but I seen what I seen. I thought to myself, *Don't we got enough troubles at Chinquapin Hill Farm?* And after Gil done gone, I seen it again. Like a moving picture in my head. Gil trying on his mama's lipsticks, saying them color names: *Whisper Pink, Peach Sunset, Victory Red.* Gil sleeping in his mama's nightgown when she away. Gil trying on your pink swimsuit and twirling on his toes. I get a sick feeling inside. Like when bad weather be on its way. And you know it ain't just gonna rain when it rains. The storm is gonna wash everything you own away.

Why?

Gil

people want to ask me. *Why did you become a woman?* I tell them, *This is who I am.* I never say what I really think. That God makes everyone a little bit or a lot wrong—on purpose. So that all their lives people go around wishing they were somehow different, or someone they aren't. Take Charlie and May Dee. They wished they were white. Take my daddy. He wished he was living in another era so he could fight the Civil War. And win it this time. And poor Mama—she wasn't born with a sound mind. She would have liked to have had ten babies when she could barely raise one. Sarah Jane said her mama would have stayed on in Oiselle Isle if she'd been rich instead of poor as she was. And Sarah Jane, she always wished she was a horse. And why not? I think a lot of girls wanted to be horses. Maybe they'd have been better off in the long run. Mama and Miz Lee included. I can see them now, galloping across the fields with nothing on their minds—just the wind whistling in their long soft ears.

Thief

Sarah Jane

I like to tease Gil whenever he calls me on the telephone. I say to him, *I know you miss us. I know you wish you was still living in the land of red clay, June bugs, copperheads, and your daddy.* And he says that as a matter of fact he does miss us. Sometimes. And besides, he adds, he let his bygones be bygone, and he might as well have. His mama is long dead. And his daddy is as old and dried up now as an earthworm in the sun. But Gil don't ever talk about him. He asks after May Dee instead. He says all he has to do is shut his eyes, and he can feel her arms, heavy on his skin. He can hear May Dee, too, singing and singing, her notes so warm, they could make the roses bloom. And sometimes, he says he dreams he's in his mama's bedroom, painting his toenails or trying on her lipsticks. And when he looks in the mirror, he sees the thief his mama always imagined. She's all dressed up in her finery and jewels.

All Grown

May Dee

I never picture Gil all grown like he is. I still see my boy, Gilbo, when he calls on the telephone, asking for Miss May Dee, here at the nursing home I stays in. Calls me once a week on Sundays, and I waits all week for his calls. He all I got now. And Miss Sarah Jane. She stop in on special days: Thanksgiving, Easter, Christmas. She done married every rich fella in Lessington before she married old Mr. Wood who died of a stroke and left her his horse farm. She say she has her horses now. Don't need no men. And Gil, or Doreen he calls hisself, he off in New York City, writing books I don't hardly understand. Fairy tales, what he calls them. But they ain't like fairy tales I ever known. He tells me one tale he wrote about a lady who catches fire when no one's looking. And this other about a boy who turns into a ice cube when he gets lonesome. But the story I like is about a girl who glows in the dark. Bugs light on her skin, just like she a light bulb. Beside that girl, everybody else looks dim. I know he's writing about Sarah Jane. She always did look lit up with her yellow hair up around her head. Gil loved that girl something awful. Still do. They twin souls, Gil and Sarah Jane.

Fairy Tale

Gil

Once upon a time there were two sisters who didn't know they were sisters. They both had yellow hair, freckles, and doorknob knees. One was so
homely, so pale, folks looked away rather than meeting her gaze. One was
so pretty, the birds sang a little louder when she walked past. The sisters
sat side by side on the porch swing on hot summer days, sipping sweet
tea and watching hummingbirds rise and dip around the honeysuckle
blooms. One sister said, *Let's go on down to the crick and catch crawdads.*
The other said, *Naw. There's no sense in getting dirty. Let's play inside where
it's cool and hide.* It took a long time for anyone to find the hidden sister
who curled up in the darkness like a snapshot in a drawer.

Writer's Note

I have been told many times to write about my childhood, to follow the dictum, *Write what you know*. But I have been hesitant, in part because of the racism that hovered like a dark cloud over my past. In my childhood memories, racism is omnipresent. Racism is a character in the corner of every scene, if not center stage. Racism is the janitor in our all-white schools, the cooks and servers in our all-white country clubs as well as in the steak houses and bars where only whites dined or drank. Racism is the black nanny, maid, and cleaning lady in our Confederate homes where the Civil War was often referred to as The War of Northern Aggression. In those days racism was as much a part of life as the sweet tea we drank, the buttered grits we ate, the hot, wet air we breathed on summer days.

Writing this, I thought of my childhood friends who told me, *Oh come on. It wasn't that bad.* Then I thought of other friends who said, *It was much worse than what you describe.* I sometimes think racism is like arsenic—you can become desensitized to it when you've sipped it over time. When I was working on my MFA, several of my mentors suggested that I avoid the topic altogether, reasoning that for me to write about racism would be comparable to a Nazi descendant writing about the Holocaust. After all, my father's ancestors fought for the Confederate army, and owned hundreds of slaves. My mother's family is from the North, and, as a girl, I sometimes thought there was a Civil War in our own home. My parents held very different political views, but I would not want to suggest that racism is unique to the South. Or that not talking or writing about racism is the right choice, although it is an easier one.

But it wasn't just racism that worried me. I also worried about how I might write about the layers of society that coexisted in my childhood—from the very wealthy to the poor, rural men and women of both races who worked on the farms outside of town, including the unkempt farm where I grew up. I had friends whose parents employed armies of servants and who lived on the manicured, white-fenced horse farms outside of Charlottesville, Virginia. I had other friends whose parents worked on these farms, and still others, mostly brought in by the university, who were new to town and to the Virginia way of life. Some, like me, went to the all-white private schools that opened as soon as integration became law. Others attended the public schools. And still others, including some of our farmhands' children, rarely went to school.

The characters in this book, Sarah Jane Lee, Gil Simmons, and May Dee are amalgamations of my childhood friends and their nannies. The city, Lessington, where the book takes place, is also an amalgamation of Virginia towns. In this book, I have composed a collection of prose poems that work together to tell stories about the South in the late fifties and early sixties. Although the stories are based on memories of my past, the book is entirely a work of fiction.

The seeds for this book were planted many years ago, when I was a farm girl and spent so much time with the farmhands and their children, I started to sound like them. My father scolded me, *Stop talking like you were raised in the barnyard*. I also imitated my African American nanny, Mary, who sang like Mahalia Jackson, loved me more than my parents did, and was one of the most racist people I've ever met. An exile from the black community, she was forever praising the Lord and using the n-word to describe all African Americans as well as anyone else she disliked. When I misbehaved, she called me *little pickaninny*.

But the formative memory for the collection took place in grade school, back when I had two pale, blond boy friends who looked very much alike, one who became a cross-dresser and wanted to be a girl, and another who was my first crush. In my head, I called them my gil-friends, meaning my almost-girl friends. (I was averse to the idea of having an actual boyfriend back then, even if I already liked boys very much.)

I remember the first time I had a play date at one of their homes. I rang the doorbell of a huge, white-pillared mansion at noon. A black nanny, dressed in a white uniform, opened the door and quickly ushered me inside. *Don't be ringing that bell again*, she said. *The missus is still in bed. We don't want to be waking her now, do we?* Gil (as I will call him here for convenience) came down the carpeted steps, still dressed in his pajamas.

You woke Mama, he said with a frown. I heard his mother calling, *Who's there?* Gil led me upstairs to his mother's room and introduced me. His mother, dressed in a peach satin robe, propped up on pillows in a four-poster bed, sat smoking her first cigarette of the day. An owl stared out of its cage on her bedside table. *Let Hermes out for his exercise, will you, dear?* Gil opened the birdcage, and the owl swooped around the room before landing on a bedpost and staring down at us, one by one, as if it wanted us gone. Then it defecated. *Don't worry*, Mrs. Simmons (or rather, the woman I fictionalized as Mrs. Simmons) said. *The maid will clean that up.* Then she turned to me. *You must be one of Ben's girls.* She blew out a puff of smoke and leaned back in the pillows. *Your father is a good man. Did you know he helped us start Belfield School when integration became law? If it hadn't been for men like your daddy, you'd be going to the public school with colored children.*

Before that day, I didn't think that Belfield, the school I attended, was started to avoid integration. I never asked my father if this was true. Mrs. Simmons informed me that private schools sprouted like mushrooms all over the South in the fifties. *Because no well-bred Southerners want to send their children to school with the negroes,* she said, adding, *It's a crying shame that the South lost the War.* Her black maid, Edna, entered the room just then. Mrs. Simmons turned to ask her, *Don't you agree, Edna? We'd all be better off if the South had won the War?* Edna nodded, *Yes'm,* before cleaning the bird shit off the floor.

Acknowledgments

Anthem: "A Melon Seed," "The Death of Charlie Dee," "Fishing," "God's Mistake," "Lucky Sarah Jane," "May Elsa Dee," "Taradiddles"

Ides of March, An Anthology of Ohio Poets: "Superstitions"

The Indiana Review: "Hair Spray and God's Minions"

KYSO: "Red Buckle Shoes"

Nothing to Declare: A Guide to the Flash Sequence: "The Year Prayer Wasn't Enough," "Confederate Gil," "Twin Souls," "Hide and Seek," "Hair Spray and God's Minions," "My Father's Research," "Practicing Snow," "Snow," "Not One Lick" (published under the title "Magic")

Sixth Finch: "Not One Lick" (published under the title "Magic")

Story Scape: "Crazy Mama," "Hide and Seek," "The Year Prayer Wasn't Enough," "My Father's Research"

I want to thank Peter Johnson, Kathleen McGookey, Sammy Greenspan, Karen Schubert, Rick Bursky, Shivani Mehta, and Nicole Santalucia for their friendship, help, and support. I also want to thank Christine Howey, Samsun Knight, and Baron Wormser for their editorial advice, insights, and careful readings of the text.

Other Books in the Notable Voices Series

CavanKerry's Mission

CavanKerry Press is committed to expanding the reach of poetry to a general readership by publishing poets whose works explore the emotional and psychological landscapes of everyday life.